THE
ONE-DISH
COOKBOOK

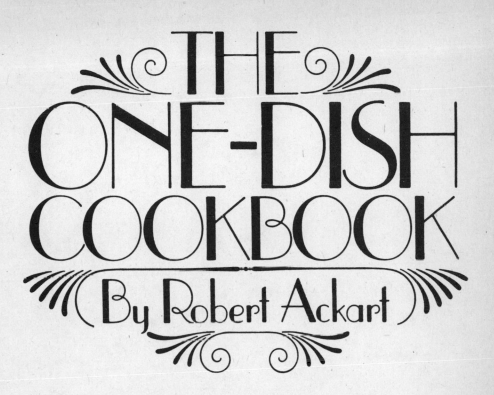

THE ONE-DISH COOKBOOK

By Robert Ackart

Drawings by Marjorie Zaum

Grosset & Dunlap Publishers New York

For my father
and for my friend
Edna Jardine Whitman

Contents

INTRODUCTION

There are two ways of dealing with today's bewildering and discouraging food economy. We may merely cope, doggedly and determinedly, with increasing prices and decreasing inspiration. Or we can rise to the challenge and, for a modest cost, easy on the weekly food budget, offer family and friends entrées that are unusual, tasty, attractive, and frequently elegant. I for one prefer to meet the challenge: I take a certain pride in achievement over these odds. I have discovered the joy of creating attractive dishes from inexpensive and simple ingredients, and I happily admit to the vanity of enjoying praise for my efforts. Thus I feel that preparing main dishes on a limited budget can be — no, *is* — fun. And that is what this book is all about.

The book offers recipes for entrées made with less expensive meat or poultry or fish, some from foreign cuisines and some from my own experimenting in the kitchen. If a single recipe does not constitute the entire entrée — although it very often does — a suggestion is made for some accompanying food to complement the main course. Recipes for these side dishes are given in chapter 8. To round out the meal, a salad may be offered, or a simple dessert of your choice: fruit, a pudding, perhaps pie or cake. Readers will find only a few recipes made with veal; they will find none for calf's liver, sweetbreads, or seafood — all notoriously costly.

Ask your butcher what he has of special interest. If, for example, his answer is "Lamb kidneys," or "Veal shanks," rejoice and buy them — as many as you feel you can use. Once your treasure is safely home, freeze it — whatever economy meat it may be. This suggestion also applies to poultry parts and giblets. Home-freezing of fish is perhaps a bit risky; while excellent for some purposes, frozen fish often suffers by comparison with fresh fish in both taste and texture.

May I urge you to become personally acquainted with your butcher? You will find that doing so produces at bargain prices various meats you had not dreamed of. Butchers in independent meat markets are there largely because they enjoy "old-time" contact with their customers; if wages were their only concern, they would do better in a supermarket, and they know it — they are independent butchers by choice. Even the impersonal atmosphere of chain store or supermarket can be altered by your making friends with the butcher hidden behind his mirrored barricade; he will welcome the opportunity to do something personal for you and he will be glad of the chance to change his usual routine. In the case of both kinds of butcher, independent or supermarket, they thrive — like actors and opera singers — on friendly appreciation.

The entrée cost is also kept down by imaginative use of cooking constituents. In "beating the economy at its own game" it would be folly to suggest dishes made with stewing meat and, at the same time, call for mushrooms and wine — delectable as these more costly ingredients are.

Hence these recipes, even some classic ones adapted for inclusion here, utilize less expensive ingredients *throughout*. Margarine rather than butter is listed as a staple ingredient, and such items as wine, artichoke hearts, avocados, and mushrooms — to name but a few expensive delights — are always indicated as options or variants, should the cook wish to use them.

In place of wine as a cooking liquid, water flavored with bouillon cubes, properly seasoned, substitutes very well indeed. My pleasure in using herbs and spices derives from growing my own — in the garden in summer, in pots in winter — and from a sense of adventure in experimenting with them. Both pleasure and experimenting have found their way into these recipes. Effort is also made to use the most common, least seasonal vegetables, ones that are always available, always reasonably priced: cabbage, carrots, onions, potatoes, squash, turnips, and so forth. I am amazed at the variety of tastes and textures of which such pleasantly homely foods are capable.

A word about utensils: not measuring cups and spoons but the principal utensil in which the recipe is prepared and cooked. Whenever possible, preparation *and* cooking are done in a single utensil. If this technique is not feasible, the ingredients, readied separately, are assembled in a single utensil for cooking. (If more than one utensil is used, you will do well to wash up as you go along. In my kitchen I play a game wherein the one rule is that, at the moment of serving, all utensils not required for the presentation of the meal have been washed, dried, and put away. The game adds to the fun of cooking, and the pleasure of working in a clean, uncluttered kitchen increases the satisfaction of preparing a meal.)

Casseroles, baking dishes, electric skillets, all cook-and-serve utensils are available today in attractive designs, pleasant to look at and easy to clean. Cooking using inexpensive ingredients can produce an elegant-looking meal. Careful preparation of the ingredients is, of course, the first contributing factor in making an eye-appealing dish. Second in importance is the utensil used to present the recipe at table. Treat yourself and treat your family and friends to the genial pleasures of elegant dining by making these recipes attractive to the eye as well as to the taste. Incidentally, the particular utensil called for in the recipe is merely one that I found to work well; you may have your own preference, and if so, follow it. When the utensil must be flameproof, this is always stated.

Each entrée is designed to serve six persons. The feasibility of refrigerating or freezing the fully cooked dish is given and when possible it has also been indicated when a recipe can be doubled. For the convenience of the reader, the length of time required to prepare the recipe and the length of time required to cook it are stated. A point is indicated of where in the recipe one "may stop and continue later"; thus the dish may be made in one session or, if desired, in two. (See the Glossary for further explanation of the terms, "Preparation," "Cooking," and "At this point you may stop and continue later.") If the recipe is oven-cooked, the temperature setting is given at the outset, so that the oven will be ready when the dish is to go into it. Each chapter is introduced by a brief description and illustration of the meats used. These short sections are, I feel, helpful in showing the cook how meats in one recipe may easily be used in another, thus yielding additional entrées. Ingredients are listed in the order of their use and, for cooks who (like me) arrange their spice shelf from A to Z, seasonings (apart from salt and pepper) are always listed alphabetically.

By this time the reader will have rightly surmised that I find cooking a very personal, highly creative experience. That is true; I do. And for this reason I take pleasure in sharing with you comments on various of the main dishes, and in indicating the country of their origin, when dishes have a particularly national flavor. I should add here, however, that the recipes, having been adapted to the specific purposes of this book — economy and ease of preparation — are more honestly "foods without a country"; assigning them national or ethnical origin is done more for the interest of the cook and for the enjoyment of menu-making.

These recipes have been prepared for and offered to family and friends in the hope that they would give enjoyable satisfaction. I hold the same hope for you: may these unusual and economical main dishes prove as attractive to your budget, taste, and eye as they have done at my table; and may they give you the same pleasure as they have given me in creating them.

Katonah, New York   Robert Ackart
1975

GLOSSARY

The few terms which follow, used throughout this book, may possibly be unfamiliar to some cooks; hence their definitions.

"At this point you may stop and continue later": This indication, included for the convenience of the cook, assumes that no longer than four hours will pass between the two interrupted steps of preparation and/or cooking. The ingredients should be covered and left at room temperature. Longer periods of culinary inactivity should be safeguarded by refrigeration. However, this step is not advised, because refrigerated ingredients should be given sufficient time to return to room temperature before continuing with the recipe.

Bouquet garni: In French cooking, a mixture of herbs, usually bay leaf, marjoram, parsley, and thyme, tied together in cheesecloth to facilitate their removal from the cooked dish (a metal tea infuser is convenient if dried herbs are used). The *bouquet garni* may be varied according to your taste.

Cooking: In general, cooking time refers to that period required to finish the assembled dish. The cooking of onion, for example, as an ingredient in the recipe, is rather a part of the preparation time than of the cooking period. Cooking times given in the recipes usually refer to that period of cooking following the suggestion, "At this point you may stop and continue later." See Preparation below.

Julienne: Meat or vegetables cut in thin strips about 2 inches long. The uniformity of size adds to the attractiveness of the dish. We commonly find the term on menus offering "Chef's salad with julienne of ham and chicken."

Pasta: Any of various forms of flour (usually semolina) mixed with eggs and water to yield a firm raw "dough," which is then boiled, baked, stuffed, or served with either a sauce or melted butter. Spaghetti, noodles, fettucini, etc., are offered as a first course or, as suggested by this book, as a side dish.

Preparation: The preparation time of a given recipe includes the browning of meat, the peeling, chopping, and cooking of vegetables used as ingredients in the recipe, the readying of the cooking liquid, etc. It is assumed that, when possible, two or three steps in the preparation will be simultaneously undertaken, for example, as meat is browning, onions, vegetables, and other ingredients are being readied. See Cooking above.

Roux: In French cooking, a mixture of equal parts melted fat and flour, cooked together over gentle heat and used as the thickening agent of a sauce.

Seasoned flour: In a waxed-paper bag, shake together ⅔ cup flour, 1½ teaspoons salt, and ¼ teaspoon pepper; add the meat called for by the recipe, a few pieces at a time, and shake the bag to coat it evenly. Reserve any remaining flour; it may be useful in completing the sauce for the dish.

Scalding: Do not boil milk (doing so makes cleaning the pan difficult); instead, heat the milk, either over direct heat or over boiling water in a double boiler, until the surface of the milk shimmers.

Stir-frying: The Chinese technique for rapid cooking of chopped meats and prepared vegetables by stirring them constantly in a small amount of oil over high heat; the method yields tender-crisp dishes with little change in the color of the vegetables.

Tenderized dried fruit: Differ from dried fruit which require soaking before being cooked slowly for a reasonably long period of time. Tenderized dried fruit are available packaged rather than in bulk and have been treated so that the time required to cook them is considerably reduced. In this book, recipes call for *tenderized* dried fruit in order to reduce the cooking time of the dish.

Wok: A round-bottomed, two-handled pan used in Chinese cookery and particularly in the rapid stir-frying process. Available in iron or aluminum, woks come equipped with a metal ring base to prevent their tipping when used on conventional kitchen ranges.

Zest: The outer part of the peel of citrus fruits containing the flavorful oils. A vegetable peeler is the best utensil to use in cutting the peel. Zest has none of the white pith attached to it; the pith is bitter and has no taste of the parent fruit.

BEEF AND VEAL

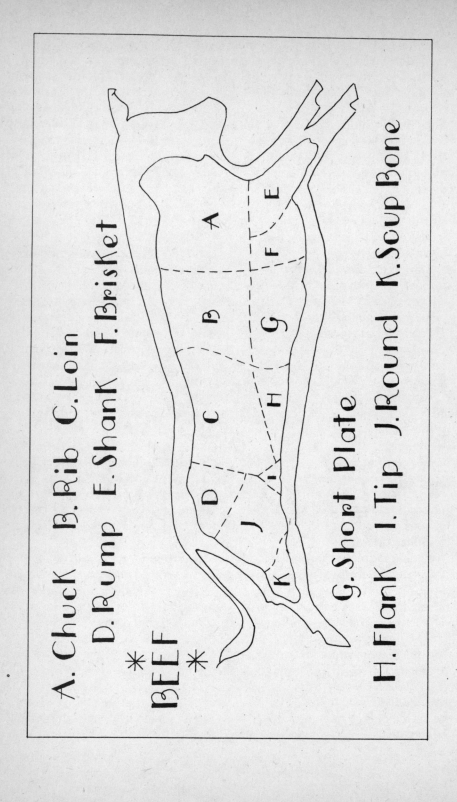

BEEF

A. Chuck   B. Rib   C. Loin
D. Rump   E. Shank   F. Brisket
G. Short Plate
H. Flank   I. Tip   J. Round   K. Soup Bone

Of all meats, beef is probably the most fortifying and nourishing. It is graded in three categories, depending upon its firmness and fine-grained texture, together with its proportion of sinews and fat. The first category includes filet, sirloin, top of the rump, and inner parts of the flank and round; this book does not concern itself with this category. The second category, including the top of the sirloin, plate, top ribs, shoulder, and chuck, does find a place in some of these recipes, as does the third category: flank, brisket, leg, neck, shin, and tail. There are eight U.S. Department of Agriculture classifications of beef according to its quality. In order of descending desirability, they are: prime, choice, good, standard, commercial, utility, cutter, and canner. Wherever *U.S.* appears in front of the classification, one is assured that the beef conforms to the standard set and indicated by the Department of Agriculture.

Americans are the largest meat-eaters in the world. Our average consumption is 175 pounds a year per person. The greater part of this amount is beef, the leading food in U.S. households. The English, known worldwide as "Beefeaters," consume an average of 110 pounds of meat per person a year; the French eat only one half as much as the English.

The best beef comes from five- to six-year-old grass- and corn-fed oxen. Cow's meat is for the most part inferior to that of the ox. As an energy food, beef contains an average of 15 to 20 percent of protein and a considerable quantity of easily digested fats.

American beef has earned the reputation of being equal to the world's best. This quality results from improvements in recent years in breeding, feeding, and shipping the processed meat. The fabled longhorn Texas steer, once our standard beef cattle, is now virtually obsolete because of crossbreeding with fine imported stock. Range feeding has been augmented by scientifically controlled grain feeding, particularly during the period prior to slaughter. It is curious and confusing, however, that throughout the United States there may be several names for the same cut of beef. For this reason, the accompanying diagram is included to aid the cook in purchasing.

Veal, the dressed carcass of a calf or young cow, is more difficult to keep than beef. It requires gentle, slow cooking to develop its nutritive qualities. Milk-fed calves, six weeks of age or younger, produce the best veal. The finest, most costly category comprises the round, rump, loin, and rib roast. The less expensive second category includes the shoulder and shoulder chops, breast, and flank. In general, however, veal tends to be expensive; for this reason, only a few recipes for it are offered here. Recipes for veal breast and shank are interchangeable with those for the same cuts of lamb. Veal should be very light pink and firm to the touch. When buying veal, avoid any grayish or reddish color, grayish bones (an indication that the calf is too old), watery-looking flesh, any flabbiness (a sign that the calf has been overfed), and yellowish outside fat.

Pot Roasts

The term *pot roast* refers to less tender cuts of beef — the brisket, chuck, or round. The meat, well browned and left in one piece to be carved at the time of serving, is cooked slowly and for a long time in a tightly covered pot with vegetables, seasonings, and only a little liquid. Traditionally cooked on top of the stove, the following pot roasts may also be cooked in the oven (tightly covered, at 300° F. for 2½ hours). Personal desire for an uncluttered kitchen leads me to a more frequent use of the oven; but the choice ultimately depends upon your preference.

The recipes lend themselves to experimentation — with herbs and seasonings and with different ingredients. For example, the flavor of any pot roast is improved by the addition of a carrot, a turnip, and a parsnip, all scraped and sliced, and a rib or two of celery with their leaves. These vegetables, known as aromatics, may be removed at the conclusion of the cooking or may be incorporated as part of the completed dish. If desired, the broth derived from the cooking may be thickened to make a sauce; for the most part, the recipes are written this way. If they are not, however, 2 tablespoons of flour mixed to a smooth paste with a little cold water may be gently stirred into the broth and cooked until the resultant sauce is thickened and smooth. Unthickened broth may be served as a sauce too, of course; and any that is left over makes a fine soup base.

Baked Pot Roast: America
Serves 6 ■ Doubles ■ Refrigerates ■ Freezes

Preparation: 30 minutes ■ Cooking: 5½ hours in a 250° F. oven

1 4-pound boneless piece
of chuck, round, or
rump
Salt
Pepper
Thyme

On a large piece of heavy duty foil, place the meat and season it with salt, pepper, and a generous sprinkling of thyme.

2 onions, grated
2 ripe tomatoes, peeled,
seeded, and chopped
(canned tomatoes,
drained, will do)

Combine the onion and tomato and spoon the mixture over the meat. Seal the edges of the foil with a double fold, so that the juices will not escape. It should not be a tight "package."

At this point you may stop and continue later.

Arrange the roast in a baking pan and cook it at 250° F. for 5½ hours.

Serve the dish with Baked White Potatoes, page 301.

Pot Roast with Sweet and Pungent Sauce: Follow the directions for
Baked Pot Roast, above, making the following changes: omit the salt and pepper when seasoning the meat; place it in an ovenproof baking dish and wrap the foil around the entire "package" — dish *and* meat; bake the pot roast as directed for 4½ hours at 250° F.; pour over Sweet and Pungent Sauce (page 311) for the final hour of cooking; refold the foil tightly.

Serve the dish with Boiled Rice, page 303.

Pot Roast with Cabbage and Potatoes: America
Serves 6 ■ Doubles ■ Refrigerates

Preparation: 30 minutes ■ Cooking: 3 hours

2 tablespoons margarine
2 tablespoons oil
1 4-pound pot roast,
   trimmed of excess fat

In a heavy kettle or flameproof casserole, heat the margarine and oil and brown the meat well on all sides. Remove it.

4 onions, chopped
3 cloves garlic, chopped
4 carrots, scraped and
   chopped
2 turnips, scraped and
   chopped
4 quarts cold water

In the remaining fat, cook the vegetables, stirring, until the onion is translucent. Replace the meat.

Add the water to the meat and vegetables; bring it rapidly to a boil, and skim the surface as necessary.

3 tomatoes, peeled,
   seeded, and chopped
   (1 1-pound can will do)
½ cup (packed) chopped
   celery leaves
1 teaspoon ground allspice
2 bay leaves
2 teaspoons chili powder
1 teaspoon marjoram
1 teaspoon thyme
2 tablespoons brown sugar
1 tablespoon salt
½ teaspoon pepper

Reduce the heat; add the tomatoes and other vegetables, together with the celery leaves and seasonings. Simmer the meat, covered, for 2½ hours, or until it is tender.

At this point you may stop and continue later.

If necessary, reheat the contents of the kettle. Transfer the meat to a serving dish and keep it warm. Strain and reserve the broth. (If desired, the vegetables may be whirled in the container of an electric blender and the purée added later to the broth.)

1 cabbage, trimmed and cut
   in sixths
12 new potatoes, washed,
   unpeeled

Bring the reserved broth to a boil, add the cabbage and potatoes and, over high heat, cook them, uncovered, for 20 minutes, or until they are tender.

Serve in soup plates: a cabbage wedge and two potatoes in each. Carve the meat across the grain and serve it. If desired, add the vegetable purée to the broth and serve the mixture separately, as a sauce.

This Creole recipe provides an unusual "boiled dinner." It requires only the accompaniment of a *good* bread, if desired, and a hearty dessert. I favor serving the dish with Dijon-style mustard, and perhaps offering for dessert apple pie with a piece of sharp cheddar cheese.

Pot Roast with Cream Sauce: America

Serves 6 ■ Doubles ■ Refrigerates ■ Freezes

Preparation: 45 minutes ■ Cooking: 3 hours

2 tablespoons margarine
2 tablespoons oil
1 4-pound pot roast, trimmed of excess fat
1 cup water

In a heavy kettle or flameproof casserole, heat the margarine and oil and brown the meat well on all sides. Add the water and simmer the meat, tightly covered, for 2½ hours, or until it is tender; more water may be added as necessary. Remove the saucepan from the heat and allow it to stand for 20 minutes.

At this point you may stop and continue later.

Reheat the meat if necessary, slice it thinly, arrange it on a serving plate, and keep it warm. Reserve any remaining broth for the sauce and for use in another dish.

4 tablespoons margarine
2 tablespoons flour
½ cup reserved broth
1 13-ounce can evaporated milk
2 cloves garlic, put through a press
¼ cup chopped parsley
Juice of 1 lemon
1½ teaspoons salt
½ teaspoon pepper

In a saucepan, melt the margarine; into it stir the flour and, over gentle heat, cook the *roux*, stirring, for a few minutes. Gradually add the broth and evaporated milk, stirring constantly until the mixture is thickened and smooth. Stir in the garlic, parsley, lemon juice, salt, and pepper. Cook the sauce, stirring it, for 2 minutes, pour it over the meat, and serve.

Serve the dish with Noodles, page 307.

Served in this manner, the brisket will assume quite an elegant appearance. The sauce is delicious on noodles.

Pot Roast with Ginger Sauce: Follow the directions above, omitting the lemon juice from the sauce and adding to the *roux* 2 teaspoons ground ginger and 1 teaspoon turmeric.

Pot Roast with Horseradish and Currant Sauce: Follow the directions above, omitting the lemon juice from the sauce and adding to it ⅓ cup currants, 1 or 2 tablespoons prepared horseradish to taste, 2 tablespoons brown sugar, 2 tablespoons vinegar, and ½ teaspoon prepared mustard. Serve the pot roast with additional horseradish.

Pot Roast with Carrots and Turnips: France
Serves 6 ■ Doubles ■ Refrigerates

Preparation: 45 minutes ■ Cooking: 2½ hours in a 300° F. oven

This traditional, eighteenth-century recipe from Provence may be made a day ahead, cooked (leave the meat in the broth), refrigerated, and defatted the next day, before reheating to serve. The dish may also be served cold, jellied.

1 4-pound pot roast, trimmed of excess fat
2 cloves garlic, split
Salt
Pepper
4 tablespoons bacon fat

Rub the meat well with the garlic and with salt and pepper to taste. In a heavy kettle or flameproof casserole, heat the bacon fat and brown the meat well on all sides.

6 onions, quartered
6 carrots, scraped and cut into 1-inch rounds
3 ribs celery, coarsely chopped
6 turnips, scraped and cut into 1-inch rounds

Add the vegetables.

At this point you may stop and continue later.

2 cups water, in which 3 beef bouillon cubes have been dissolved
3 whole cloves
5 peppercorns
Zest of 1 lemon *or* of 1 orange

To the contents of the casserole, add the bouillon and seasonings. Bring the liquid to a boil. Transfer the casserole to a 300° F. oven and cook the meat, covered, for 2½ hours, or until it is tender.

Serve the dish with Crusty Bread, page 300.

Pot Roast with Dried Fruit: Netherlands
Serves 6 ■ Doubles ■ Refrigerates

Preparation: 45 minutes ■ Cooking: 2½ hours

I say the recipe is Netherlandish only because of the beer used in it. In the Dutch and Flemish parts of Europe, beer is used as a cooking liquid just as wines are in other cuisines. If desired, six boneless flank steaks may be prepared using this recipe.

2 tablespoons margarine 2 tablespoons oil 1 4-pound pot roast, trimmed of excess fat 2 onions, chopped	In a heavy kettle or flameproof casserole, heat the margarine and oil and brown the meat well on all sides. Add the onions and cook them until translucent.
1 cup warm water 4 tablespoons honey 4 tablespoons brown sugar ¾ teaspoon ground cinnamon 1 teaspoon ground ginger 1½ teaspoons salt	Combine the water, honey, and seasonings. Pour the mixture over the meat and simmer it, tightly covered, for 2 hours, or until it is tender.
1 11-ounce package dried fruit 1 12-ounce can stale ale or beer	While the meat is cooking, soak the fruit in the ale. *At this point you may stop and continue later.*
2 tablespoons flour	Drain the fruit, reserving the ale. Mix the flour and a little of the ale to form a smooth paste; add it to the remaining ale, stirring. Add the mixture to the contents of the saucepan, stirring gently.
6 medium potatoes, peeled and halved, *or* 12 whole new potatoes, unpeeled Reserved dried fruit	Arrange the potatoes and fruit around the meat. Continue to simmer the dish for 30 minutes, or until the potatoes are tender and the sauce is thickened. (The final cooking time will depend upon your choice of potatoes.)

Pot Roast with Eggplant and Peppers: Greece
Serves 6 ■ Doubles ■ Refrigerates

Preparation: 45 minutes ■ Cooking: 2½ hours

In Greece, eggplants are very small — and very good. Be sure to get a good-sized one for this recipe.

2   tablespoons margarine
2   tablespoons oil
1   4-pound pot roast, trimmed of excess fat
Salt
Pepper

In a heavy kettle or flameproof casserole, heat the margarine and oil and brown the meat well on all sides. Season and remove it.

2   onions, chopped
1   clove garlic, chopped

In the remaining fat, cook the onion and garlic until translucent. Replace the meat.

1   8-ounce can tomato sauce
1⅓ cups water, in which 2 beef bouillon cubes have been dissolved
1   tablespoon wine vinegar
2   tablespoons brown sugar
1   bay leaf
1   teaspoon ground cumin

Combine the tomato sauce, bouillon, and seasonings. Pour the mixture over the meat, bring it to the boil, reduce the heat, and simmer the pot roast, covered, for 2 hours, or until it is tender.

At this point you may stop and continue later.

1   eggplant, peeled and cut into bite-size pieces
2   green peppers, seeded and coarsely chopped
12 small onions, peeled

To the contents of the kettle, add the eggplant, pepper, and onions. Continue to simmer the dish, covered, for 30 minutes, or until the eggplant and onions are tender.

Serve the dish with Boiled Rice, page 303.

Pot Roast with Lima Beans and Barley: Israel
Serves 6 ■ Doubles ■ Refrigerates ■ Freezes

Preparation: 45 minutes ■ Cooking: 5 hours (in a 250° F. oven, if desired)

Cholent, this Jewish Sabbath one-dish meal, is very hearty. Note that the potatoes may be omitted if desired. The recipe may also be made with short ribs; allow about 5 pounds of short ribs for 6 servings.

1 cup dried lima beans,
    soaked overnight in
    2 quarts water

1 4-pound pot roast, trimmed of excess fat	In a heavy kettle or flameproof casserole, arrange the meat. Add the onion, garlic, beans, barley, and potatoes.
2 onions, chopped	
1 clove garlic, chopped	
Reserved beans	
½ cup pearl barley	
6 medium-sized potatoes, peeled and quartered (optional)	
2 tablespoons flour	Combine the flour and seasonings and sprinkle the mixture over the contents of the kettle.
1 tablespoon salt	
½ teaspoon pepper	
1 teaspoon ground ginger	
1 tablespoon paprika	
Reserved bean water	Bring the water to a boil, and pour it over the meat. Simmer the dish, tightly covered, over very gentle heat, for 5 hours, or cook it in the oven, as suggested.

Corned Beef with Vegetables: America

Serves 6 ■ Doubles ■ Refrigerates

Preparation: 45 minutes ■ Cooking: 3¾ hours

New England Boiled Dinner, perhaps the most celebrated classic of American one-dish meals, came to this country from Tudor England, brought by the colonists. As we eat it today, it was enjoyed by Shakespeare and by Queen Elizabeth herself, who enjoyed a tankard of good ale with her meals.

1 4-pound corned brisket of beef, trimmed of excess fat

Under cold water, rinse the meat to remove surface brine. In a heavy kettle or flameproof casserole, arrange the meat, cover it with cold water, and bring the water to a boil; allow it to boil vigorously for 5 minutes. Reduce the heat, remove the scum, and simmer the meat, covered, for 3 hours, or until it is tender.

6 medium-sized potatoes, peeled and halved
6 carrots, scraped and cut into 1-inch rounds
3 turnips, scraped and cut into 1-inch rounds
1 medium-sized cabbage, cut into sixths

Prepare the vegetables. Reserve the potatoes in cold water to prevent their darkening.

At this point you may stop and continue later.

Remove the meat from the broth. Add the potatoes, carrots, and turnips, and cook them for 15 minutes. Add the cabbage and continue to cook all the vegetables for 20 minutes longer, or until they are tender. Replace the meat to heat it through.

Arrange the meat in a serving dish with the vegetables around it. Serve the dish with horseradish or a good Dijon mustard.

Flank Steak with Onion: Brazil

Serves 6 ■ Doubles ■ Refrigerates

Preparation: 45 minutes ■ Cooking: 2¼ hours in a 350° F. oven

This recipe may also be made with breast of lamb or veal.

1 3-pound flank steak Salt Pepper	Season the meat to taste. Roll it with the grain and tie it.
2 tablespoons margarine 2 tablespoons oil	In a heavy kettle or flameproof casserole, heat the margarine and oil and brown the meat well on both sides. Remove it.
2 onions, chopped 1 clove garlic, chopped 1 rib celery, chopped	In the remaining fat, cook the onion, garlic, and celery until the onion is translucent. Replace the meat.
5 cups hot water in which 3 beef bouillon cubes have been dissolved	Pour the bouillon over the meat. Bake it, tightly covered, at 350° F. for 2 hours, or until it is tender. If desired, the meat may be simmered on top of the stove. *At this point you may stop and continue later.*
2 tablespoons olive oil 4 onions, chopped 2 teaspoons ground cumin	In a skillet, heat the oil and in it cook the onion until translucent. Stir in the cumin and cook the mixture, stirring, for a few minutes. Spread the onion over the meat and bake the dish, uncovered, at 400° F. for 15 minutes, or until the onion is lightly browned. The meat may be sliced and served from the kettle or casserole. If desired, the sauce may be thickened (see *Roux*, page 17), using 3 tablespoons of flour.

Serve the dish with Mashed White Potatoes, page 302.

Southern-Style Meat Hash: America

Serves 6 ■ Doubles ■ Refrigerates ■ Freezes

Preparation: 30 minutes ■ Cooking: 1 hour

This homely and satisfying recipe is contributed by James Litton, a friend of nearly twenty years. Of the hash, James writes: "In parts of the South, it is served on buttered toast, or on leftover biscuits that have been split, toasted, and buttered. I find the recipe a good way to use frozen bits and pieces of leftover meats — all kinds — in a tasty dish. Indeed, I make a large casserole and use it for several meals. Don't worry about overcooking or reheating it — it gets better each time."

If desired, the hard-boiled egg may be omitted and each serving of hash topped with a poached egg.

4 tablespoons butter
4 onions, chopped
2 or 3 cups leftover cooked beef, lamb, pork, veal, or chicken (or a combination of your choice), diced
4 potatoes, peeled and diced
1 10½-ounce can condensed beef broth
1 tablespoon Worcestershire sauce
Salt
Pepper

In a large skillet or flameproof casserole, heat the butter and in it cook the onion until translucent. Add the meat, potatoes, broth, Worcestershire sauce, and salt and pepper to taste. Bring the liquid to a boil, reduce the heat, and simmer the mixture, covered, for ½ hour.

Uncover the hash and continue to cook it for ½ hour, or until most of the liquid is absorbed.

At this point you may stop and continue later. (Cover the hash to keep it moist.)

2 hard-boiled eggs, chopped (optional)
Leftover gravy
Leftover cooked vegetables (beans, carrots, peas, etc.)

Stir the egg, gravy, and any vegetables into the hash. Heat the dish, covered, until it is of desired serving temperature.

Swiss Steak with Tomato Sauce
Serves 6 ■ Doubles ■ Refrigerates ■ Freezes

Preparation: 30 minutes ■ Cooking: 2½ hours in a 300° F. oven

The classic "Swiss Steak" — is it from Switzerland? I honestly do not know and cannot find out! It is, in any case, a hearty, savory dish.

Seasoned flour
1 2½- or 3-pound rump, round, or chuck of beef, cut 1½ inches thick
2 tablespoons margarine
2 tablespoons oil

In the seasoned flour, dredge the meat. To tenderize it, beat the flour in with a meat hammer. In a heavy skillet or flameproof casserole with tight-fitting lid, heat the margarine and oil and brown the meat well on both sides. Sprinkle over the meat any remaining flour.

2 onions, sliced
1 teaspoon basil
½ teaspoon marjoram

Over the meat, arrange a layer of the onion and sprinkle it with the herbs.

At this point you may stop and continue later.

1 8-ounce can tomato sauce
½ cup water, in which 1 beef bouillon cube has been dissolved

Pour the liquids over the meat. Simmer the dish, tightly covered, for 2½ hours, or until it is tender. (If desired, it may be cooked in the oven at 300° F. for 2½ hours.)

Serve the dish with Mashed Sweet Potatoes, page 302.

Short Ribs

Short ribs, lying under the rib roast, are rather loaflike in shape. The rib end is encased by the meat. Short ribs are either braised or marinated to tenderize them before roasting or barbecuing. If you purchase lean short ribs, or prepare the recipe a day in advance, so that any fat may be easily removed from the refrigerated dish, short ribs may be used in the recipes for pot roasts, pages 23 to 31. The cooking time is 2½ hours, either at a simmer or in a 300° F. oven. You should allow 1 pound of short ribs per serving.

Braised Short Ribs: America
Serves 6 ■ Doubles ■ Refrigerates ■ Freezes

Preparation: 45 minutes ■ Cooking: 2½ hours (in a 300° F. oven, if desired)

2 tablespoons margarine
2 tablespoons oil
2 cloves garlic, peeled
   and split
6 pounds lean short ribs,
   trimmed of excess fat
Seasoned flour

In a heavy kettle or flameproof casserole, heat the margarine and oil and cook the garlic until it is golden; remove and discard it. Dredge the short ribs in the seasoned flour and, in the flavored fat, brown them well on both sides.

12 small onions, peeled
6   carrots, scraped and
    cut into 1-inch rounds
3   ribs celery, cut into
    1-inch pieces
1   green pepper, seeded
    and coarsely chopped
    (optional)

Arrange the vegetables over and around the meat. Prepare the bouillon mixture. Sprinkle over the herbs.

At this point you may stop and continue later.

1½ cups water, in which
    2 beef bouillon cubes
    have been dissolved
1   bay leaf, crumbled
1   teaspoon marjoram
1   teaspoon thyme

Pour the bouillon over the contents of the kettle, bring it rapidly to a boil, reduce the heat, and simmer the short ribs, tightly covered, for 2½ hours, or until they are tender. (If desired, you may cook the dish in the oven.)

The recipe may be varied by arranging the floured short ribs side by side in a roasting pan and browning them at 500° F. on the middle shelf of the oven for 25 minutes. In this way, any excess fat may be discarded at once. Transfer the meat to a kettle or casserole and deglaze the drained roasting pan with the bouillon mixture before adding it to the other ingredients. This technique reduces the cooking time slightly.

In addition to, or in place of, the vegetables listed here, you may use 6 medium potatoes, peeled and halved, 3 parsnips, scraped and cut in 1-inch rounds, and 3 turnips, scraped and cut in 1-inch rounds.

Short Ribs with Chick-Peas: Turkey
Serves 6 ■ Doubles ■ Refrigerates ■ Freezes

Preparation: 45 minutes ■ Cooking: 2½ hours (in a 300° F. oven, if desired)

2 tablespoons margarine
2 tablespoons oil
6 pounds lean short ribs, trimmed of excess fat
Salt
Pepper

In a heavy kettle or flameproof casserole, heat the margarine and oil and brown the short ribs well on both sides; season them. Remove and reserve. Discard all but 3 tablespoons of the fat.

2 onions, chopped
2 ribs celery, chopped, with their leaves
4 teaspoons flour

In the reserved fat, cook the onion and celery until translucent. Stir in the flour. Replace the short ribs.

2 cups water, in which 3 beef bouillon cubes have been dissolved
1 teaspoon dried mint
½ teaspoon oregano

Over the contents of the kettle, pour the liquid and sprinkle the seasonings; bring the bouillon to a boil, reduce the heat, and simmer the short ribs, tightly covered, for 2½ hours, or until they are tender. (If desired, you may cook the dish in the oven.)

At this point you may stop and continue later.

1 20-ounce can chick-peas, drained

Add the chick-peas and continue to cook the dish only long enough to heat them through.

Serve the dish with Tomato Pilaf, page 306.

Savory Short Ribs: England
Serves 6 ■ Doubles ■ Refrigerates ■ Freezes

Preparation: 30 minutes ■ Cooking: 10 minutes in a 450° F. oven, followed by 1¼ hours in a 400° F. oven

No need to "stop and continue later" in this recipe. A delicious entrée for a wintry evening.

Seasoned flour
6 pounds lean short ribs, trimmed of excess fat

In the seasoned flour, dredge the short ribs heavily. On a greased rack in a roasting pan, arrange the meat and bake it at 450° F. for 10 minutes.

1 tablespoon margarine, melted
1 tablespoon Worcestershire sauce
Dash of cayenne
1 teaspoon curry powder
1 teaspoon dry mustard
1 teaspoon salt
1 teaspoon sugar

Meanwhile, in a mixing bowl, combine these seven ingredients. Reduce the heat to 400° F., brush the ribs with the sauce, and continue to bake them, brushing often with the sauce, for 1¼ hours, or until they are tender.

Serve the dish with Mashed Turnips, page 296.

Short Ribs with Sweet Peppers
Serves 6 ■ Doubles ■ Refrigerates

Preparation: 40 minutes ■ Cooking: 3 hours in a 300° F. oven

Made with sweet red *and* green peppers, this dish is colorfully appetizing. Regardless of the color combination, however, it is satisfyingly tasty.

2 tablespoons margarine
2 tablespoons oil
5 pounds short ribs, cut into 3-inch lengths
Salt
Pepper

In a flameproof casserole, heat the margarine and oil and brown the short ribs well on all sides; season them. Remove them to absorbent paper and reserve them.

4 green and/or sweet red peppers, seeded and cut into 2-inch julienne
2 onions, chopped
1 clove garlic, chopped

In the remaining fat, cook the pepper until it is barely tender. Remove and reserve it. To the fat add the onion and garlic and cook them until translucent.

1 cup water, in which 1 beef bouillon cube has been dissolved
2 teaspoons Worcestershire sauce
1 tablespoon cornstarch
Water

Add the bouillon to the onion. Mix together the Worcestershire sauce and cornstarch, adding a little water as needed to make a smooth paste; add the mixture to the casserole and, over medium heat, cook it, stirring constantly, until it is thickened and smooth. Replace the meat.

Bake the casserole, covered, at 300° F. for 3 hours, or until the short ribs are tender.

At this point you may stop and continue later.

Reserved peppers

Add the reserved peppers and continue cooking the dish for 5 minutes, or until the peppers are heated through.

Serve the dish with Rice en Casserole, page 303.

Stews

There are so many beef stews! The selection here comprises one classic recipe with variants, and several others, rather original in their ingredients and tastes. In these recipes you may use any of the less expensive cuts: chuck, flank, brisket, or neck. I prefer lean chuck, which I always pick over fussily, removing any excess fat and cutting the pieces into generous bite-size pieces. Pieces cut too small tend to shrivel and "dry" even though cooked in liquid. The recipes lend themselves to alteration and experimentation, and because one aim of this book is to evoke a sense of fun and adventure in cooking, I urge you to explore — with different vegetables, herbs, whatever and wherever your fancy dictates. If desired, these recipes may be prepared a day in advance of serving, cooked, and refrigerated overnight; in this way any excess fat is easily removed the next day before reheating the dish. The following dishes may also be made with stewing veal; in this case, use chicken bouillon cubes and reduce the cooking time by nearly half.

Old-Fashioned Beef Stew
Serves 6 ■ Doubles ■ Refrigerates ■ Freezes

Preparation: 35 minutes ■ Cooking: 2½ hours (in a 300° F. oven, if desired)

2 tablespoons margarine 2 tablespoons oil 3 pounds lean chuck, cut into bite-size pieces Salt Pepper	In a heavy skillet or flameproof casserole, heat the margarine and oil and brown the meat well on all sides; season it. Remove and reserve it.
2 onions, chopped 1 clove garlic, chopped 3 tablespoons flour	In the remaining fat, cook the onion and garlic until translucent. Stir in the flour. Replace the meat.
6 carrots, scraped and cut into 1-inch rounds 12 small onions, peeled and quartered 1 10-ounce package frozen peas, fully thawed to room temperature 6 medium-sized potatoes, peeled and quartered	Prepare the vegetables. Reserve the potatoes in cold water to prevent their darkening.
3 cups water, in which 3 beef bouillon cubes have been dissolved	Prepare the bouillon.
1 bay leaf, crumbled 2 whole cloves ½ teaspoon celery seed 1 teaspoon marjoram ½ teaspoon oregano ½ teaspoon rosemary ½ teaspoon thyme ½ teaspoon pepper 2 teaspoons sugar ¼ cup chopped parsley	To the contents of the kettle, add the seasonings. *At this point you may stop and continue later.* Over the contents of the kettle, pour the bouillon; bring it rapidly to a boil, reduce the heat, and simmer the meat, tightly covered, for 2 hours.

Add the reserved carrots, onions, and potatoes. Continue to simmer the stew, covered, for 25 minutes. Add the peas and cook them, covered, for 5 minutes longer, or until the beef and vegetables are tender.

If desired, the stew may be cooked in the oven.

Serve the dish with Crusty Bread, page 300.

SAVORY

I cannot give a nationality for the recipe on pages 42–43; it is legion throughout the Western world since time immemorial. This is my version of the basic formula. Here follow some variations.

Beef Stew with Ale — *Flanders:* Use ale as the cooking liquid. Render ¼ pound salt pork, diced; remove the dice to absorbent paper and reserve them. In the fat, brown the meat; remove and reserve it. Cook the chopped onion and garlic and add the flour. Replace the pork dice and meat. Omit the potatoes and peas. As seasonings, use 1 teaspoon salt, 1 teaspoon sugar, 2 tablespoons mustard, and 2 tablespoons cider vinegar. Use 2 cans stale ale as the liquid ingredient, or, if preferred, 1 can stale ale and water to equal 3 cups. Cook the stew as directed and serve it with Boiled White Potatoes, page 301.

Beef Stew with Figs — *India:* Brown the meat and season it with 2 teaspoons ground cinnamon. Omit the seasonings as listed. Sprinkle over the flour. Add the bouillon and simmer the meat for 1½ hours. Combine ½ cup honey, ¼ cup wine vinegar, 2 teaspoons salt, and 1 teaspoon pepper. Add this mixture to the kettle and continue simmering the meat for ½ hour, or until it is tender. Add the carrots and quartered onions and cook them for ½ hour, or until they are tender. Omit the potatoes. Add 1 17-ounce can of figs, drained, 1 cup of golden raisins, and, if desired, 1 cup of slivered almonds. Cook only long enough to heat the figs. Garnish the stew generously with chopped parsley and serve it with Boiled Rice, page 303.

Beef Stew with Grapes — *Rumania:* Dredge the meat in seasoned flour before browning it in a skillet; remove it to a heavy skillet or flameproof casserole. In the remaining fat, cook 3 thickly sliced onions and 2 cloves garlic, chopped, until translucent; add them to the casserole. With 1 cup of water deglaze the skillet and add the liquid to the casserole. Add the potatoes and carrots; omit the small onions, but add 1 small eggplant, cut in chunks, 1 green pepper, coarsely chopped, and 3 ribs celery, coarsely chopped. Add the bay leaf, marjoram, oregano, thyme, and parsley; omit the other seasonings. Add 2 cups of water in which 3 beef bouillon cubes have been dissolved. Cook the stew as directed for 2¼ hours. Add 3 tomatoes, peeled, seeded, and chopped (canned tomatoes, drained, will do) and 2 cups seedless grapes, stemmed, rinsed, and drained on absorbent paper. Continue cooking the dish for 15 minutes, or until the beef is tender. Serve the stew with Crusty Bread, page 300.

Beef Stew with Horseradish — *Bulgaria:* Stir into the finished stew 4 or 5 tablespoons of prepared horseradish. A very good dish for those who enjoy horseradish — as I do.

Beef Stew with Peas — *Turkey:* Follow first two steps up to replacing the meat; then 2 packages of frozen peas are used and the other vegetables omitted. Prepare the bouillon. Of the seasonings, only the bay leaf, marjoram, rosemary, thyme, and sugar are used; add, however, 2 tablespoons dillweed. Cook the stew as directed, adding the peas for the final 5 minutes of cooking. If desired, 2 pounds of fresh peas may be used in place of the frozen ones; the cooking time will be increased. Serve the dish with Tomato Pilaf, page 306.

Beef and Onions: France

Serves 6 ■ Doubles ■ Refrigerates ■ Freezes

Preparation: 30 minutes ■ Cooking: 2½ hours in a 300° F. oven

This recipe is a classic French dish dating from the eighteenth century. If desired, it may be made a day in advance of serving, refrigerated, and any excess fat removed before reheating.

¼ pound salt pork, diced

In a flameproof casserole, render the salt pork until it is golden and crisp. Remove the dice to absorbent paper and reserve them.

18 small onions, peeled

In the fat, glaze the onions. Remove and reserve them.

3 pounds stewing beef, trimmed of excess fat and cut into bite-size pieces
2 tablespoons flour

In the fat, brown the beef well and sprinkle it with the flour. Replace the pork dice and onions.

1 bay leaf, crumbled
½ teaspoon marjoram
½ teaspoon savory
½ teaspoon thyme
2 ribs, celery, chopped, with their leaves
1½ teaspoons salt
¼ teaspoon pepper
2¼ cups water

Add the seasonings and water.

At this point you may stop and continue later.

Bake the casserole, covered, at 300° F. for 2½ hours, or until the meat is tender.

If desired, ¼ cup brandy and 1 cup dry red wine may be substituted for 1¼ cups of the water.

Serve the dish with Boiled White Potatoes, page 301.

Beef with Sour Cream: Rumania
Serves 6 ■ Doubles ■ Refrigerates ■ Freezes

Preparation: 40 minutes ■ Cooking: 2½ hours (in a 300° F. oven, if desired)

6 slices bacon, diced,
   or ¼ pound salt pork,
   diced
3 pounds lean chuck, cut
   into bite-size pieces

In a heavy kettle or flameproof casserole, render the bacon, remove it to absorbent paper, and reserve. In the remaining fat, brown the beef; remove and reserve it. Discard all but 4 tablespoons of the fat.

4 onions, chopped
2 cloves garlic, chopped
2 tablespoons flour
¾ teaspoon marjoram
2 teaspoons salt
¼ teaspoon pepper

In the fat, cook the onion and garlic until translucent. Stir in the flour. Add the seasonings. Replace the meat and bacon bits.

At this point you may stop and continue later.

1 cup water, in which 1
   beef bouillon cube has
   been dissolved
2 cups sour cream
Chopped parsley

To the contents of the kettle, add the bouillon and sour cream. Bring the liquid to a boil; reduce the heat, and simmer the meat, tightly covered, for 2½ hours, or until it is tender. Garnish the dish with chopped parsley.

Serve the dish with Noodles, page 307.

Very easy and rather elegant. If desired, fresh lemon juice may be added, to taste, just before serving.

Hungarian Goulash: Follow first step of previous recipe as directed; in second step, increase the onions to 6, omit the garlic, and stir into the onion, together with the flour, 2 tablespoons paprika, or more, to taste; omit the marjoram, but add the salt and pepper. Follow next step as described; the parsley is optional. A three-meat goulash may be made by using 1 pound each stewing lamb, pork, and veal; reduce the cooking time by about half. A delicately flavored dish. Goulash is traditionally served with Noodles, page 307.

Beef with Sweet and Pungent Sauce
Serves 6 ■ Doubles ■ Refrigerates

Preparation: 20 minutes ■ Cooking: 10 minutes

3 tablespoons oil
1½ to 2 pounds lean
   boneless chuck,
   trimmed of excess
   fat and cut into
   2-inch julienne
Oregano

In a wok or flameproof casserole, heat the oil and in it stir-fry the beef for 3 minutes. Season it with a sprinkling of oregano.

Add Sweet and Pungent Sauce, page 311; when it is hot, serve the dish.

Serve the dish with Baked Acorn Squash, page 294.

Beef and Vegetables: Norway

Serves 6 generously ■ Doubles ■ Refrigerates

Preparation: 30 minutes ■ Cooking: 4 hours

What a wonderful recipe this is! It yields virtually an entire meal. Serve the broth as a first course, garnished with chopped parsley. Serve the beef and vegetables, once again garnish with chopped parsley, if desired, as the main dish of the meal.

3 pounds beef marrow bones
3 quarts water

In a soup kettle, boil the beef bones in the water for 1½ hours. Remove and discard the bones; reserve the marrow.

3 pounds stewing beef, trimmed of excess fat and cut into bite-size pieces
2 bay leaves
3 cloves
1 teaspoon rosemary
2 teaspoons salt
½ teaspoon pepper

To the broth, add the beef and seasonings. Simmer the meat, covered, for 2 hours, or until it is tender. Remove and reserve the meat. Sieve the broth; chill it and remove and discard the fat. Return the meat to the soup kettle, together with the reserved marrow; add the broth, reserving 1 cup of it.

6 carrots, scraped and cut into ¼-inch slices
1 medium-sized head cabbage, cut into eighths

Bring the kettle to a boil. Add the vegetables and cook them, covered, for 20 minutes, or until they are just tender.

At this point you may stop and continue later.

From the hot broth, remove the meat and vegetables. Arrange them in a serving dish and keep them warm.

1 onion, chopped
Reserved broth
¼ cup cider vinegar
1 tablespoon brown sugar
1 tablespoon flour mixed until smooth with 3 tablespoons cold water
Salt
Pepper

Meanwhile, simmer the onion in the broth for 5 minutes. Add the vinegar, sugar, and flour mixture, stirring constantly until the sauce is thickened and smooth. Adjust the seasonings. Pour the sauce over the meat and vegetables.

Curried Beef Stews

Curried Beef Stews provide a pleasant change from the blander flavors of more standard recipes. The amounts of curry powder may vary from very small, for a hint of flavor, to large, for those experienced in Far Eastern cuisines. The amounts suggested here are for the average eater who enjoys curry and who, at the same time, wishes to retain the roof of his mouth. Curry powder, incidentally, as I am sure many readers already know, is not a single spice, but rather a combination of spices — sometimes as many as fifty — in different combinations and quantities. A good grade of commercial curry powder available in the supermarket blends fifteen different spices. If you are able to buy Madras curry, do so; it has a fuller, more aromatic flavor than many others. Any reputable brand of curry powder, however, will do well in these dishes, which are at their best served with rice and the various traditional condiments for curries, namely: chutneys of different kinds, chopped sweet pickle, raisins, chopped hard-boiled egg, chopped scallions, peanuts (preferably unsalted), pineapple tidbits, shredded coconut, and thin-sliced banana, all served in small side dishes. Presented in this way, curried beef stews make for a festive and colorful meal. Incidentally, these recipes may also be made with stewing lamb; merely adjust the simmering time to 1½ hours and the oven, if used, to 350° F. I find that all curried stews improve by being made 24 hours in advance of serving, then cooled, refrigerated, and the excess fat removed before reheating (be careful not to overcook at this time). Not only is the stew a "leaner" dish for this operation but also the flavors mellow and meld.

Curried Beef I: America
Serves 6 ■ Doubles ■ Refrigerates ■ Freezes

Preparation: 30 minutes ■ Cooking: 2½ hours (in a 300° F. oven, if desired)

Seasoned flour
3   pounds boneless stewing
    beef, trimmed of excess
    fat and cut into 1-inch
    cubes
2   tablespoons margarine
2   tablespoons oil

In the seasoned flour, dredge the meat well. In a heavy kettle or flameproof casserole, heat the margarine and oil and brown the meat. Remove it.

6   onions, chopped
2   teaspoons curry powder
    or more, to taste

In the fat, cook the onion until translucent. Stir in the curry powder. Replace the meat.

½   cup tomato juice
1   cup water, in which 2
    beef bouillon cubes have
    been dissolved

Prepare the liquid ingredients.

At this point you may stop and continue later.

Over the contents of the casserole, pour the bouillon, bring it rapidly to a boil; reduce the heat and simmer the meat, tightly covered, for 2½ hours, or until it is tender.

Serve the dish with Boiled Rice, page 303, and condiments for curries, page 50.

A very simple recipe, but a good one for people who would like to be introduced to curried dishes. If desired, 1 green pepper, cut in julienne, may be added for the final 30 minutes of cooking. Also, if desired, 1 cup sour cream may be stirred into the dish at the time of serving; this stretches the sauce but makes it more bland.

Curried Beef II: India
Serves 6 ■ Doubles ■ Refrigerates ■ Freezes

Preparation: 30 minutes ■ Cooking: 2½ hours (in a 300° F. oven, if desired)

A one-dish meal of curried beef, very easy to prepare.

2 tablespoons margarine 3 onions, sliced 2 cloves garlic, chopped	In a heavy kettle or flameproof casserole, heat the margarine and in it cook the onion and garlic until translucent.
½ teaspoon ground cardamom 1 tablespoon ground coriander 1 teaspoon ground cumin 1 teaspoon dry mustard 1½ teaspoons salt ¼ teaspoon pepper 2 tablespoons cider vinegar	Combine the dry seasonings and stir them into the onion. Stir in the vinegar.
3 pounds boneless stewing beef, trimmed of excess fat and cut into 1-inch cubes 3 tomatoes, peeled, seeded, and chopped (canned tomatoes, drained, will do)	Add the beef and tomatoes. Simmer the mixture, tightly covered, for 1 hour. *At this point you may stop and continue later.*
3 cups water, in which 3 beef bouillon cubes have been dissolved 1½ cups raw natural rice	Add the bouillon and continue to simmer the meat for 1 hour longer. Stir in the rice and cook the dish, tightly covered, for 30 minutes, or until the beef and rice are tender and the liquid is absorbed.

Serve the dish with condiments for curries, page 50.

Curried Beef with Fruit — *South Africa:* In a mixing bowl, combine 1 cup dried apple, coarsely chopped, ½ cup dried tenderized prunes, coarsely chopped, and ½ cup golden raisins; add 2 cups water and allow the fruit to stand 1 hour. Omit the seasoned flour, but brown 2 pounds of beef as directed (the fruit "stretches" the meat). Remove the meat and, in the fat, cook 3 chopped onions, until translucent. Stir in 1 tablespoon curry powder, or more to taste. Replace the meat. Drain and reserve the fruit. Add the fruit water to the kettle, and bring it rapidly to a boil; reduce the heat and simmer the beef, tightly covered, for 2 hours. Add the reserved fruit and the juice of 1 lemon; continue simmering the curry for ½ hour, or until the meat is tender. This curry should be moist, but not liquid.

LAMB

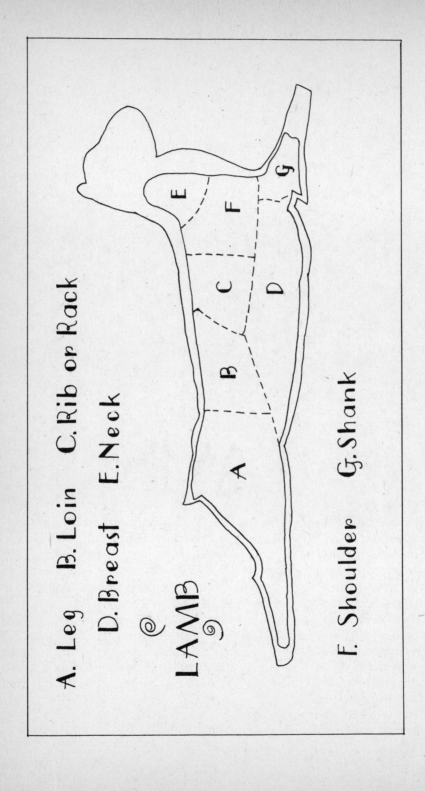

A. Leg   B. Loin   C. Rib or Rack

D. Breast   E. Neck

LAMB

F. Shoulder   G. Shank

One of our oldest sources of meat, the lamb is referred to in Exodus as a significant sacrificial offering. Indeed, the use of lamb as a table food has traditionally been related to its importance in religious observances. The role of lamb in the celebration of the Jewish Passover is another instance in point and, as a matter of fact, the widespread use of lamb as a popular food may have resulted very directly from religio-ethnic tradition.

The modern lamb, bred for nutritional value, offers more protein and far less fat than did its forefathers even fifty years ago; it is also a good source of the B vitamins and iron. "Spring" or young lamb is never more than a year old; now available year round, it should be light to medium pink and of a smooth and fine texture. Any fat should be firm. Lamb may be safely stored in the refrigerator, sealed with wrap, for up to five days; it may be safely frozen for three to four months. Once cooked, it should be tightly covered to prevent loss of moisture.

Lamb Breast

Sometimes called, rather preciously, "riblets," lamb breast is delicious braised. It is bony, but an excellent proof of the old saw about the sweetest meat lying nearest the bone.

Roast Stuffed Breast of Lamb: Syria

Serves 6 ■ Refrigerates

Preparation: 1¼ hours ■ Cooking: 2 hours in a 350° F. oven

5 pounds breast of lamb
Salt
Water

Soak the breast of lamb in salted water to cover for 1 hour. Dry the meat and sprinkle it lightly with salt.

4 tablespoons margarine
½ cup pine nuts
(optional)
1½ cups raw natural rice

In a large saucepan, heat the margarine and in it cook the pine nuts and rice, stirring, until they are very lightly browned.

1 teaspoon ground cinnamon
½ teaspoon ground cumin
½ teaspoon nutmeg
1½ teaspoons salt
½ teaspoon pepper
3 cups water
¼ cup chopped parsley
1 teaspoon dried mint
3 tablespoons margarine, melted

Stir the five seasonings into the rice mixture. Add the water and bring the liquid to a boil. Reduce the heat and simmer the rice, covered, for 15 minutes, or until it is tender and the liquid is absorbed. Toss the rice with the parsley and mint. With this mixture, stuff the lamb breast. Skewer it. Arrange the meat in a roasting pan and brush it liberally with the melted margarine.

At this point you may stop and continue later.

Roast the breast of lamb at 350° F. for 2 hours, or until it is tender. Baste the dish with the pan juices. Remove the lamb to a serving dish and carve it as you would a roast.

The stuffing absorbs the meat juices and is delightfully flavored. If desired, 1 20-ounce can chick-peas, drained, may be used in the stuffing; in this case, reduce the rice to 1 cup and the water to cook it to 2 cups.

Breast of Lamb with Orange Sauce: America
Serves 6 ■ Doubles ■ Refrigerates ■ Freezes

Preparation: 30 minutes ■ Cooking: 1½ hours
(in a 325° F. oven, if desired)

A dish simply made and refreshing to the taste.

Seasoned flour
4 pounds breast of lamb, separated and trimmed of excess fat
2 tablespoons margarine
2 tablespoons oil

In the seasoned flour, dredge the meat. In a heavy kettle or flameproof casserole, heat the margarine and oil and brown the meat. Remove and reserve it.

1 onion, chopped
½ teaspoon ground allspice
½ teaspoon thyme
1 tablespoon sugar
Grated rind of 1 orange

In the remaining fat, cook the onion until translucent. Stir in the seasonings. Replace the meat.

At this point you may stop and continue later.

2 cups orange juice

Over the contents of the casserole, pour the orange juice. Bring the liquid to a boil, reduce the heat, and simmer the dish, covered, for 1½ hours, or until the meat is tender.

Serve the dish with Baked or Boiled Sweet Potatoes, page 301.

Breast of Lamb with Peaches
Serves 6 ■ Doubles ■ Refrigerates

Preparation: 15 minutes ■ Cooking: 2 hours in a 325° F. oven;
5 minutes under a hot broiler

4 to 6 pounds lamb breast
1 clove garlic, split

Rub the meat with the garlic. Place it, fat side up, on a rack in a roasting pan. Bake it at 325° F. for 2 hours, or until it is tender; remove it from the oven. Pour the pan drippings into a saucepan and allow the fat to separate; remove and discard the fat.

½ cup water, in which 1 chicken bouillon cube has been dissolved
2 tablespoons soy sauce
½ cup brown sugar
1 teaspoon dry mustard

In a mixing bowl, combine the bouillon and soy sauce. Mix the sugar and mustard and add the mixture to the liquid.

At this point you may stop and continue later.

1 29-ounce can peach halves, drained

Around the meat, arrange the peach halves, so that their seed cavities face up. Spread the sauce over the meat and peaches. Under a hot broiler, cook the dish for 5 minutes, or until the sugar is melted and the peaches are hot. Meanwhile, heat the defatted pan drippings and serve them separately.

Serve the dish with Baked Acorn Squash, page 294.

If desired, 1 teaspoon curry powder, or more, to taste, may be used in place of the dry mustard.

Breast of Lamb with Rice: Turkey
Serves 6 ■ Doubles ■ Refrigerates ■ Freezes

Preparation: 30 minutes ■ Cooking: 1½ hours (in a 325° F. oven, if desired)

I am very fond of meat and rice dishes; the flavor of meat enhances rice, and rice absorbs the "fattiness" that meats sometimes have. This dish is a happy example of this complementary partnership.

2 tablespoons margarine
2 tablespoons oil
4 pounds breast of lamb, separated and trimmed of excess fat
Salt
Pepper

In a heavy kettle or flameproof casserole, heat the margarine and oil and brown the lamb pieces; season them. Remove and reserve them.

2 onions, chopped
1½ cups raw natural rice
½ teaspoon ground cardamom
½ teaspoon ground cinnamon
¼ teaspoon ground ginger
½ teaspoon ground nutmeg
¼ teaspoon pepper
1 teaspoon salt
⅓ cup currants

In the remaining fat, cook the onion until translucent. Add the rice, stirring to coat each grain. Stir in the seasonings. Replace the meat and sprinkle the currants over it.

1 8-ounce can tomato sauce
2 cups water, in which 1 beef bouillon cube has been dissolved

Combine the liquid ingredients.

At this point you may stop and continue later.

¼ cup chopped parsley

Over the contents of the kettle, pour the liquid and bring it to a boil; reduce the heat and simmer the dish, tightly covered, for 1½ hours, or until the meat and rice are tender and the liquid is absorbed. Garnish the dish with parsley.

Breast of Lamb with Vegetables: America
Serves 6 ■ Doubles ■ Refrigerates

Preparation: 30 minutes ■ Cooking: 1½ hours in a 325° F. oven

Such an easy dish! And a very savory one, redolent of many flavors.

6   carrots, scraped and cut into 1-inch rounds
1   medium eggplant, cut into 1-inch chunks
2   onions, thickly sliced
3   potatoes, peeled and quartered
3   zucchini, cut into 1-inch rounds
1   28-ounce can tomatoes, drained
2   bay leaves, crumbled
1   clove garlic, chopped
1   teaspoon marjoram
¼   cup chopped parsley
½   teaspoon savory
2   teaspoons salt
½   teaspoon pepper

In a casserole or large baking dish, toss together the vegetables and seasonings.

4   pounds breast of lamb, separated and trimmed of excess fat

In the vegetable mixture, stand the meat pieces in a circle.

At this point you may stop and continue later.

Bake the casserole, covered, at 325° F. for 1¼ hours; remove the cover and continue to bake it for 15 minutes longer.

Lamb Shanks

Lamb shanks are among my favorite meats. They seem capable of infinite variety — of taste, color, even of texture — depending upon the ingredients cooked with them. They are easily served. They are satisfying to the hungry eater but do not cause satiety in the finicky diner. The following recipes and their variants are ruthlessly selected from a group of nearly five times their number; not an easy task for one who would gladly have included them all! If desired, recipes for lamb shanks may be made with veal shanks, more expensive and more delicately flavored. The cooking time remains the same.

Lamb Shanks with Lentils: America
Serves 6 ■ Doubles ■ Refrigerates ■ Freezes

Preparation: 30 minutes ■ Cooking: 1½ hours in a 325° F. oven

2 tablespoons margarine
2 tablespoons oil
3 cloves garlic, split
6 lamb shanks
Salt
Pepper
3 onions, chopped

In a heavy kettle, heat the margarine and oil and cook the garlic until it is golden; then discard it. In the fat, brown the lamb shanks and season them. Remove them to a roasting pan and bake them at 325° F. for 1½ hours, or until they are tender. In the fat, cook the onion until translucent.

3 cups water, in which 3
   beef bouillon cubes
   have been dissolved
3 cups lentils, washed
   and drained
1 bay leaf, crumbled
½ teaspoon rubbed sage
1 teaspoon salt
¼ teaspoon pepper
3 tablespoons lamb
   drippings
3 scallions, chopped, with
   as much green as possible
¼ cup chopped parsley

Meanwhile, to the onion, add the first six ingredients. Bring the bouillon to the boil; reduce the heat and simmer the lentils, covered, for 1 hour, or until they are tender and the liquid is absorbed. Stir in the lamb drippings, scallions, and parsley.

To serve the dish, arrange the lentils in the middle of a large plate and place the lamb shanks around them, like the spokes of a wheel.

Lamb Shanks with Vegetables: Hungary
Serves 6 ■ Doubles ■ Refrigerates ■ Freezes
Preparation: 30 minutes ■ Cooking: 2 hours in a 325° F. oven

This recipe serves as a basis upon which several variations may be made.

Seasoned flour
6 lamb shanks
2 tablespoons margarine
2 tablespoons oil

In the seasoned flour, dredge the lamb shanks; reserve any excess flour. In a flameproof baking dish, heat the margarine and oil and brown the meat. Remove and reserve it.

2 onions, chopped
1 clove garlic, chopped
½ teaspoon oregano
1 tablespoon paprika, or more, to taste
2 tablespoons reserved seasoned flour

In the remaining fat, cook the onion and garlic until translucent. Stir in the oregano, paprika, and flour. Replace the meat.

6 new potatoes, scrubbed
12 small onions, peeled
6 carrots, scraped and cut into ¾-inch rounds

Prepare the vegetables and reserve them.

At this point you may stop and continue later.

1 1-pound can tomato sauce
1 cup water
1 cup sour cream

Combine the three liquid ingredients and pour the mixture over the meat. Bake the dish, covered, at 325° F. for 1½ hours. Add the reserved vegetables and continue cooking the lamb shanks 30 minutes longer, or until the meat and vegetables are tender.

Lamb Shanks with Celery — *Germany:* In first step, render 6 slices bacon, diced; drain them on absorbent paper and reserve them. In the fat, brown the flour-dredged lamb shanks. In next step, omit the paprika. With vegetables, add 6 ribs celery, chopped. For the cooking liquid, use 3 cups water in which 3 beef bouillon cubes have been dissolved. Add the liquid and continue as directed.

Lamb Shanks with Horseradish — *Sweden:* Follow first step as directed. Decrease the paprika to 1 teaspoon, and add ½ teaspoon rosemary, ¼ cup chopped parsley, and 3 or 4 tablespoons prepared horseradish. Omit the vegetables. For the cooking liquid, combine 1½ cups water, in which 1 beef bouillon cube has been dissolved, with 1 cup sour cream. Add the liquid and continue as directed. Serve the dish with Noodles, page 307.

Lamb Shanks with Lemon — *Italy:* In first step, brown the flour-dredged lamb shanks in 4 tablespoons olive oil. In next step, omit the paprika. Omit the vegetables. Add ¼ cup parsley, chopped, and the zest of 1 lemon, cut in fine julienne. For the cooking liquid, combine 2 cups water, in which 2 chicken bouillon cubes have been dissolved, and the juice of 1 lemon. Add the liquid and continue as directed. Serve the dish with Spaghetti, page 307.

Lamb Shanks with Pimiento — *Mexico:* In first step discard the fat after the meat has been browned. Omit next two steps; instead, add to the casserole 3 onions, sliced, 1 bay leaf, crumbled, 2 teaspoons chili powder, ½ teaspoon cinnamon, 2 teaspoons unsweetened cocoa, and ¼ teaspoon pepper. For the cooking liquid, combine 1½ cups water, in which 2 chicken bouillon cubes have been dissolved, with 1 1-pound can tomato sauce and 1 tablespoon Worcestershire sauce. Add the liquid, garnish the dish with 1 4-ounce jar pimientos, chopped, and continue as directed. Serve the dish with Boiled Sweet Potatoes, page 301.

Lamb Shanks with Rice — *Bulgaria:* Follow first step as directed. Increase the onions to 4 and omit the oregano and paprika; to the onions, add 1½ cups rice and cook the mixture, stirring, until each grain is coated; omit the additional reserved flour. Replace the lamb shanks, spooning the grain around them. Over the contents of the casserole, sprinkle 2 teaspoons dillweed, or more, to taste. Omit entirely the vegetables. For the cooking liquid, combine 2 cups water, in which 3 beef bouillon cubes have been dissolved, 1 cup sour cream, and the juice of 1 lemon. Add the liquid and continue as directed. This recipe may also be made with veal neck.

Lamb Shanks with Tomatoes: Arab States
Serves 6 ■ Doubles ■ Refrigerates

Preparation: 45 minutes ■ Cooking: 1¼ hours, starting in a 450° F. oven

4   tablespoons olive oil
6   lamb shanks
4   onions, thickly sliced

In a heavy skillet, heat the oil and brown the lamb shanks; remove them. In the fat, cook the onion until translucent.

1¼ teaspoons ground
     allspice
1   teaspoon nutmeg
1   teaspoon salt
½   teaspoon pepper
1   28-ounce can tomatoes

In a baking dish, arrange the lamb shanks in a single layer. Bake them, uncovered, at 450° F. for 30 minutes; turn them occasionally so that they color evenly. Add the onion and sprinkle over the seasonings. Spread the tomatoes evenly over all.

At this point you may stop and continue later.

Bake the dish, covered, at 325° F. for 30 minutes; remove the cover, and continue to bake it for 15 minutes longer, or until the shanks are tender.

Serve the dish with Dried Bean Casserole, page 309.

Lamb Shanks with Yogurt: Greece
Serves 6 ■ Doubles ■ Refrigerates

Preparation: 30 minutes ■ Cooking: 20 minutes in a 500° F. oven

So quick and so easy. There is no need for a "stop and continue later" point.

6 lamb shanks
Oregano
Thyme
Salt
Pepper

Rub the lamb shanks liberally with the oregano and thyme; add salt and pepper to taste. Arrange the shanks on a rack and broil them at 500° F. for 20 minutes (the meat should be moist and pink).

1 cup yogurt
1 tablespoon flour
Juice of ½ lemon, or
  more, to taste

In a saucepan, combine the yogurt and flour, stirring the mixture until it is smooth. Add the lemon juice, and, over gentle heat, cook the yogurt, stirring constantly, for a few minutes.

Reserved pan juices

Arrange the lamb shanks on a serving dish. Stir the pan juices with the yogurt. Serve the sauce separately.

Serve the dish with Tomato Pilaf, page 306.

Lamb Shanks with Sweet and Pungent Sauce: Follow the directions for Lamb Shanks with Yogurt, above. Follow first step as directed; omit next step; when serving the lamb shanks, pour over them hot Sweet and Pungent Sauce, page 311. Serve the dish with Boiled Rice, page 303.

Lamb Stews

Perhaps the most luxurious meat for lamb stews is cut from the shoulder — cheaper than the leg, but not as inexpensive as what the supermarket labels "stewing lamb." It is with this *latter* grade of lamb that these recipes are prepared. Before using the meat as directed, remove and discard any excess fat. Also, as is often suggested here, you will do well to make a dish of your choice one day in advance of serving it; let it cool, refrigerate it overnight, remove and discard the solidified fat, allow the dish to come fully to room temperature, and then reheat it gently, to avoid overcooking. For special occasions, a lamb stew made with boned shoulder is very pleasant; for more ordinary times, stewing lamb, with or without bones in it (do not remove the bones, for they add to the nutrition of the dish), is more economical and, I feel, even tastier.

Lamb and Barley Soup

Serves 6 ▪ Doubles ▪ Refrigerates ▪ Freezes

Preparation: 30 minutes ▪ Cooking: 2½ hours

A dish satisfying to both stomach and taste. If desired, it may be made with *un*boned lamb pieces, for the meat will fall from the bones when the soup is cooked. If prepared a day in advance of serving and refrigerated, any excess fat may be easily removed before the soup is reheated.

3 tablespoons margarine
2½ pounds lean stewing lamb, trimmed of excess fat and cut into 1-inch cubes
Salt
Pepper

In a heavy kettle, heat the margarine and in it brown the lamb: season it. Remove it to absorbent paper. Discard all but 3 tablespoons of the fat.

3 onions, sliced
¾ cup medium-sized pearl barley
3 ribs celery, chopped, with their leaves
3 cups coarsely chopped parsley
1 bay leaf
1½ teaspoons salt
¼ teaspoon pepper

In the fat, cook the onion until translucent. Replace the meat and add the barley, celery, parsley, and seasonings.

At this point you may stop and continue later.

6 cups water

To the contents of the kettle, add the water. Bring the liquid to a boil, reduce the heat, and simmer the meat, covered, for 2½ hours, or until it is very tender. Adjust the seasoning.

Serve the soup with Crusty Bread, page 300.

Traditional Lamb Stew

Serves 6 ■ Doubles ■ Refrigerates ■ Freezes

Preparation: 30 minutes ■ Cooking: 1¾ hours

If desired, this traditional stew may be made with pieces of *un*boned lamb; the meat will fall from the bones when the dish is cooked. If desired, 1 cup of dry sherry may be substituted for 1 cup of the water.

2 tablespoons margarine 2 tablespoons oil 2½ pounds stewing lamb, trimmed of excess fat and cut into bite-size pieces Salt Pepper	In a heavy kettle, heat the margarine and oil and brown the lamb; season it. Remove and reserve it.
2 onions, sliced 4 tablespoons flour	In the remaining fat, cook the onion until translucent. Stir in the flour and, over gentle heat, cook the mixture, stirring it often, for 5 minutes. Replace the meat.
3 cups water, in which 3 beef bouillon cubes have been dissolved	Add the bouillon, bring it to a boil, reduce the heat, and simmer the meat, covered, for 1 hour. *At this point you may stop and continue later.*
3 medium-sized potatoes, peeled and cut into chunks 3 large carrots, scraped and cut into 1-inch rounds 1½ teaspoons dillweed ¾ teaspoon thyme	Add the potatoes, carrots, and seasonings, and continue to cook the stew, covered, for 30 minutes, or until the vegetables are tender.
1 10-ounce package frozen peas, fully thawed to room temperature ¼ cup chopped parsley	Add the peas and cook the stew for 15 minutes longer. Garnish it with the parsley.

Serve the stew with Crusty Bread, page 300.

Irish Stew: A variant of this recipe: Grate 3 potatoes, peel and leave whole 6 others. Peel and slice 6 large onions. In a heavy kettle or flameproof casserole, put the grated potatoes. Add the onion in a single layer. Add the lamb; do not brown it. Sprinkle over the dillweed, thyme, 1½ teaspoons salt, and ½ teaspoon pepper. Add the whole potatoes. Over the contents of the kettle pour 3 cups of water. Cover the kettle very tightly. Simmer it for 2½ hours (or, if desired, cook it in a 350° F. oven for the same length of time).

Lamb Stew with Cranberries: Follow first step of Traditional Lamb Stew recipe, as directed. In second step, use 4 onions and 2 cloves of garlic, chopped. For the liquid ingredient, combine 1 6-ounce can tomato paste, 1 cup water, and 1½ cups cider or apple juice. Season the liquid with 1¼ teaspoons ground ginger and 1 teaspoon oregano. Cook the stew as directed. Omit vegetables and herbs, but add 2 cups whole cranberry sauce for the final hour of cooking. 15 minutes before serving, thicken the dish by mixing 3 tablespoons cornstarch in a little cold water and gently stirring it into the simmering stew. Serve the dish with Boiled Rice, page 303.

MINT

Lamb with Dried Beans: France
Serves 6 ■ Doubles ■ Refrigerates ■ Freezes

Preparation: 30 minutes ■ Cooking: 3 hours in a 300° F. oven

This soup-stew, and the variants that follow, should be offered in soup plates. A good bread is a nice accompaniment. The stew may be flavored with a variety or combination of herbs: basil, cumin, dill, marjoram, oregano, rosemary, tarragon, and thyme.

6 cups cold water
1 pound dried navy or pea beans
1½ tablespoons salt
1 onion, stuck with 3 cloves
1 bay leaf, broken
½ teaspoon thyme

In a large saucepan, combine the water and beans. Bring the water rapidly to a boil; cook the beans for 5 minutes, remove them from the heat, and allow them to stand, tightly covered, for at least 1 hour. Add the salt, onion, and seasonings and simmer the beans, covered, for 2½ hours, or until they are tender.

Seasoned flour
3 pounds stewing lamb, trimmed of excess fat and cut into bite-size pieces
3 tablespoons margarine
Bouquet garni, page 16
1 onion, stuck with 3 cloves
2 cups hot water, in which 2 beef bouillon cubes have been dissolved

Meanwhile, in the seasoned flour, dredge the lamb. In a flameproof casserole, heat the margarine and in it brown the lamb. Add the *bouquet garni*, the onion, and the bouillon. Bake the meat, covered, at 300° F. for 2 hours.

At this point you may stop and continue later.

Drain the beans, discarding the onion and bay leaf. Add them to the simmering lamb and continue cooking the dish for 30 minutes longer.

Lamb with Chick-Peas — *Turkey:* Omit first step entirely; in next step, add 1 6-ounce can tomato paste to the cooking liquid. Use 2 20-ounce cans chick-peas, drained and rinsed, added to the lamb for the final 30 minutes of cooking; adjust the seasoning.

Lamb with Fava Beans — *Greece:* In first step, use 1 pound large dried fava beans; in second step, brown the lamb in olive oil, use as the cooking liquid 1 35-ounce can Italian tomatoes, and season the sauce with 1½ teaspoons dried mint, crumbled; follow last step as directed.

Lamb with Lima Beans: In first step, use a 1-pound package dried lima beans (their simmering time will be between 30 and 45 minutes); in second step, omit the margarine, but render until crisp 3 slices of bacon, diced; use this fat to brown the meat, and garnish the completed dish with the bacon bits; follow last step as directed.

Lamb with Green Beans: Arab States
Serves 6 ■ Doubles ■ Refrigerates

Preparation: 30 minutes ■ Cooking: 1½ hours in a 325° F. oven

4 tablespoons olive oil
2 pounds stewing lamb, trimmed of excess fat and cut into bite-size pieces
Salt
Pepper

In a skillet, heat the oil and in it brown the lamb well on all sides; season it. Remove and reserve it. Discard all but 3 tablespoons of the fat.

4 onions, sliced thin
1 clove garlic, chopped
1½ tablespoons flour
½ teaspoon ground allspice
¾ teaspoon nutmeg
½ teaspoon thyme

In the fat, cook the onion and garlic until translucent. Stir in the flour and seasonings.

2 pounds green beans, stemmed and cut into 2-inch lengths
1 20-ounce can Italian tomatoes

Over the bottom of a baking dish or casserole, arrange a level layer of the beans. Over the beans, arrange the lamb pieces. Over the lamb, arrange a level layer of the onion mixture. Over all, pour the tomatoes.

At this point you may stop and continue later.

Bake the dish, covered, at 325° F. for 1½ hours, or until the lamb is tender.

Serve the dish with Crusty Bread, page 300.

Lamb with Cabbage — *Norway:* In place of the beans, use 1 medium-sized cabbage, cut into sixths and arranged on top of the onion layer. In place of the tomatoes, use 2 cups water, in which 2 beef bouillon cubes have been dissolved. Serve the dish with Boiled White Potatoes, page 301.

Lamb with Carrots and Onions: In place of the seasonings suggested in the second step, use 1 tablespoon chili powder and 1 teaspoon ground coriander; in place of the beans, 6 carrots, scraped and cut into ½-inch rounds, and 12 to 18 small white onions, peeled.

Lamb with Okra: In place of the beans, use 1½ pounds fresh okra, trimmed and cut into 1-inch lengths, added to the stew for the final ½ hour of cooking.

NUTMEG

Lamb with Lima Beans
Serves 6 ■ Doubles ■ Refrigerates

Preparation: 25 minutes ■ Cooking: 10 minutes

The secret of this very simple Chinese-type recipe is to have everything — ingredients and utensils — ready before you start cooking. The dish is improved by cooking with ingredients at room temperature.

2 pounds lean boneless lamb, cut into 2-inch julienne
2 packages frozen baby Lima beans

Prepare the lamb. Cook the Lima beans as directed on the package, taking care not to overcook them. Drain them well.

Vegetable oil
2 cloves garlic, to be put through a press
Soy sauce

Ready these ingredients.

At this point you may stop and continue later.

In a flameproof casserole or wok, heat 2 tablespoons of the oil. Into it press the garlic cloves. Add the reserved lamb and stir-fry it for 3 minutes. Remove it to a serving dish and pour the pan juices over it.

In the hot casserole or wok, heat 2 tablespoons oil. Add the reserved beans and stir-fry them for 3 minutes. Into them stir 2 tablespoons soy sauce. Arrange the beans around the lamb and serve.

Serve the dish with Carrots, page 295.

Lamb with Dill Sauce: Sweden

Serves 6 ■ Doubles ■ Refrigerates ■ Freezes

Preparation: 30 minutes ■ Cooking: 1½ hours

3 pounds stewing lamb, trimmed of excess fat and cut into bite-size pieces
Cold water

In a heavy kettle, arrange the lamb, measure cold water just to cover, bring it to a boil, uncovered, and skim the surface. Reduce the heat to simmer.

1 bay leaf
6 sprigs fresh dill, if available
6 sprigs parsley
1½ teaspoons salt
6 peppercorns
1 teaspoon sugar

To the simmering kettle, add the seasonings and cook the meat, covered, for 1½ hours, or until it is tender. Remove the bay leaf and dill and parsley sprigs.

At this point you may stop and continue later.

If necessary, reheat the kettle. Drain the meat, reserving the broth. Arrange the lamb on a serving platter and keep it warm.

2 tablespoons margarine
2 tablespoons flour
2 cups reserved stock

In a saucepan, heat the margarine, stir in the flour, and, over gentle heat, cook the mixture for a few minutes. Gradually add the stock and cook the sauce, stirring constantly, until it is thickened and smooth.

¼ cup fresh dill or 1 tablespoon dried dillweed
1 teaspoon white vinegar (optional)
2 teaspoons sugar
Juice of ½ lemon
1 egg yolk, lightly beaten

To the sauce, add the dill, vinegar, sugar, and lemon juice, stirring to blend the mixture well. Into the egg yolk, stir a little of the sauce, then stir the yolk mixture into the bulk of the sauce; do not allow it to boil. Pour the sauce over the warm lamb and serve.

Serve the dish with Boiled White Potatoes, page 301.

Lamb with Cucumber
Serves 6 ■ Doubles ■ Refrigerates

Preparation: 30 minutes ■ Cooking: 1½ hours in a 325° F. oven

This recipe is my combination of two recipes for lamb with cucumber—one from the West Indies and the other from Australia. I find the dish fresh and light, pleasant summer fare.

2   tablespoons margarine
2   tablespoons oil
3   pounds stewing lamb, trimmed of excess fat and cut into bite-size pieces
Salt
Pepper
½ teaspoon rosemary, crushed

In a flameproof casserole, heat the margarine and oil and brown the lamb; season it. Remove and reserve it. Discard all but 3 tablespoons of the fat.

3   onions, chopped
1   clove garlic, chopped
2   ribs celery, chopped
1   green pepper, seeded and chopped
1   sweet red pepper, seeded and chopped (optional)

In the reserved fat, cook the vegetables until the onion is translucent. Replace the meat.

2   cups hot water, in which 2 chicken bouillon cubes have been dissolved

To the contents of the casserole, add the bouillon and bake the lamb, covered, at 325° F. for 1½ hours, or until the lamb is tender.

At this point you may stop and continue later.

3   tablespoons cornstarch, mixed with a little cold water
2   cucumbers, peeled, sliced lengthwise, seeded, and coarsely grated

Remove the excess fat from the surface of the simmering lamb. Add the cornstarch, stirring gently but constantly until the sauce is thickened and smooth. Stir in the grated cucumber and cucumber slices and heat them through (the sauce will thin

2 cucumbers, peeled, sliced lengthwise, seeded and cut into thick slices

somewhat with the addition of the cucumber).

Serve the dish with Crusty Bread, page 300.

Lamb with Eggplant: Turkey
Serves 6 ■ Doubles ■ Refrigerates

Preparation: 30 minutes ■ Cooking: 1½ hours

Seasoned flour
3 pounds stewing lamb, trimmed of excess fat and cut into bite-size pieces
4 tablespoons olive oil

In the seasoned flour, dredge the lamb. In a heavy kettle, heat the oil and in it brown the meat on all sides. Remove it in order to discard any remaining fat; replace the lamb.

2 onions, chopped
1 bay leaf
¼ teaspoon ground clove
½ teaspoon ground cinnamon
¼ teaspoon nutmeg
1½ teaspoons salt
1 cup hot water, in which 1 beef bouillon cube has been dissolved
Juice of 1 lemon

To the meat, add the onions, seasonings, bouillon and lemon juice. Bring the kettle to a boil, reduce the heat, and simmer the meat, covered, for 45 minutes.

At this point you may stop and continue later.

1 medium-sized eggplant, cubed
1 green pepper, seeded and cut into julienne (optional)
2 tomatoes, peeled, seeded, and chopped

To the kettle, add the eggplant, pepper, and tomatoes. Continue simmering the stew, covered, for 45 minutes.

Serve the dish with Crusty Bread, page 300.

Curried Lamb with Eggplant: In first step, remove the browned meat and, in the remaining fat, sauté for 5 minutes 1 eggplant, diced, 3 onions, chopped, 2 tart apples, peeled, cored, and diced, and 3 ribs celery, chopped; sprinkle over 1 tablespoon curry powder, or more, to taste; replace the meat. In second step, omit the onion and seasonings. In last step, omit the pepper. Serve the dish with Tomato Pilaf, page 306.

Lamb Chops with Eggplant — *Italy:* In first step, use 6 or 12 shoulder lamb chops, browning them as directed; arrange them in a level layer in a baking dish; follow the remainder of the recipe as directed and bake the dish, covered, at 325° F. for each 45 minutes designated.

Lamb with Pasta: Greece
Serves 6 ■ Doubles ■ Refrigerates ■ Freezes

Preparation: 40 minutes ■ Cooking: 1¼ hours

Orzo is a pasta shaped like rice grains; it is available at supermarkets. It is commonly used in Greece, where it is called *kritharaki*. I found this dish at a restaurant on the island of Kos, surely one of the loveliest spots in the Aegean. The restaurant, where I ate out of doors, overlooked the forum built by the Romans in their days of conquest.

4 tablespoons olive oil 3 pounds stewing lamb, cut into bite-size pieces	In a large heavy saucepan or kettle, heat the olive oil and in it brown the lamb. Remove and reserve the meat.
2 onions, chopped 2 cloves garlic, chopped 1 teaspoon basil 1 bay leaf, crumbled 1 teaspoon thyme 2 teaspoons salt ½ teaspoon pepper Juice and zest of 1 lemon	In the fat, cook the onion and garlic until translucent. Replace the lamb and add the seasonings.
2 ripe tomatoes, peeled, seeded, and chopped (canned tomatoes, drained, will do)	Prepare the tomatoes. *At this point you may stop and continue later.*
1 6-ounce can tomato paste 6 cups water	To the contents of the saucepan add the prepared tomatoes, tomato paste, and water. Bring the liquid to a boil, reduce the heat, and simmer the lamb, covered, for 1 hour, or until it is fork-tender. Remove it to a large serving bowl and keep it warm.
1 1-pound box *orzo*	Over high heat, return the sauce to a boil. Add the pasta, stirring. Cook it, uncovered, stirring often, for 12 minutes. Pour the sauce over the lamb.

Serve the dish with Crusty Bread, page 300.

Lamb and Onions: Greece
Serves 6 ■ Doubles ■ Refrigerates

Preparation: 30 minutes ■ Cooking: 1½ hours (in a 325° F. oven, if desired)

Stifado (meat and onion stew) is a popular dish in Greece. This recipe is my own, culled from a summer's touring of the Greek islands. The recipe may also be made with stewing veal or chicken parts (for the latter, the cooking time is 1 hour).

4 tablespoons olive oil
3 pounds stewing lamb, trimmed of excess fat and cut into bite-size pieces
Salt
Pepper
¾ teaspoon thyme

In a heavy kettle (or flameproof casserole, if you wish to cook the stew in the oven), heat the oil and in it brown the meat on all sides; season it. Remove and reserve it.

4 tablespoons olive oil
18 white onions, peeled

To the casserole add the olive oil. When the fat is very hot, add the onions, stirring gently, and glaze them well. Remove and reserve them. Discard any remaining fat.

2 tomatoes, peeled, seeded, and chopped
1 6-ounce can tomato paste
2 cloves garlic, chopped
2 tablespoons wine vinegar
1 bay leaf
1 3-inch piece cinnamon stick
6 whole cloves
2 teaspoons salt
¼ teaspoon pepper

In the kettle, mix together the tomatoes, tomato paste, garlic, vinegar, and seasonings. Replace the meat and over it arrange the onions.

At this point you may stop and continue later.

Cold water

To the contents of the kettle add cold water barely to cover. Bring it to a boil, reduce the heat, and simmer the stew, covered, for 1½ hours, or until the meat is tender.

Serve the dish with Boiled Rice, page 303.

Lamb with Onions and Honey — *Morocco:* In first step, omit the thyme, but add ½ teaspoon ground ginger; in third step, omit the tomato paste, vinegar, and bay leaf; in last step, over the contents of the casserole pour 4 tablespoons honey before adding the water as directed; for the final 30 minutes of cooking, remove the lid of the kettle so that the sauce will cook down.

Lamb with Peanut Sauce: Mexico
Serves 6 ■ Doubles ■ Refrigerates ■ Freezes

Preparation: 40 minutes ■ Cooking: 1½ hours in a 325° F. oven

The dish may also be made with chicken. The cooking time for this is 1 hour in a 350° F. oven.

4 tablespoons olive oil
3 pounds stewing lamb, trimmed of excess fat and cut into bite-size pieces
Salt
Pepper

In a flameproof casserole, heat the olive oil and in it brown the lamb; season it. Remove and reserve it. Discard all but 3 tablespoons of the fat.

2 onions, chopped
1 clove garlic, put through a press
3 tomatoes, peeled, seeded, and chopped
1 tablespoon sugar

In the reserved fat, cook the onion until translucent. Add the garlic, tomatoes, and sugar, and cook the mixture until the tomato liquid has evaporated.

1½ cups unsalted peanuts
¼ cup chopped parsley
½ teaspoon nutmeg
¼ teaspoon oregano
¼ teaspoon thyme

In the container of an electric blender, grind the peanuts until quite fine. Add them to the tomato-onion mixture, together with the parsley and seasonings.

1½ cups hot water, in which 2 chicken bouillon cubes have been dissolved

Add the bouillon, stirring.

At this point you may stop and continue later.

Replace the lamb. Bake the casserole, covered, at 325° F. for 1½ hours, or until the meat is tender.

Serve the dish with Boiled Rice, page 303.

Lamb with Rice: Italy

Serves 6 ■ Doubles ■ Refrigerates

Preparation: 30 minutes ■ Cooking: 1½ hours

2 tablespoons margarine
2 tablespoons oil
3 pounds stewing lamb, trimmed of excess fat and cut into bite-size pieces
Salt
Pepper

In a heavy kettle, heat the margarine and oil and brown the lamb on all sides; season it. Remove and reserve it. Discard all but 4 tablespoons of the fat.

2 onions, chopped
1½ cups raw natural rice

In the remaining fat, cook the onion until translucent. Add the rice, stirring to coat each grain; toast the rice in the fat for several minutes. Replace the lamb, spooning the rice over it.

1 1-pound can Italian tomatoes
2 cups hot water, in which 2 chicken bouillon cubes have been dissolved
¾ teaspoon basil
½ teaspoon oregano
¼ cup chopped parsley

Combine the tomatoes, bouillon, and seasonings.

At this point you may stop and continue later.

To the contents of the kettle, add the cooking liquid, bring it to a boil, reduce the heat, and simmer the dish, covered, for 1½ hours, or until the lamb and rice are tender and the liquid is absorbed.

Grated Parmesan cheese

When serving, offer the cheese separately.

Serve the dish with Mixed Green Salad, page 298.

Lamb with Barley and Orange: Follow first step as directed; in next step, use 1½ cups pearl barley in place of the rice; in third step, omit the tomatoes, reduce the water to 1½ cups, adding only bouillon cube; add 1½ cups orange juice mixed with the juice of 1 lemon; in fourth step, add for the final 30 minutes of cooking 2 oranges, sliced paper-thin and seeded, arranged over the top of the ingredients. When serving, omit cheese.

PORK

A. Ham B. Fatback C. Loin D. Flank
E. Spareribs F. Shoulder Butt G. Picnic Shoulder

PORK

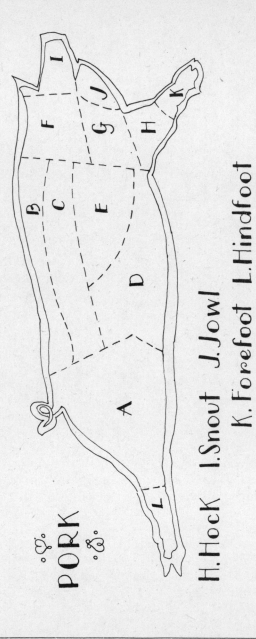

H. Hock I. Snout J. Jowl
K. Forefoot L. Hindfoot

Introduced to the New World when de Soto landed off the Florida coast, the hog is perhaps the first animal to have been domesticated by man; records of its use go back several thousand years before Christ. Pork was an important part of the Pilgrim diet and by 1700 pork-packing ("barreled" pork) was an item of trade between New England and the West Indies.

A fine source of protein and vitamin B_2, pork, as produced today, is highly digestible — despite old-fashioned beliefs to the contrary. China is the largest hog producer; the United States is the second "hog butcher to the world" with approximately 10 billion pounds of pork products processed annually. In America, the "pigsty" is a thing of the past; hogs no longer wallow in mud and feed on waste. Their quarters are sanitary and acclimatized; their diet, recommended by the Department of Agriculture, is scientifically formulated.

Pork is graded by numbers, 1 through 3. Number 1 is best, a pinkish gray meat of fine texture with a thin outer layer of white fat. The pork hog is at its gastronomic prime from 4½ to 6 months of age. The meat is sweet and tender — some people feel it is the *supreme* meat; Shakespeare refers to it, and Charles Lamb, in his essay "On Roast Pig," eulogizes pork as few foods have ever been praised.

Fresh pork should be promptly stored in the refrigerator and cooked within two days. It can be safely frozen for as long as three months.

Pork Chops

Recipes for pork chops suggest using 6 shoulder chops. These are cheaper than loin chops and just as flavorful; in this way, they fulfill the economical purposes of this book. Shoulder chops are, however, bonier and less meaty than loin chops; therefore, it may be well to allow 2 chops per serving for the heavier eaters in your family.

Pork Chops with Knackwurst and Potatoes: Germany

Serves 6 ■ Doubles ■ Refrigerates

Preparation: 30 minutes ■ Cooking: 45 minutes in a 350° F. oven

A fine *bauer* meal for winter suppers. Offer it with a good beer.

Seasoned flour
6   shoulder pork chops
2   tablespoons margarine
2   tablespoons oil

In the seasoned flour, dredge the chops. In a flameproof casserole, heat the margarine and oil and brown the chops thoroughly. Remove and reserve them.

1   pound knackwurst, cut into ¼-inch rounds
3   onions, chopped
1   carrot, scraped and thinly sliced
1   rib celery, chopped, with its leaves

In the fat, cook the knackwurst and vegetables, stirring often, for 5 minutes. Replace the chops.

At this point you may stop and continue later.

1½ cups hot water, in which 2 chicken bouillon cubes have been dissolved
6   medium-sized potatoes, peeled and thinly sliced
1   1-pound can tomatoes

To the contents of the casserole add the bouillon. Arrange the potatoes over the chops. Over all, pour the tomatoes and their liquid. Bake the casserole, tightly covered, at 350° F. for 45 minutes, or until the chops and potatoes are tender.

Serve the dish with Cabbage, page 294.

Pork Chops with Paprika and Dill Sauce: Hungary
Serves 6 ■ Doubles ■ Refrigerates ■ Freezes

Preparation: 30 minutes ■ Cooking: 45 minutes

Seasoned flour
6 shoulder pork chops
4 tablespoons margarine

In the seasoned flour, dredge the chops. In a skillet or flameproof casserole, heat the margarine and in it brown the chops. Remove and reserve them.

4 onions, chopped
2 cloves garlic, chopped

In the remaining fat, cook the onion and garlic until translucent.

2 tablespoons paprika, or more, to taste
1 cup hot water, in which 1 chicken bouillon cube has been dissolved

Into the onion, stir the paprika. Add the bouillon to the onion mixture and, over high heat, deglaze the pan.

At this point you may stop and continue later.

Replace the chops, bring the liquid to a boil, reduce the heat, and simmer the chops, covered, for 45 minutes, or until they are tender. Remove them to a platter and keep them warm.

1 cup sour cream
2 tablespoons reserved seasoned flour
1 tablespoon dillweed

Into the sour cream stir the flour. When the mixture is smooth, stir in the dill. Add the sour cream to the contents of the skillet and, over medium heat, cook the sauce, stirring constantly, until it is thickened and smooth. Pour the sauce over the chops and serve.

Serve the dish with Noodles, page 307.

Pork Chops with Prunes
Serves 6 ■ Doubles ■ Refrigerates

Preparation: 30 minutes ■ Cooking: 45 minutes

2 tablespoons margarine 2 tablespoons oil 6 shoulder pork chops Salt Pepper	In a large skillet or flameproof casserole, heat the margarine and oil and brown the chops; season them. Remove and reserve them. Discard all but 2 tablespoons of the fat.
2 onions, chopped	In the remaining fat, cook the onion until translucent.

1 cup hot water, in which
    2 chicken bouillon cubes
    have been dissolved
Grated rind and juice of
    1 lemon
	Add the bouillon to the onion and, over high heat, deglaze the casserole. Stir in the lemon rind and juice.

18 tenderized pitted dried
    prunes, six stuck with
    1 clove
	Prepare the prunes.

	At this point you may stop and continue later.
	Replace the chops and around them arrange the prunes. Bring the liquid to a boil, reduce the heat, and simmer the chops, tightly covered, for 45 minutes, or until they are tender. Remove them and the prunes to a serving platter and keep them warm.

1½ teaspoons cornstarch,
    mixed with 2
    tablespoons
    cold water
	Add the cornstarch to the hot liquid and, over medium heat, cook the sauce, stirring constantly, until it is thickened and smooth. Pour the sauce over the meat and serve.

Serve the dish with Boiled Rice, page 303.

Pork Chops with Rice: Italy
Serves 6 ■ Doubles ■ Refrigerates

Preparation: 30 minutes ■ Cooking: 45 minutes

A dish discovered at a restaurant in Rome where, on a summer evening, I dined on a square in Trastevere and listened to the carillon of a nearby church.

6 large shoulder pork chops	Trim the chops of any excess fat.
3 tablespoons olive oil	In a flameproof casserole, heat the oil and in it brown the chops on both sides. Add more oil as necessary. Remove the chops and reserve them.
1½ cups raw natural rice 1 teaspoon oregano ½ teaspoon sage 1½ teaspoons salt ½ teaspoon pepper	In the remaining fat, cook the rice, stirring to coat each grain. Add the seasonings. Replace the chops, spooning the rice over them. *At this point you may stop and continue later.*
3 cups hot water in which 3 chicken bouillon cubes have been dissolved	Over the contents of the casserole, pour the bouillon. Bring it to a boil, reduce the heat, and simmer the dish, covered, for 45 minutes, or until the chops and rice are tender and the liquid is absorbed.

Pork Chops with Sour Cream: America
Serves 6 ■ Doubles ■ Refrigerates

Preparation: 30 minutes ■ Cooking: 1 hour in a 350° F. oven

This recipe, my version of a New England classic, is pleasant party fare.

2 tablespoons margarine
2 tablespoons oil
6 shoulder pork chops
Salt
Pepper

In a flameproof casserole, heat the margarine and oil and brown the chops well; season them. Remove and reserve them. Discard all but 3 tablespoons of the fat.

3 onions, chopped
1 green pepper, seeded and cut into julienne
2 tablespoons flour

In the reserved fat, cook the onion and pepper until the onion is translucent. Stir in the flour.

1 cup sour cream
½ cup milk
½ cup hot water, in which 2 chicken bouillon cubes have been dissolved

Add the sour cream and liquids to the onion mixture and, over medium heat, cook the sauce, stirring constantly, until it is thickened and smooth. Replace the chops, spooning the sauce over them.

At this point you may stop and continue later.

¼ cup chopped parsley

Bake the chops, tightly covered, at 350° F. for 1 hour, or until they are tender. When serving, garnish them with parsley.

Serve the dish with Mashed White Potatoes, page 302.

Spareribs

Spareribs are delectable but are bony; you will need a full pound per serving. Loin ribs, meatier than "regular" ribs, are more expensive, but you will need fewer per serving. Because they are usually served with a sauce, spareribs go well with rice, which soaks up any extra sauce easily and tastily.

Basted and baked, spareribs are universally popular. Use your favorite barbecue sauce and proceed in the following way: have the spareribs cut into pieces of 2 ribs each. Season them to taste with a salt and pepper. Arrange them on a rack in a baking pan. Bake them at 350° F. for 1½ hours, turning them occasionally so that they will cook evenly, and basting them often with the sauce of your choice.

Spareribs with Fruit
Serves 6 ■ Doubles ■ Refrigerates

Preparation: 30 minutes ■ Cooking: 2 hours in a 325° F. oven, followed by 15 minutes in a 425° F. oven

A delicious and fresh way to prepare a "heavy" meat. More orange juice may be added as necessary.

6 pounds spareribs, cut into pieces of 2 ribs each
Salt
Pepper

Prepare the spareribs and, in a large skillet, over medium-high heat, brown them well on both sides. Drain them and arrange them in a roasting pan. Season them with salt and pepper.

12 to 18 tenderized pitted dried prunes
12 to 18 tenderized dried apricot halves
1 cup orange juice
¼ cup brown sugar

Around the spareribs arrange the fruit. Combine the orange juice and brown sugar. Pour the mixture over the spareribs.

At this point you may stop and continue later.

Bake the spareribs, tightly covered, at 325° F. for 2 hours. Remove the cover, skim off any excess fat, and brown the spareribs for 15 minutes in a 425° F. oven.

Serve the dish with Boiled Rice, page 303.

Spareribs with Fruit Sauce
Serves 6 ■ Refrigerates ■ Freezes

Preparation: 20 minutes ■ Marination: 2 hours
Cooking: 1½ hours in a 350° F. oven

6 pounds spareribs, cut into pieces of 2 ribs each

Prepare the spareribs.

¾ cup soy sauce
¾ cup orange marmalade
1 6-ounce can pineapple juice
Juice of 1 lemon
Juice of 1 orange
2 cloves garlic, put through a press
1 piece of ginger root the size of a walnut, grated
½ teaspoon rosemary, crumbled
½ teaspoon thyme

In the container of an electric blender, combine these nine ingredients and, on medium speed, whirl them until the mixture is smooth.

Arrange the spareribs in a shallow pan or baking dish. Over them, pour the marinade and allow them to stand for at least 2 hours.

At this point you may stop and continue later.

Drain and dry the spareribs; reserve the marinade. Arrange the spareribs on a rack in a baking pan. Roast them at 350° F. for 1½ hours, basting them frequently, until they are glazed and golden. Remove the ribs to a serving dish and keep them warm.

Cornstarch
Cold water

Sieve the remaining marinade, measure it, and, for each cup mix 2 teaspoons cornstarch in ¼ cup cold water. In a saucepan, combine the marinade and cornstarch and, over high heat, cook the sauce, stirring constantly, until it is thickened and smooth. Serve the sauce separately.

Serve the dish with Boiled Rice, page 303.

Spareribs with Sauerkraut
Serves 6 ■ Doubles ■ Refrigerates

Preparation: 30 minutes ■ Cooking: 1½ hours in a 350° F. oven

6 pounds spareribs, cut into pieces of 2 ribs each
Salt
Pepper

On a rack in a broiler pan, arrange the spareribs; season them. Under the broiler, brown them well on both sides. Drain them on absorbent paper and discard all fat.

2 pounds sauerkraut, rinsed, drained, and pressed dry in a colander
2 bay leaves, broken
3 tart apples, peeled, cored, and diced
3 tablespoons brown sugar
2 onions, finely chopped
1 tablespoon caraway seed (optional)

In a large casserole, arrange a bed of the sauerkraut. Insert the bay leaves. Add a layer of the diced apple and sprinkle it with the brown sugar. Sprinkle over the onion and caraway seed.

1½ cups hot water, in which 1 chicken bouillon cube has been dissolved

Over the contents of the casserole, arrange the spareribs. Prepare the bouillon.

At this point you may stop and continue later.

Add the bouillon and bake the casserole, tightly covered, at 350° F. for 1½ hours, or until the spareribs are very tender.

Serve the dish with Boiled White Potatoes, page 301.

The dish may be made with 6 pork hocks, *un*browned (first step); if desired, omit the apples, brown sugar, and caraway seed; use water *to cover*; increase the cooking time to 2 hours.

Spareribs with Sweet and Pungent Sauce
Serves 6 ■ Doubles ■ Refrigerates

Short ribs may also be prepared in the same manner.

Follow the basic directions for baked spareribs, page 98, omitting your favorite barbecue sauce. When the ribs are done, arrange them in a baking dish, pour over them Sweet and Pungent Sauce, page 311, and bake the dish, uncovered, at 325° F. for 15 minutes. Serve the dish with Boiled Rice, page 303.

Pork Hocks and Pig's Feet

Pork or ham hocks, that section of the foreleg immediately above the foot, together with the feet, are economical cuts of meat which, carefully prepared, produce very appetizing dishes. They are available fresh or corned and are interchangeable in these recipes. Before being used in a particular recipe, they should be well scrubbed and rinsed under cold water. Allow 1 ham hock or 1 pig's foot per serving.

Ham Hock and Bean Soup: America
Serves 6 ▪ Doubles ▪ Refrigerates ▪ Freezes

Preparation: 30 minutes ▪ Cooking: 2¾ hours

Water
1 pound dried navy beans

In water to cover by 1 inch, soak the beans overnight. Drain them, reserving the bean water. Add more water, if necessary, to equal 6 cups.

Reserved beans
6 ¾-pound ham hocks (or, if desired, 1 3- or 4-pound ham butt)
3 onions, chopped
3 ribs celery, chopped, with their leaves
2 bay leaves
1 tablespoon salt
½ teaspoon pepper

In a soup kettle, arrange the beans, the ham hock, onion, celery, bay leaves, salt, and pepper.

Reserved 6 cups water

Add the reserved water, bring the liquid to a boil, reduce the heat, and simmer the soup, covered, for 2½ hours, or until the meat falls from the bone.

At this point you may stop and continue later.

1 28-ounce can tomatoes

Remove the ham hocks, strip the meat from them; dice the meat and reserve it. If desired, mash the beans a little. Stir in the tomatoes. Replace the meat. Heat the soup for 15 minutes, or until it reaches serving temperature. Adjust the seasoning.

Serve the soup with Cabbage, page 294.

This Creole dish, satisfying to the hungriest soup-lover, is capable of pleasant variations:

Ham Hock and Bean Casserole: Soak the beans overnight; follow second step as above; next, use only enough reserved bean water just to cover the ingredients (more reserved bean water may be added as necessary, but do not allow the ingredients to become soupy); dice the meat as directed, but omit the tomatoes and, when replacing the meat, stir in 2 teaspoons dry mustard mixed until smooth with ¼ cup molasses. Spoon the mixture into a large baking dish or casserole and bake it, uncovered, at 325° F. for 45 minutes, or until the beans are fully tender, the liquid is absorbed, and the top is crusty.

Ham Hock and Black-Eyed Pea Soup: Use 1 pound dried black-eyed peas in place of the beans.

Ham Hock and Lentil Soup: Use 1 pound lentils in place of the beans.

Ham Hocks with Vegetables
Serves 6 ■ Doubles ■ Refrigerates

Preparation: 30 minutes ■ Cooking: 2½ hours

6 ¾-pound ham hocks
   (or, if desired, 1 3-
   or 4-pound ham butt)
2 cloves garlic, split
1 bay leaf
8 peppercorns
Cold water

In a heavy kettle, arrange the ham hocks; add the seasonings and the cold water to cover.

Bring the liquid to a boil, reduce the heat, and simmer the meat, tightly covered, for 2 hours, or until it is tender.

6 large carrots, scraped
   and cut into ¼-inch
   rounds
6 medium-sized potatoes,
   peeled and quartered
6 onions, peeled
1 small cabbage, cut into
   sixths

Prepare the vegetables. Reserve the potatoes in cold water to prevent their discoloring.

At this point you may stop and continue later.

To the contents of the simmering kettle add the vegetables in order. Increase the heat slightly and gently steam the vegetables, covered, for 25 minutes, or until they are tender.

Arrange the meat and vegetables on a platter. Serve the dish with a good mustard.

Sieve the cooking liquid and use it as stock or as the liquid in which to cook other vegetables.

Pig's Feet: Germany
Serves 6 ■ Doubles ■ Refrigerates ■ Freezes

Preparation: 15 minutes ■ Cooking: 2 hours

No need to "stop and continue later," because the preparation is so fast and the cooking so simple that you will feel very free of kitchen work. Sieve the broth to use for cooking vegetables.

6 pig feet
2 onions, sliced
3 cloves garlic, split
1 bay leaf
8 peppercorns
2 tablespoons salt
Cold water

In a heavy kettle, arrange the pig feet. Add the onions, garlic, bay leaf, peppercorns, and salt. Add cold water just to cover.

Bring the liquid to a boil, reduce the heat, and simmer the pig feet, covered, for 2 hours, or until the meat is tender enough nearly to fall from the bone.

Serve the pig feet sprinkled with a little vinegar or lemon juice, if desired.

Serve the dish with Hot Potato Salad, page 302.

Pig's Feet with Chick-Peas: Turkey
Serves 6 ■ Doubles ■ Refrigerates ■ Freezes

Preparation: 3 hours ■ Final cooking: 15 minutes

6 pig feet
2 onions, quartered
3 cloves garlic, split
2 ribs celery, with
   their leaves
1 lemon, quartered
6 parsley sprigs
1 bay leaf
4 whole cloves
1 teaspoon marjoram
1 teaspoon thyme
1 tablespoon salt
½ teaspoon pepper
1 teaspoon sugar
4 quarts (16 cups) cold
   water

In a soup kettle, combine these thirteen ingredients and add the water; bring the liquid to a boil, reduce the heat, and simmer the pig feet, covered, for 2½ hours, or until the meat is easily removed from the bones.

Remove the pig feet from the broth; strip them of their meat and dice it. Discard the bones and reserve the meat. Meanwhile, reduce the broth to 3 cups. Sieve and reserve it.

At this point you may stop and continue later.

2 tablespoons margarine
2 onions, finely chopped
1 6-ounce can tomato paste

In the kettle, heat the margarine and in it cook the onion until translucent. Add the tomato paste, stirring, and, over gentle heat, cook the mixture for 8 minutes.

2 20-ounce cans chick-peas,
   drained and rinsed
Reserved diced meat
Reserved 3 cups broth
Salt
Pepper

To the tomato mixture add the chick-peas, the reserved meat, and the broth, stirring gently. Adjust the seasoning.

Serve the dish in bowls, accompanied by a side dish of Eggplant made with yogurt, page 295.

Pig's Feet with Sauerkraut: America

Serves 6 ■ Doubles ■ Refrigerates

Preparation: 20 minutes ■ Cooking: 2½ hours

This hearty Pennsylvania Dutch classic makes a fine and easy meal. Have on hand a good mustard and, if desired, well-chilled beer.

2 pounds sauerkraut, rinsed, drained, and pressed dry in a colander
2 onions, chopped
1 bay leaf, broken
3 whole cloves
½ teaspoon thyme
1 teaspoon sugar
½ teaspoon salt
½ teaspoon pepper
6 pig feet
1 cup hot water, in which 1 chicken bouillon cube has been dissolved

In a heavy kettle, arrange a bed of the sauerkraut. Over the sauerkraut, sprinkle the onion and seasonings. On the sauerkraut bed, arrange the pig feet. Add the bouillon.

Bring the liquid to a boil, reduce the heat, and simmer the dish, very tightly covered, for 2½ hours, or until the pig feet are tender enough so that the meat falls easily from the bones.

Serve the dish with Dumplings, page 307.

Pork Stews

Pork is a fine meat for stewing and braising; it yields a tender, succulent main dish, slightly sweet when compared with other meats. In this book the recipes for stews of beef, lamb, and pork are interchangeable; merely adjust the cooking times to the particular meat you are using. (Specifically, beef cooks *en casserole* in a 300° F. oven or at the simmer for 2 to 2½ hours; lamb cooks *en casserole* in a 325° F. oven or at the simmer for 1½ hours; and pork cooks *en casserole* in a 350° F. oven or at the simmer for 1¾ hours.)

Pork with Beans: Hungary
Serves 6 ■ Doubles ■ Refrigerates ■ Freezes

Preparation: 1½ hours ■ Cooking: 1½ hours

1 pound dried navy beans
Cold water

In a saucepan, cover the beans with water, bring them to a boil, and cook them, uncovered, for 5 minutes. Remove them from the heat and allow them to stand 1 hour. Drain them, reserving 2 cups of the water.

3 tablespoons margarine
4 onions, chopped
1½ tablespoons paprika
1 bay leaf, broken

In a heavy kettle, heat the margarine and in it cook the onion until translucent. Stir in the paprika and bay leaf.

2 pounds lean boneless pork butt

Into the onion, stir the beans. On the beans, arrange the pork butt.

Reserved bean water
2 chicken bouillon cubes

In the reserved water, dissolve the bouillon cubes.

At this point you may stop and continue later.

Over the contents of the kettle, pour the liquid; bring it to a boil, reduce the heat, and simmer the dish, covered, for 1¼ hours. Remove the cover and continue cooking for 15 minutes, or until the meat and beans are tender and the sauce is reduced to your desired consistency.

Serve the dish with Mixed Green Salad, page 298.

Cassoulet of Pork with Black-Eyed Peas
Serves 6 ■ Doubles ■ Refrigerates ■ Freezes

Preparation: 45 minutes (30 minutes in a 450° F. oven) ■ Cooking: 3 hours in
a 350° F. oven

Black-eyed peas are really *beans*, botanically speaking. Do not be confused
if they are so called at your supermarket.

1 pound dried black-eyed
  peas
Water

In a saucepan, soak the black-eyed
peas overnight in water to cover.
Then simmer the peas for 30 minutes.
Drain them, reserving 2 cups of the
water.

1 3-pound fresh pork
  shoulder

Meanwhile on a rack in a roasting
pan, bake the pork shoulder at 450° F.
for 30 minutes.

2 cloves garlic, finely
  chopped
1 bay leaf, broken
¾ teaspoon thyme
¼ teaspoon pepper
12 small onions, peeled

In a casserole, arrange the pork shoulder. Into the peas stir the garlic, bay
leaf, thyme, and pepper. Spoon the
peas around the meat. Arrange the
onions over the peas.

2 cups reserved water
2 beef bouillon cubes
1 tablespoon
  Worcestershire sauce

In the reserved water, dissolve the
bouillon cubes; stir in the Worcestershire sauce.

*At this point you may stop and continue
later.*

Over the contents of the casserole,
pour the liquid. Bake the dish, covered, at 350° F. for 3 hours, or until
the meat and peas are very tender.

Serve the dish with Cabbage, page 294.

Pork with Celery

Serves 6 ■ Doubles ■ Refrigerates

Preparation: 30 minutes ■ Cooking: 1¾ hours

What a pleasant complement the tang of celery is to the sweetness of pork. A particularly attractive main dish, I feel.

Seasoned flour
2½ pounds lean boneless pork, cut into bite-size pieces
4 tablespoons olive oil
1 clove garlic, finely chopped

In the seasoned flour, dredge the pork. In a heavy kettle, heat the oil and in it cook the garlic until the oil is flavored. Add the pork and brown it lightly.

2 cups hot water, in which 2 beef bouillon cubes have been dissolved
1 bay leaf, broken
1 teaspoon sugar

To the contents of the kettle, add the bouillon, bay leaf, and sugar. Bring the liquid to a boil, reduce the heat, and simmer the meat, tightly covered, for 1½ hours, or until it is nearly tender.

At this point you may stop and continue later.

2 cups hot water
10 to 12 ribs celery, cut into 1½-inch lengths

In a saucepan, bring the water to a boil. Add the celery and cook it, uncovered, for 10 minutes, or until it is crisp-tender. Drain it; reserve the broth for use in another dish.

3 tomatoes, peeled, seeded, and chopped

Add the celery and tomotoes to the simmering stew. Cook the dish, uncovered, for 5 minutes.

Serve the dish with Boiled Sweet Potatoes, page 301.

Pork and Celery Stew — *Greece:* After browning the pork, remove it and, adding a little more olive oil, cook 6 onions, chopped, until translucent; follow second and third steps as directed; in fourth step, omit the tomato when adding the parboiled celery to the stew. Beat 1 egg; to it add the juice of 1 lemon; add ¼ cup of the stew sauce, stirring. Remove the casserole from the heat and gently stir in the egg-lemon mixture.

Pork with Eggplant: Italy
Serves 6 ■ Doubles ■ Refrigerates

Preparation: 35 minutes ■ Cooking: 1¼ hours in a 375° F. oven

2   tablespoons olive oil
1½ pounds lean boneless
    pork, cut into ¾-inch
    dice
Salt
Pepper

In a flameproof casserole, heat the olive oil and in it brown the pork dice; season them. Remove and reserve them.

2   onions, sliced
1   clove garlic, finely
    chopped
2   green peppers, seeded
    and cut into julienne

In the remaining fat, cook the onion, garlic, and pepper until the onion is translucent (a little olive oil may be added, if necessary).

½   cup raw natural rice
1   1-pound can Italian
    tomatoes
½   teaspoon ground
    cinnamon

Over the onion mixture, sprinkle the rice. Add the tomatoes and sprinkle them with the cinnamon.

1   medium-sized eggplant,
    diced
½   cup raw natural rice
1   10-ounce package frozen
    okra (optional)
1   1-pound can Italian
    tomatoes
½   teaspoon cinnamon

Over the tomatoes, arrange the egg-plant in a flat layer. Replace the pork in a flat layer. Over it, sprinkle the rice. If desired, add the okra in a flat layer. Add the tomatoes and sprinkle them with the cinnamon.

At this point you may stop and continue later.

Bake the casserole, covered, at 375° F. for 1 hour. Remove the cover and bake it for 15 minutes longer.

Pork with Hominy: Mexico

Serves 6 ■ Doubles ■ Refrigerates ■ Freezes

Preparation: 35 minutes ■ Cooking: 2½ hours

4   strips bacon, sliced

In a flameproof casserole, render the bacon until crisp; remove it to absorbent paper and reserve it.

Seasoned flour
2½ pounds lean boneless pork, cut into bite-size pieces
3   onions, chopped
1   clove garlic, chopped
2   tablespoons chili powder (or more, to taste)
½   teaspoon each: basil, marjoram, oregano, thyme

In the seasoned flour, dredge the pork. In the remaining bacon fat, brown it lightly. Add the onion and garlic and cook them until translucent. Stir in the chili powder and other seasonings.

3   cups hot water, in which 3 chicken bouillon cubes have been dissolved

Prepare the bouillon.

At this point you may stop and continue later.

2   20-ounce cans whole hominy, drained

Over the contents of the casserole, pour the liquid; bring it to a boil, reduce the heat, and simmer the meat, covered, for 2 hours. Add the hominy and continue cooking for ½ hour longer.

Serve the dish with Green Bean Salad, page 299.

115

Pork with Horseradish Sauce

Serves 6 ■ Doubles ■ Refrigerates ■ Freezes

Preparation: 30 minutes ■ Cooking: 1½ hours

I am very fond of horseradish and always use at least 6 tablespoonsful. You will be surprised at how its "edge" disappears in the sauce. This dish may also be made with stewing lamb, with or without bones.

Seasoned flour
2½ pounds lean boneless pork, cut into bite-size pieces
2 tablespoons margarine
2 tablespoons oil

In the seasoned flour, dredge the pork. In a heavy kettle, heat the margarine and oil and brown the meat. Remove and reserve it.

1 onion, chopped
1 carrot, scraped and thinly sliced
1 rib celery, thinly sliced
½ teaspoon powdered clove

In the remaining fat, cook the vegetables until the onion is translucent. Stir in the clove. Replace the meat.

2 cups water in which 2 beef bouillon cubes have been dissolved
½ cup cider vinegar

Prepare the liquids.

At this point you may stop and continue later.

4 tablespoons prepared horseradish (or more, to taste)

To the contents of the casserole, add the liquids; bring them to a boil, reduce the heat, and simmer the stew, covered, for 1½ hours, or until the pork is tender. Remove the casserole from the heat, stir in the horseradish, and serve the stew.

Serve the dish with Boiled White Potatoes, page 301.

Pork and Kidney Stew: Ireland

Serves 6 ■ Doubles ■ Refrigerates ■ Freezes

Preparation: 20 minutes ■ Cooking: 2 hours in a 300° F. oven

Seasoned flour

2 pork kidneys, cut into 1-inch cubes

2 pounds lean boneless pork, cut into bite-size pieces

In the seasoned flour, dredge the kidney pieces and pork.

4 onions, sliced

2 tart apples, peeled, cored, and diced

Bouquet garni (page 16)

Over the bottom of a casserole, arrange a layer of onion slices. Sprinkle the apple over it. Add a *bouquet garni*. Arrange the meats over the apple.

1½ cups hot water, in which 1 beef bouillon cube has been dissolved

Prepare the bouillon.

At this point you may stop and continue later.

3 carrots, scraped and sliced

Over the contents of the casserole, pour the liquid. Cook the dish, covered, at 300° F. for 1 hour. Add the carrots and continue cooking the stew, covered, for 1 hour longer.

Serve the dish with Mashed White Potatoes, page 302.

If desired, 3 parsnips, scraped and sliced, may be substituted for the carrots.

Pork with Sauerkraut: Hungary
Serves 6 ■ Doubles ■ Refrigerates

Preparation: 35 minutes ■ Cooking: 1 hour 45 minutes

3 strips bacon, diced
3 onions, chopped
1 clove garlic, chopped
2½ pounds lean boneless pork, cut into bite-size pieces
Salt
Pepper

In a flameproof casserole, render the bacon until crisp and brown; remove it to absorbent paper and reserve it. In the remaining fat, cook the onion and garlic until translucent. Add the pork and brown it lightly, stirring to prevent the onion from burning. Season the pork and onion.

1½ teaspoons caraway seed (optional)
1½ tablespoons paprika (or more, to taste)
1 cup water

Stir in the caraway seed and paprika and add the water. Bring the liquid to a boil, reduce the heat, and simmer the pork, covered, for 1 hour. (More water may be added as necessary.)

At this point you may stop and continue later.

2 pounds sauerkraut, rinsed, drained, and pressed dry in a colander
Water

Add the sauerkraut and only sufficient water barely to cover. Simmer the dish, covered, for 45 minutes longer.

1½ tablespoons flour
2 cups sour cream

Blend the flour and sour cream until the mixture is smooth. Add it to the stew, stirring gently, and simmer the dish, uncovered, until the sauce is slightly thickened.

Serve the dish with Noodles, page 307.

Pork with Stroganoff Sauce: Russia
Serves 6 ■ Doubles ■ Refrigerates ■ Freezes

Preparation: 40 minutes ■ Cooking: 10 minutes

A pleasant supper-party dish. Sliced mushrooms may be added, if desired.

Seasoned flour, to which 1 teaspoon paprika is added
2 or 2½ pounds lean boneless pork, cut into 2-inch julienne
4 tablespoons margarine
2 cloves garlic, split

In the seasoned flour, dredge the pork strips. In a large saucepan, heat the margarine and in it cook the garlic until the margarine is flavored. Discard the garlic. Brown the meat.

2 onions, finely chopped
1½ cups water, in which 2 chicken bouillon cubes have been dissolved
2 teaspoons Worcestershire sauce

To the contents of the saucepan, add the onion, bouillon, and Worcestershire sauce. Bring the liquid to a boil, reduce the heat, and simmer the meat, covered, for 30 minutes, or until it is tender. (More water may be added if the sauce thickens too much.)

At this point you may stop and continue later.

1½ cups sour cream
¼ cup chopped parsley

Stir in the sour cream and cook the dish only long enough to heat it through (approximately 10 minutes). Adjust the seasonings. Garnish the dish with parsley.

Serve the dish with Noodles, page 307.

Sausages

Sausage, most often the finely chopped and well-seasoned meat of beef or pork, may be bought either stuffed into animal or artificial casings or packaged much like ground beef. Sausage is also available smoked—frankfurters, or hot dogs, are a variety of smoked sausage; in their case, they have been already cooked but are more appetizing for being re-cooked, either in simmering water, hot margarine, or in combination with other foods.

Sausages trace their beginnings to ancient Rome. The Gauls also used ground meats seasoned, or preserved, with spices, and shaped by an outer casing. In the *Odyssey*, Homer mentions a kind of sausage. Today there are over two hundred different varieties; they may be made of beef, veal, pork, lamb, liver, poultry, or a mixture of these meats. There are sausages for every taste: mild or hot, moist or dry, thick or thin, small or large. Sausages are high in protein, vitamins, and minerals; their caloric count depends upon the specific sausage in question. In these recipes, packaged sausage meat is most often called for; you may vary the taste of the dishes, however, by mixing together so-called American sausage meat (flavored with sage) and Italian sweet or hot sausage meat (which each has its own distinctive taste).

Sausage and Bean Soup: Dominican Republic
Serves 6 generously ■ Doubles ■ Refrigerates

Preparation: 1 hour ■ Cooking: 1½ hours

This recipe is a much simplified — and far less rich — version of a Latin American classic. Plainer than the original though it is, you will find it a satisfying dish.

1   pound dried navy or pea beans
8   cups hot water
2   tablespoons salt

In a soup kettle, cover the beans with the water and add the salt. Bring them to a rolling boil and cook them for 5 minutes. Remove them from the heat and allow them to stand, covered, for 1 hour.

1   pound sweet sausage meat, rolled into small balls
6   slices bacon, diced

In a skillet, cook the sausage balls until golden. Drain them on absorbent paper and add them to the beans. In the remaining fat, render the bacon until crisp. Drain it on absorbent paper and add it to the beans. Discard all but 3 tablespoons of the fat.

3   onions, chopped
2   cloves garlic, chopped

In the remaining fat, cook the onion and garlic until translucent. Add the mixture to the beans.

Simmer the soup, covered, for 1 hour, or until the beans are tender.

At this point you may stop and continue later.

¼   teaspoon cayenne (or less, to taste)
2   teaspoons chili powder
1   teaspoon ground cumin
1   6-ounce can tomato paste
Grated rind and juice of 1 lemon

Add these 6 ingredients and continue simmering the soup, covered, for ½ hour.

2 or 3 ripe bananas, peeled and sliced

Add the banana and continue cooking the soup only long enough to heat the banana through.

Serve the soup with Mixed Green Salad, page 298.

Smoked Sausage and Vegetable Soup: France

Serves 6 generously ∎ Doubles ∎ Refrigerates

Preparation: 1 hour ∎ Cooking: 30 minutes

Soupe fermière aux saucisses is a substantial and flavorful peasant dish; like the other soups made with sausages, it is a one-dish meal.

2 pounds smoked sausage (wurst)
½ pound salt pork, cut into large dice
8 cups water

In a soup kettle, arrange the sausage and salt pork; add the water. Bring the liquid to a boil, reduce the heat, and simmer the meats, covered, for 1 hour.

3 medium turnips, scraped and sliced
3 carrots, scraped and sliced
6 onions, peeled and quartered
4 medium-sized potatoes, peeled and diced
1 small cabbage, cut into sixths

Meanwhile, prepare the vegetables. Reserve the potatoes in cold water to prevent their discoloring.

At this point you may stop and continue later.

1 teaspoon marjoram
1 teaspoon sage
2 teaspoons salt
½ teaspoon pepper
1 teaspoon sugar
¼ cup chopped parsley

To the contents of the soup kettle, add the prepared vegetables and seasonings. Stir the soup gently. Continue to simmer it, covered, for 30 minutes, or until the vegetables are tender. Adjust the seasoning. When serving the soup, garnish it with the parsley.

Serve the soup with Crusty Bread, page 300.

Sausage with Eggplant
Serves 6 generously ▪ Doubles ▪ Refrigerates

Preparation: 30 minutes ▪ Cooking: 1 hour in a 350° F. oven

1 pound sausage meat, rolled into small balls

In a flameproof casserole, render the sausage balls until they are crisp and browned. Remove them to absorbent paper and reserve them. Discard all but 3 tablespoons of the fat.

2 onions, chopped
¼ cup chopped parsley
½ cup hot water
2 teaspoons curry powder

In the remaining fat, cook the onion until translucent. Add the parsley, water, and curry powder, and cook the mixture, stirring, for 5 minutes.

1 large eggplant, cut into 1-inch cubes

Stir in the eggplant and reserved sausage balls. Bake the casserole, covered, at 350° F. for ½ hour.

At this point you may stop and continue later.

2 tablespoons margarine
2 tablespoons flour
1½ cups warm milk
1½ teaspoons salt
¼ teaspoon pepper
1 egg yolk

In a saucepan, heat the margarine; into it, stir the flour and, over gentle heat, cook the mixture, stirring, for 3 minutes. Gradually add the milk and cook the mixture, stirring constantly, until it is thickened and smooth. Stir in the seasonings. Stir in the egg yolk.

Over the contents of the casserole, pour the sauce. Bake the dish, uncovered, at 350° F. for 30 minutes, or until the custard is somewhat set and browned on top.

Serve the dish with Dried Bean Salad, page 309.

Italian Sausage with Beans: Italy
Serves 6 ■ Doubles ■ Refrigerates ■ Freezes

Preparation: 30 minutes ■ Cooking: 15 minutes (or, if desired, 30 minutes in a 350° F. oven)

1　pound Italian sausage meat (sweet or hot or a combination of both), rolled into small balls
2　onions, chopped

In a large skillet or flameproof casserole, brown the sausage balls. When they are crisp, remove them to absorbent paper and reserve them. Discard all but 3 tablespoons of the fat. In it, cook the onion until translucent.

1　1-pound can tomato sauce
½　teaspoon oregano
½　teaspoon salt

Stir in the tomato sauce, oregano, and salt. Cook the mixture for 5 minutes.

2　20-ounce cans kidney beans, drained

Gently fold the beans into the onion mixture. Arrange the sausage balls over the beans.

At this point you may stop and continue later.

¼　cup chopped parsley

Simmer the dish, tightly covered, for 15 minutes (or, if desired, for 30 minutes, covered, in a 350° F. oven). Garnish it with parsley.

Serve the dish with Eggplant, page 295.

If desired, 1 pound American sausage meat may be used, in place of the Italian.

If desired, 2 bay leaves and a generous pinch of rosemary, cooked with the onion, will give quite a different flavor to the sauce.

In place of the sausage meat, 4 to 6 frankfurters, cut into ¾-inch rounds and browned in 3 tablespoons margarine, may be used.

Four green peppers, seeded and cut into julienne, may be added and cooked with the onion.

Sausage with Lentils: Use 1 pound dried lentils, cooked as directed on the package.

Sausage with Lima Beans: Use 2 10-ounce packages frozen Lima beans, cooked as directed on the package.

Sausage with Split Peas: Use 1 pound yellow or green dried split peas, cooked as directed on the package.

PARSLEY

Sausage and Onion Tart
Serves 6 ■ Doubles ■ Refrigerates

Preparation: 45 minutes ■ Cooking: 10 minutes in a 450° F. oven, followed by 20 minutes in a 325° F. oven

A festive luncheon or supper dish.

1 pound sausage meat, rolled into small balls

In a skillet, render the sausage balls until they are golden; they should not, however, be "crusty." Remove them to absorbent paper and reserve them. Discard all but 4 tablespoons of the fat.

4 large onions, sliced

In the reserved fat, cook the onion, stirring gently, until the rings separate and are translucent.

Short pastry for a 9-inch, 1-crust pie

Using your favorite recipe, prepare the pastry and line the pie tin. Over the bottom of the pie shell, arrange the onion in an even layer. Over the onion, arrange the sausage balls.

3 eggs
2 cups dairy half-and-half
¼ teaspoon nutmeg
1 teaspoon salt
¼ teaspoon pepper

In the container of an electric blender, whirl these 5 ingredients for 10 seconds. (If desired, the ingredients may be combined in a mixing bowl and blended with a rotary blender.)

At this point you may stop and continue later.

Over the contents of the pie shell, pour the custard (it cooks best if used at room temperature). Bake the tart at 450° F. for 10 minutes; reduce the heat to 325° F. and continue baking for 20 minutes, or until the custard is set.

Serve the dish with Mixed Green Salad, page 298.

Sausage Pudding: America
Serves 6 ■ Doubles ■ Refrigerates ■ Freezes

Preparation: 30 minutes ■ Cooking: 20 minutes in a 350° F. oven

2 pounds sausage meat, rolled into small balls

In a skillet, render the sausage balls until they are crisp and browned. Remove them to absorbent paper and reserve them. Discard all but 4 tablespoons of the fat.

3 eggs
1½ cups milk
1½ cups flour
3 tablespoons reserved sausage fat
½ teaspoon basil
½ teaspoon thyme
½ teaspoon salt
¼ teaspoon pepper

In the container of an electric blender, whirl these 8 ingredients on medium speed until the mixture is smooth.

1 tablespoon reserved sausage fat

With the fat, lightly grease a 2-quart baking dish. Arrange the sausage balls in it.

At this point you may stop and continue later.

Over the sausage balls, pour the pudding batter and bake it, uncovered, at 350° F. for 20 minutes, or until it is golden brown and puffed.

Serve the dish with Cabbage, page 294.

Sausage with Rice and Chicken: France
Serves 6 ▪ Doubles ▪ Refrigerates ▪ Freezes

Preparation: 45 minutes ▪ Cooking: 1 hour in a 350° F. oven

Two pieces of chicken per serving should be sufficient, when added to the sausage. This Basque recipe may be made with almost any part of the chicken — legs, wings, hearts, or gizzards.

1 pound Italian hot sausage, cut into ½-inch rounds

In a flameproof baking dish or casserole, brown the sausage rounds; remove them to absorbent paper and reserve them. Discard all but 4 tablespoons of the fat.

2 onions, chopped
1 clove garlic, chopped
2 green peppers, seeded and chopped

In the fat, cook the onion, garlic, and pepper until the onion is translucent.

1½ cups raw natural rice
1 teaspoon oregano
2 teaspoons paprika
Grated rind of 1 orange
1 1-pound can tomatoes, drained and chopped (reserve the liquid)

To the contents of the baking dish, add the rice, stirring to coat each grain. Stir in the seasonings and tomatoes. Stir in the reserved sausage.

Two pieces of chicken each for 6 persons (see preceding note)

Add the chicken, spooning the rice mixture over and around them.

Juice of 1 orange
Reserved tomato liquid
Hot water
3 chicken bouillon cubes

Combine the orange juice and tomato liquid, add water to equal 3 cups, and into the mixture, crumble the bouillon cubes.

At this point you may stop and continue later.

Pour the hot liquid over the contents of the dish and bake it, covered, at 350° F. for 1 hour, or until the chicken and rice are tender and the liquid is absorbed.

Sausage with Rice and Eggplant: America
Serves 6 generously ■ Doubles ■ Refrigerates

Preparation: 45 minutes ■ Cooking: 45 minutes in a 350° F. oven

This substantial Creole dish is unusually tasteful. If desired, the ingredients may be prepared and mixed and the recipe baked in an ovenproof crockery dish.

1 pound sweet sausage meat
1 pound hot sausage meat

Roll the sausage meat into small balls and, in a large flameproof casserole, brown them well. Remove the balls to absorbent paper and reserve them; discard all but 4 tablespoons of the fat.

3 onions, chopped
2 cloves garlic, chopped
1 green pepper, seeded and chopped
3 ribs celery, chopped
1½ cups raw natural rice
1 large eggplant, unpeeled and cubed

In the reserved fat, cook the onions and garlic until translucent. Add the pepper and celery and cook them, stirring often, for 5 minutes. Add the rice, stirring the mixture to coat each grain. Finally add the eggplant and the reserved sausage balls, stirring to blend the mixture well.

1 6-ounce can tomato paste
Water
3 beef bouillon cubes
1 teaspoon salt

In a saucepan, add to the tomato paste water to equal 3 cups. Add the bouillon cubes.

At this point you may stop and continue later.

Bring the liquid to a boil, stirring; pour it over the contents of the casserole. Bake the dish, covered, at 350° F. (or, if desired, simmer it, covered) for 45 minutes, or until the rice is tender and the liquid is absorbed.

Sausage Risotto: Italy

Serves 6 ■ Doubles ■ Refrigerates

Preparation: 30 minutes ■ Cooking: 45 minutes in a 350° F. oven

1 pound sweet Italian sausage meat	In a flameproof casserole, render the sausage meat until it is crisp and browned. With a fork, crumble it so that it cooks evenly. Remove it to absorbent paper and reserve it.
3 onions, chopped 3 ribs celery, chopped 1 green pepper, seeded and chopped	In the remaining fat, cook the onion, celery, and pepper until the onion is translucent.
1½ cups raw natural rice ½ cup grated Parmesan cheese (optional)	Add the rice, stirring to coat each grain. Replace the sausage, add the cheese, and, using two forks, toss the mixture lightly. *At this point you may stop and continue later.*
3 cups hot water, in which 3 beef bouillon cubes have been dissolved	Over the contents of the casserole, pour the liquid. Bake the dish, covered, at 350° F. for 45 minutes, or until the rice is tender and the liquid is absorbed.

Serve the dish with Green Bean Salad, page 299.

Sausage with Sweet and Pungent Sauce

Serves 6 ■ Doubles ■ Refrigerates

Preparation: 25 minutes ■ Cooking: ½ hour in a 350° F. oven

1½ pounds sausage meat, rolled into small balls
Dillweed or nutmeg

In a heavy skillet, render the sausage balls until they are crisp and brown. Drain them on absorbent paper. Season them with dillweed or nutmeg.

Sweet and Pungent Sauce (page 311)

In a baking dish, arrange the sausage balls. Over them, spoon the Sweet and Pungent Sauce. Bake the dish, covered, at 350° F. for 30 minutes.

Serve the dish with Boiled Rice, page 303.

Sausage Sauce for Pasta: Italy
Serves 6 ■ Doubles ■ Refrigerates

Preparation: 30 minutes ■ Cooking: 1½ hours

1 pound Italian sausage meat (sweet or hot, or a combination of both), rolled into small balls

In a skillet, render the sausage balls until they are crisp and brown. Remove them to absorbent paper and reserve them. Discard all but 3 tablespoons of the fat.

2 onions, chopped
1 clove garlic, chopped
1 rib celery, chopped
1 6-ounce can tomato paste
1 35-ounce can Italian tomatoes

In the reserved fat, cook the onion, garlic, and celery until translucent. Stir in the tomato paste and then add the tomatoes.

¼ cup chopped parsley
1½ teaspoons basil
½ teaspoon marjoram
1½ teaspoons sugar
Salt

Add the parsley, seasonings, sugar, and salt to taste. Stir in the reserved sausage balls. Simmer the sauce, gently, for 1½ hours, or until it is thickened.

At this point you may stop and continue later.

Reheat the sauce and spoon it over cooked pasta of your choice (spaghetti, linguine, or noodles). Allow 1½ pounds of uncooked pasta for 6 persons.

Serve the dish with Zucchini, page 296.

Frankfurters and Noodles
Serves 6 ■ Doubles ■ Refrigerates

Preparation: 30 minutes ■ Cooking: 15 minutes in a 425° F. oven

3 tablespoons margarine
3 tablespoons flour
2 cups hot water, in which
  2 chicken bouillon cubes
  have been dissolved
1 5⅓-ounce can
  evaporated milk
1 onion, grated
Salt
Pepper

In a saucepan, heat the margarine and in it, over low heat, cook the flour, stirring, for 3 minutes. Gradually add the bouillon, stirring, and then the evaporated milk and onion. Cook the sauce, stirring constantly, until it is thickened and smooth. Season it to taste with salt and pepper.

1 pound frankfurters, cut
  into ½-inch rounds

Add the frankfurters and simmer the mixture for 10 minutes, stirring it often.

At this point you may stop and continue later.

1 ½-pound package
  noodles

Cook the noodles, *al dente,* as directed on the package. Drain them and arrange them in a 2½-quart baking dish.

½ cup grated Parmesan
  cheese

Over the noodles, spoon the frankfurter mixture. Sprinkle the cheese over the top. Bake the dish at 425° F. for 15 minutes, or until the top is golden brown.

Serve the dish with Zucchini, page 296.

Frankfurters with Sauerkraut: Hungary
Serves 6 ■ Doubles ■ Refrigerates

Preparation: 45 minutes ■ Cooking: 10 minutes

4 tablespoons margarine
6 frankfurters, cut into
    ½-inch rounds
2 onions, chopped

In a deep skillet or flameproof casserole, heat the margarine and in it lightly brown the frankfurters. Add the onion and cook it until translucent.

2 pounds sauerkraut,
    rinsed, drained, and
    pressed dry in a colander

Add the sauerkraut and, over medium heat, simmer it, covered, for 20 minutes.

1½ cups sour cream
1½ teaspoons flour
1 tablespoon paprika
¼ teaspoon salt

Beat together until smooth the sour cream, flour, and seasonings.

At this point you may stop and continue later.

Over the simmering contents of the skillet, pour the sour cream mixture. Over medium heat, cook the dish, uncovered, for 10 minutes, or until the sauce is heated and slightly thickened.

Serve the dish with Crusty Bread, page 300.

This simple and tasty recipe is capable of several variations:

Six strips bacon, diced, may be rendered, removed to absorbent paper, and reserved; use the bacon fat in place of the margarine and garnish the completed dish with the bacon bits.

In place of the frankfurters, use 1½ pounds American or Italian sausage meat, rolled into small balls, rendered until crisp and brown, and removed to absorbent paper and reserved. Discard all but 4 tablespoons of the fat and use this in place of the margarine. Toss together the sauerkraut and sausage balls before simmering the sauerkraut.

Bratwurst or knackwurst may be used in place of the frankfurters.

Two tart apples, peeled, cored, and chopped, may be tossed with the sauerkraut.

Caraway or dill seeds may be sprinkled over the sauerkraut, to taste, before simmering the dish.

Sausage with Pork in Sour Cream — *Russia:* Brown 1 pound fresh pork shoulder, diced, in the fat remaining from rendering until crisp and browned 1 pound sausage meat rolled into small balls. Omit the sauerkraut, but simmer the meats and onion as directed, adding a little water as necessary. Follow rest of steps as directed. Serve the dish with Noodles, page 307.

Frankfurter and Corn Chowder

Serves 6 ■ Doubles ■ Refrigerates

Preparation: 30 minutes ■ Cooking: 10 minutes

A festive-looking soup, attractive — and economical — for informal supper parties.

4 tablespoons margarine 3 onions, sliced 3 ribs celery, chopped, with their leaves 3 medium-sized potatoes, peeled and diced	In a soup kettle, heat the margarine and in it cook the onion and celery until translucent. Add the potatoes and, over medium heat, cook them, stirring, for 5 minutes.
3 cups water 6 frankfurters, cut into ¼-inch rounds 1 bay leaf 3 whole cloves 1 teaspoon thyme 1½ teaspoons salt ½ teaspoon pepper	To the vegetables add the water, frankfurters, and seasonings. Bring the liquid to a boil, reduce the heat, and simmer the mixture for 20 minutes, or until the potatoes are just tender. *At this point you may stop and continue later.*
1 10-ounce package frozen whole-kernel corn, fully thawed to room temperature 1 1-pound can cream-style corn	Add the frozen and canned corn and cook them, stirring, for 5 minutes.
3 tablespoons flour 1 cup cold milk 2 cups hot milk 1 10-ounce package frozen peas, fully thawed to room temperature	Shake together until smooth the flour and cold milk. Add mixture to the soup, stirring. Add the hot milk and the peas, stirring. Cook the chowder for 5 minutes longer.

Serve the chowder with Crusty Bread, page 300.

GROUND MEATS

Americans are the largest meat-eaters in the world, and the greatest amount of the meat we consume is ground meat. Usually, ground meat is assumed to be ground beef, either chuck or round, and known to us as "hamburger," a term which, until recently, no German would have even vaguely understood.

In addition to ground beef, however, there are also ground veal and ground pork, and together the three (and sometimes lamb) are the most commonly used ground meats. In combination, they produce meat loaves of greater delicacy and subtlety than is possible by using only one variety of ground meat and are frequently sold, packaged together, as "Meat Loaf Mix" at supermarkets. The comparatively low price of ground meats is the reason for the numerous recipes here.

Ground meats are used in cooking all over the world, as the following recipes will show you — in meat loaves, soups, pilafs, exotic stews, and in combination with various fruits and vegetables. Sometimes, especially in Far Eastern cuisines, minced meat is called for — that is, meat cut into the finest possible pieces. For the purposes of this book, and with awareness of the time schedule of the cook, all such recipes have been adapted to products direct from your butcher or supermarket.

Meat Loaves

Meat Loaf — Basic Recipe
Serves 6 ■ Doubles ■ Refrigerates ■ Freezes

Preparation: 30 minutes ■ Cooking: 1 hour in a 350° F. oven

1½ pounds meat-loaf
   mixture (page 138)
   or 1½ pounds
   ground beef
½ cup milk
2 onions, grated
¾ cup bread crumbs
1 egg, beaten
1½ teaspoons salt
¼ teaspoon pepper

In a mixing bowl, combine these 7 ingredients. Knead the mixture until it is blended.

Margarine

With the margarine, grease an 8- or 9-inch loaf pan. In it pack the meat mixture evenly.

At this point you may stop and continue later.

Bake the meat loaf at 350° F. for 1 hour. Drain off any excess liquid (and reserve it for use in some other dish). To serve the loaf, unmold it onto a serving platter and slice it at the table.

Serve the dish with Mashed White Potatoes, page 302, or "Dressed-up" Canned Baked Beans, page 310.

This recipe lends itself to several variations:

Meat Loaf with Carrot: In first step, add 1 cup finely shredded carrot, increase the eggs to 2, and add 2 teaspoons Worcestershire sauce; follow the remainder of the recipe as directed.

Meat Loaf with Cheese: In first step, add ½ cup grated Parmesan or finely chopped Swiss cheese.

Meat Loaf with Cottage Cheese: In first step, reduce the milk to ¼ cup; add 1 6-ounce can tomato paste and 1 small green pepper, seeded and chopped. In second step, pack half of the meat mixture in an 8- by 8-inch baking dish, lightly greased. Combine ½ cup cracker crumbs with 1½ cups cottage cheese and ¼ cup chopped parsley: spread this mixture over the meat. Spread the remaining meat on top. In last step, allow the meat loaf to stand several minutes before draining it. Serve the dish with Dried Bean Salad, page 309.

Meat Loaf with Dill: In first step, add 1 clove garlic, put through a press, and 2 tablespoons dillweed; follow the remainder of the recipe as directed. (If desired, 1½ teaspoons ground allspice may also be added to the meat mixture — an exotic flavor combination.)

Meat Loaf with Dressing: In first step, use only ⅓ cup bread crumbs; add ¼ cup chopped parsley; in second step, arrange a layer of the meat mixture, then a layer of 1½ or 2 cups prepared poultry dressing, and finish with a layer of the rest of the meat; follow the remainder of the recipe as directed. Serve the dish with Cabbage, page 294.

Meat Loaf with Herbs: In first step, add ½ teaspoon each of basil, marjoram, oregano, rosemary, sage, and thyme; follow the remainder of the recipe as directed.

Meat Loaf with Oatmeal — *Scotland:* In first step, use, in place of the bread crumbs, ¾ cup uncooked oatmeal; increase the milk to 1¼ cups, season the mixture with 1½ teaspoons prepared mustard, and increase the eggs to 2; follow the remainder of the recipe as directed.

Meat Loaf with Sweet Peppers: In first step, add 1 sweet red and 1 green pepper, seeded and finely chopped; follow the remainder of the recipe as directed.

Meat Loaf with Sausage: In first step, add ¼ pound sausage meat and 4 tablespoons tomato paste; follow the remainder of the recipe as directed.

Meat Loaf with Spices: In first step, add ½ teaspoon each ground allspice and cinnamon, ¼ teaspoon ground clove, and 1 teaspoon nutmeg, and use, in place of the milk, ½ cup orange juice; follow the remainder of the recipe as directed.

Meat Loaf with Tomato: In first step, in place of the milk, use 3 tomatoes, peeled, seeded, and chopped, together with their juices; in last step, add 1 tomato, peeled and sliced thinly, arranged over the top of the meat loaf, for the final 30 minutes of cooking.

All meat loaves may be attractively made in a ring mold, the center hole then being filled with mashed potato, baked beans, rice, or any other side dish of your choice.

Steamed Beef Loaf
Serves 6 ■ Doubles ■ Refrigerates

Preparation: 25 minutes ■ Cooking: 15 minutes

1½ pounds ground beef
6   scallions, chopped
2   cloves garlic, put
    through a press
2   eggs, lightly beaten
½   cup bread crumbs
½   cup chopped parsley
Grated rind and juice of 1
    lemon
1   teaspoon sugar
1½ teaspoons salt
¼   teaspoon pepper

In a mixing bowl, combine and blend thoroughly these 11 ingredients.

Pack the meat mixture into a ring mold. Unmold it on a heatproof serving platter or baking dish.

At this point you may stop and continue later.

Place the platter on a rack in the bottom of a covered roasting pan. Add water to just below the level of the rack. Bring the water to a boil, reduce the heat, and steam the meat, covered, for 15 minutes, or until the meat is cooked to your taste.

Serve the dish with Tomato Pilaf, page 306, arranged in the middle of the meat ring.

Ground Beef with Eggplant: Iran
Serves 6 ■ Doubles ■ Refrigerates

Preparation: 30 minutes ■ Cooking: 30 minutes in a 350° F. oven

1 large eggplant, cut into ½-inch slices Olive oil	In a skillet, brown the eggplant slices in olive oil, adding more oil as necessary. Remove and reserve the eggplant.
1½ pounds ground beef 2 onions, chopped	In the skillet, brown the beef, breaking it up with a spoon so that it is uniformly cooked. Discard any excess fat. Add the onion and cook the mixture, stirring until the onion is translucent.
2 tomatoes, peeled, seeded, and chopped 1 teaspoon ground cumin 1½ teaspoons salt ½ teaspoon pepper ½ cup raisins ½ cup pine nuts (optional)	Stir in the tomatoes, then add the seasonings and, last, the raisins and pine nuts. In a 2-quart oiled baking dish, arrange alternate layers of the meat mixture and eggplant slices. *At this point you may stop and continue later.* Bake the dish, uncovered, in a 350° F. oven for 30 minutes.

Meat Loaf with Eggplant: Peel and slice the eggplant, but do not brown it. Do not brown the meat. In a large mixing bowl, combine the meat, 1 egg, the onion, tomatoes, seasonings, raisins, and pine nuts; blend the mixture well. Oil the casserole, arrange the ingredients in layers as directed, and bake the dish, uncovered, at 350° F. for 1 hour; let it stand 10 minutes, discard any liquid that has risen to the top, and serve.

Ground Beef with Lentils: Turkey
Serves 6 ■ Doubles ■ Refrigerates ■ Freezes

Preparation: 30 minutes ■ Cooking: 30 minutes

4 cups boiling water 1½ cups lentils	In the boiling water, cook the lentils for 20 minutes. Drain and reserve them.
2 tablespoons margarine 2 onions, chopped 1 clove garlic, finely chopped	In a deep skillet, heat the margarine, and in it cook the onion and garlic until translucent.
1½ pounds ground chuck	To the onion add the meat and brown it well.
1½ cups hot water, in which 2 beef bouillon cubes have been dissolved	Add the bouillon and simmer the meat for 10 minutes.
Reserved lentils 2 tablespoons raw natural rice ⅓ cup water 1 teaspoon sugar 1 teaspoon ground cumin ½ teaspoon pepper	To the contents of the skillet add the reserved lentils, rice, water, and seasonings. Stir the mixture to blend it. *At this point you may stop and continue later.*
1 tablespoon vinegar	Bring the liquid to a boil, reduce the heat, and simmer the dish, covered, for 30 minutes, or until the lentils and rice are tender and the liquid is nearly absorbed. Stir in the vinegar.

Serve the dish with Eggplant made with yogurt, page 295.

Casseroles

Ground Beef with Macaroni I

Serves 6 ■ Doubles ■ Refrigerates

Preparation: 30 minutes ■ Cooking: 30 minutes in a 350° F. oven

1 8-ounce package elbow macaroni	Cook the macaroni as directed on the package.
1 tablespoon margarine 1 onion, chopped 1 pound ground chuck	In a heavy saucepan, heat the margarine and in it cook the onion until translucent. Add the meat and brown it.
2 tablespoons flour 1½ tablespoons paprika 1 cup hot water, in which 2 beef bouillon cubes have been dissolved 1 cup sour cream	Into the meat, stir the flour and paprika. Gradually add the bouillon and cook the mixture, stirring constantly, until it is thickened and smooth. Stir in the sour cream.
Reserved macaroni Paprika	Into the macaroni, gently stir the meat mixture. Arrange the combined ingredients in a lightly greased 2-quart baking dish and sprinkle them with paprika. *At this point you may stop and continue later.* Bake the dish, uncovered, at 350° F. for 30 minutes.

Serve the dish with Spinach, page 296.

Ground Beef with Macaroni II: Greece
Serves 6 generously ■ Doubles ■ Refrigerates ■ Freezes

Preparation: 1 hour ■ Cooking: 45 minutes in a 350° F. oven

Pastitso is a popular dish in Greece. Its flavor is very subtle, despite the quantity of cinnamon called for. It is well worth the effort of its preparation. This recipe for *pastitso* — there are several variants — comes from a restaurant in the harbor of the island of Kea where for two days I was stranded by high winds.

6 quarts hot water, salted 1 pound macaroni	In a large kettle, bring the water to a rolling boil and in it cook the macaroni for 12 minutes, or until it is just tender. Drain and rinse it with hot water. Allow it to cool to lukewarm.
2 tablespoons margarine 2 tablespoons flour 1 teaspoon salt 1 teaspoon cinnamon 4 cups milk, scalded	In a saucepan, melt the margarine, stir in the flour, and, over gentle heat, cook the *roux* for 3 minutes. Stir in the seasonings. Gradually add the milk, stirring constantly to assure a smooth sauce; cook the mixture until it boils and is thickened and smooth. Allow it to cool.
4 tablespoons olive oil 3 onions, chopped 1½ pounds ground beef 2½ teaspoons cinnamon ¾ teaspoon nutmeg 2 teaspoons salt ¼ teaspoon pepper	In a skillet, heat the oil and in it cook the onion until translucent. Add the meat and brown it. Discard the excess fat. Stir in the seasonings and simmer the mixture 5 minutes.
3 eggs, beaten	To the cooked macaroni, add the eggs. Blend the mixture well (I use my hands, thus preventing the macaroni from breaking).

1 tablespoon margarine
Mild grated cheese

With the margarine, grease a 9- by 13-inch baking pan. In it, arrange a layer of one half of the macaroni. Add the meat mixture in one layer. Add the remaining pasta and a sprinkling of the cheese. Pour over the white sauce.

At this point you may stop and continue later.

Bake the dish, uncovered, at 350° F. for 45 minutes, or until it is set and the top is golden brown.

Moussaka: Greece
Serves 6 generously ∎ Doubles ∎ Refrigerates

Preparation: 45 minutes ∎ Cooking: 45 minutes in a 350° F. oven

A recipe deriving from my summer spent among the Greek islands and one that I believe you will enjoy. A pleasant variation results from using one-half eggplant and one-half zucchini.

2 medium eggplants, cut into ½-inch slices
Olive oil

On a broiling rack, arrange the eggplant slices, brush them with olive oil, and broil them for 5 minutes on each side.

1½ pounds ground chuck
2 onions, chopped
3 tomatoes, peeled, seeded, and sliced (canned tomatoes, drained, will do)
1 teaspoon cinnamon
Salt
Pepper

In a large skillet, brown the meat and onion. Add the tomatoes and cinnamon, and cook the mixture until it is moist but not watery. Season it.

Grated Parmesan cheese (optional)

In a greased baking dish, arrange a layer of the meat mixture and then a layer of the eggplant. Repeat. If desired, sprinkle each layer with grated cheese.

6 tablespoons margarine
6 tablespoons flour
4 cups milk, scalded
4 eggs, beaten
Grated Parmesan cheese

In a saucepan, heat the margarine and in it, over gentle heat, cook the flour for 3 minutes. Gradually add the milk, stirring constantly until the mixture is thickened and smooth. Blend a little of the sauce with the eggs. Then, away from the heat, blend the egg mixture into the sauce. Over the contents of the baking dish, pour the sauce. Sprinkle it liberally with the cheese.

At this point you may stop and continue later.

Bake the dish, uncovered, at 350° F. for 45 minutes, or until the top is golden brown.

Ground Beef Risotto: Italy
Serves 6 ■ Doubles ■ Refrigerates

Preparation: 30 minutes ■ Cooking: 30 minutes

3 tablespoons olive oil 1 cup raw natural rice 1 pound ground beef 2 onions, chopped	In a large skillet, heat the olive oil and in it cook the rice, beef, and onion until the meat is browned and the onion translucent.
1 green pepper, chopped 1 rib celery, chopped	Add the pepper and celery and, over gentle heat, cook the mixture for 5 minutes.
1 1-pound can Italian tomatoes ¾ cup water ¼ cup chopped parsley 1 teaspoon oregano 2 teaspoons sugar 1½ teaspoons salt ¼ teaspoon pepper	To the contents of the skillet add these 7 ingredients, stirring to blend the mixture. *At this point you may stop and continue later.*
Grated Parmesan cheese	Bring the liquid to a boil, reduce the heat, and simmer the dish, covered, for 30 minutes, or until the rice is tender and the liquid is absorbed. Stir the dish occasionally during the cooking. When serving the risotto, offer the cheese separately.

Serve the dish with Green Bean Salad, page 299.

Stuffed Cabbage Rolls
Serves 6 ■ Refrigerates

Preparation: 30 minutes ■ Cooking: 45 minutes in a 375° F. oven

12 large cabbage leaves
Boiling salted water

In a shallow dish, arrange the cabbage leaves in a flat layer. Over them pour the water to cover fully. Allow the leaves to stand for 5 minutes. Drain and dry them on absorbent paper.

¾ pound ground beef
¾ pound ground lamb
2 onions, chopped
2 ripe tomatoes, peeled, seeded, and chopped
½ cup raw natural rice
3 tablespoons chopped parsley
1 teaspoon cinnamon
1 tablespoon mint

In a mixing bowl, combine and blend thoroughly these 8 ingredients. In the center of each cabbage leaf, spoon an equal amount of the meat mixture. Fold the opposite edges over the meat, roll the leaves into a cylindrical shape, and secure them with toothpicks. In a baking dish, arrange the rolls in a single layer.

At this point you may stop and continue later.

1 cup hot water, in which 1 beef bouillon cube has been dissolved

Over the cabbage rolls, pour the bouillon. Bake the dish, covered, at 375° F. for 45 minutes, or until the cabbage is tender.

Serve the dish with Noodles, page 307.

152

The suggested filling is of Greek origin. Other fillings are equally appetizing:

1½ pounds ground beef, ⅓ cup quick-cooking oatmeal, 1 onion, chopped, ¼ cup parsley, 1 egg, lightly beaten, ½ cup hot water (in which 1 beef bouillon cube has been dissolved), 1 teaspoon salt, and ¼ teaspoon pepper. Proceed with last step as directed.

1½ pounds ground meat (or meats) of your choice, browned in 4 tablespoons margarine, together with 3 onions, chopped. Blend this mixture with ¾ cup raw natural rice and ⅓ cup currants, 1½ teaspoons sugar, 1 tablespoon dillweed, 1 teaspoon salt, ¼ teaspoon pepper, and ½ cup hot water, in which 1 beef bouillon cube has been dissolved. Proceed with last step as directed.

If desired, a pleasant sauce may be made from the cooking liquid: with a slotted spoon, remove the cooked cabbage rolls to a serving dish and keep them warm. In a saucepan, make a *roux* of 1 tablespoon margarine and 1 tablespoon flour; gradually add the reserved liquid from the baking dish. Stir the mixture constantly until it is thickened and smooth. Stir in milk until the sauce is of the consistency desired and season it to taste with salt and pepper. Pour the sauce over the cabbage rolls.

Stuffed Eggplant: Italy
Serves 6 ■ Doubles ■ Refrigerates

Preparation: 40 minutes ■ Cooking: 25 minutes in a 325° F. oven

3 small eggplants

Trim the stem end of the eggplants. With a grapefruit knife, cut out the center flesh; do not cut the shells. Chop the flesh.

3 tablespoons olive oil
1½ pounds ground chuck
Reserved chopped eggplant

In a heavy skillet, heat the oil and in it brown the meat and chopped eggplant.

1 1-pound can Italian tomatoes
1 8-ounce can tomato sauce
½ teaspoon garlic salt
½ teaspoon oregano

Stir into the meat mixture these 4 ingredients. Simmer them, uncovered, stirring often, for 25 minutes, or until most of the liquid has evaporated.

½ cup grated Parmesan cheese

Stir in the cheese. With this mixture fill the eggplant shells. Stand them in a baking dish.

At this point you may stop and continue later.

Bake the dish, uncovered, at 325° F. for 25 minutes, or until the eggplant shells are tender. Before serving the stuffed eggplants, halve them lengthwise.

Serve the dish with Dried Bean Salad, page 309.

Meatballs with Chinese Vegetables

Serves 6 ■ Doubles ■ Refrigerates (adequately only)

Preparation: 30 minutes ■ Cooking: 15 minutes

This "Chinese" dish comes from China by way of my own kitchen, where it was invented in order to offer a meal to unexpected friends.

1½ pounds ground beef
2 eggs
½ teaspoon ground cumin
1½ teaspoons salt
¼ teaspoon pepper

Mix well these 5 ingredients and shape them into 36 small balls.

3 tablespoons oil

In a wok or large deep-sided skillet or casserole, heat the oil and brown the meatballs. Remove them to absorbent paper and reserve. Reserve the meat drippings in the skillet.

6 or 8 scallions, sliced diagonally, with as much green as possible
2 cups chopped Chinese celery cabbage
1 10-ounce package frozen snow peas, fully thawed to room temperature
1 8-ounce can bamboo shoots, drained
3 tablespoons preserved ginger, chopped (optional)

Prepare all the remaining ingredients.

At this point you may stop and continue later.

Reheat the meat drippings and in them cook the scallions and celery cabbage, stirring constantly, for 2 minutes. Add the remaining vegetables and cook them, stirring constantly, for 2 minutes. Add the reserved meatballs.

1½ cups hot water, in which 2 beef bouillon cubes have been dissolved
1 teaspoon sugar

Add the bouillon and sugar. Rapidly bring the liquid to the boil.

2 tablespoons cornstarch
¼ cup soy sauce

Mix the cornstarch and soy sauce and add to the boiling liquid. Cook the dish, stirring constantly, for 3 minutes, or until the sauce is thickened and smooth.

Serve the dish with Boiled Rice, page 303.

Meatballs with Eggplant: Italy
Serves 6 ■ Doubles ■ Refrigerates

Preparation: 30 minutes ■ Cooking: 30 minutes

1½ pounds ground chuck ½ cup bread crumbs 1 egg ¼ cup chopped parsley 1 teaspoon salt ¼ teaspoon pepper	In a mixing bowl, combine and blend thoroughly these 6 ingredients. Roll the mixture into 24 balls.
3 tablespoons olive oil	In a large skillet, heat the oil and in it evenly brown the meatballs. Remove and reserve them.
2 onions, chopped 1 clove garlic, chopped 1 medium-sized eggplant, peeled and cubed Reserved meatballs	In the remaining fat, cook the onion and garlic until translucent. Stir in the eggplant and add the meatballs.
1½ teaspoons sugar 1 teaspoon ground cumin 1 1-pound can Italian tomatoes	Over the contents of the skillet, sprinkle the sugar and cumin; pour over the tomatoes. *At this point you may stop and continue later.* Simmer the dish, uncovered, for 30 minutes. Stir it gently from time to time.

Serve the dish with Spaghetti, page 307, buttered and sprinkled with grated Parmesan cheese.

Meatballs with Sauerkraut
Serves 6 ■ Doubles ■ Refrigerates

Preparation: 30 minutes ■ Cooking: 40 minutes

1½ pounds meat-loaf mix, page 138
1 egg
⅓ cup bread crumbs
½ teaspoon thyme
1 teaspoon salt
¼ teaspoon pepper

In a mixing bowl, combine and blend thoroughly these 6 ingredients. Roll the meat into 24 balls.

2 tablespoons margarine

In a deep skillet, heat the margarine and in it brown the meatballs. Remove them to absorbent paper and reserve them.

2 onions, chopped
2 tart apples, peeled, cored, and diced
2 pounds sauerkraut, rinsed and thoroughly drained

In the remaining fat, cook the onion and apple until the onion is translucent. Add the sauerkraut and toss the mixture to blend it. Replace the meatballs.

At this point you may stop and continue later.

3 tablespoons brown sugar
1 6-ounce can apple juice

Mix the sugar and apple juice. Pour the liquid over the contents of the skillet. Simmer the dish, covered, for 40 minutes, or until the sauerkraut is tender.

Serve the dish with Boiled Sweet Potatoes, page 301.

Meatballs with Peas: Italy
Serves 6 ■ Doubles ■ Refrigerates

Preparation: 30 minutes ■ Cooking: 30 minutes in a 300° F. oven

This recipe is contributed by my good friend Edward Giobbi, extraordinary artist and superb cook, in whose kitchen-dining room many companionable evenings have been spent with Ed and his gracious wife and delightful children. His *Italian Family Cooking*, illustrated by the children, is a delightful and original cookbook.

1½ pounds meat-loaf mix, page 138; *or* 1½ pounds ground chuck	In a mixing bowl, combine and blend thoroughly these 10 ingredients. Roll the mixture into 18 balls.
1 cup bread crumbs, soaked in ½ cup milk and squeezed dry	
2 onions, chopped	On a greased tray, broil the meatballs, turning them so that they brown evenly. Arrange them in an oven-proof serving dish and keep them warm.
½ cup seedless raisins	
½ cup grated Parmesan cheese	
½ cup chopped parsley	
2 eggs, lightly beaten	
1 teaspoon thyme	
1½ teaspoons salt	
¼ teaspoon pepper	

3	tablespoons olive oil	In a saucepan, heat the oil and in it cook the onion and garlic until translucent. Add the tomatoes and oregano. Simmer the mixture, covered, for 10 minutes.
3	onions, chopped	
1	clove garlic, chopped	
3	large ripe tomatoes, peeled, seeded, and chopped (canned tomatoes, drained, will do)	
1	teaspoon oregano	
1	10-ounce package frozen peas, fully thawed to room temperature	Add the peas and simmer them in the sauce, covered, for 8 minutes, or until they are tender.

At this point you may stop and continue later.

Over the meatballs, pour the sauce and bake the dish, covered, for 30 minutes in a 300° F. oven.

Serve the dish with Molded Rice, page 305.

A variation of this recipe from India: In first step, omit the onion, cheese, and thyme; season the mixture with 1 teaspoon ground cinnamon, 1 tablespoon curry powder, and 1 teaspoon ground ginger. Omit the garlic and oregano.

Meatballs with Spinach in Orange Sauce

Serves 6 ■ Doubles ■ Refrigerates ■ Freezes

Preparation: 40 minutes ■ Cooking: 20 minutes

1½ pounds ground beef 2 onions, grated ½ teaspoon cinnamon 1 teaspoon salt ¼ teaspoon pepper	In a mixing bowl, combine and blend thoroughly these 5 ingredients. Roll the meat into 36 small balls.
4 tablespoons oil	In a large skillet, heat the oil and in it brown the meatballs. Remove them to absorbent paper and reserve. Discard the fat.
2 tablespoons margarine 1 10-ounce package fresh spinach, rinsed, dried, and finely chopped ¼ cup chopped parsley	In the skillet, heat the margarine and in it cook the spinach and parsley, stirring often, for 10 minutes. Replace the meat. *At this point you may stop and continue later.*
1 cup orange juice Juice of ½ lemon 1 tablespoon cornstarch	Combine the orange and lemon juice with the cornstarch. Add the mixture to the meatballs and, over low heat, cook the dish, stirring gently but constantly, for 20 minutes, or until the sauce is thickened and the meat is heated through.

Serve the dish with Boiled Rice, page 303.

Ground Beef with Squash: Turkey
Serves 6 ■ Doubles ■ Refrigerates

Preparation: 25 minutes ■ Cooking: 30 minutes in a 325° F. oven

6 summer squash (yellow or zucchini), quartered crosswise
Boiling salted water

Cook the squash in the boiling water for 3 minutes. Drain it and, in a lightly greased baking dish, arrange it in a single layer.

2 tablespoons olive oil
1 pound ground beef
2 onions, chopped

In a skillet, heat the oil and in it brown the meat and onion. Stir the mixture often.

3 tomatoes, peeled, seeded, and chopped (canned tomatoes, drained, will do)
1 green pepper, chopped
1 tablespoon dillweed
1 tablespoon mint
¼ teaspoon pepper

To the meat, add the tomato and pepper and cook the mixture for 5 minutes. Stir in the seasonings. Spread the meat over the squash.

At this point you may stop and continue later.

½ cup hot water, in which 1 beef bouillon cube has been dissolved

Over the contents of the baking dish, pour the bouillon. Bake the dish, uncovered, at 325° F. for 30 minutes.

Serve the dish with Noodles, page 307.

Meatball Stew
Serves 6 ■ Doubles ■ Refrigerates ■ Freezes

Preparation: 30 minutes ■ Cooking: 1 hour in a 350° F. oven

1½ pounds ground chuck
1   onion, grated
½   cup bread crumbs
1   egg
1½ teaspoons salt
¼   teaspoon pepper

In a mixing bowl, combine and blend thoroughly these 6 ingredients. Roll the mixture into 1-inch balls.

2   tablespoons olive oil

In a flameproof casserole, heat the oil and in it brown the meatballs. Remove them to absorbent paper and reserve them. Discard all but 3 tablespoons of the fat.

3   tablespoons flour
1   1-pound can Italian
    tomatoes
1   cup water
1   teaspoon basil
1   bay leaf
½   teaspoon thyme
2   teaspoons sugar
½   teaspoon salt

Into the reserved fat, stir the flour and, over gentle heat, cook the mixture for 3 minutes. Add the tomatoes, water, and seasonings and cook the mixture, stirring constantly, until it is thickened and smooth.

3   potatoes, peeled and
    diced
3   large carrots, scraped
    and sliced
3   onions, quartered
3   stalks celery, chopped

Add the vegetables and cook them for 10 minutes.

At this point you may stop and continue later.

To the contents of the casserole add the reserved meatballs, stirring gently to blend the ingredients. Bake the stew, covered, at 350° F. for 1 hour, or until the vegetables are tender.

Serve the stew with Crusty Bread, page 300.

Ground Beef with Sweet and Pungent Sauce

Serves 6 ■ Doubles ■ Refrigerates

Preparation: 25 minutes ■ Cooking: ½ hour in a 350° F. oven

1½ pounds ground round
½ teaspoon ground
    allspice
Salt
Pepper
3 tablespoons margarine

Season the meat. Roll it into small balls. In a skillet, heat the margarine and in it brown the meatballs. Drain them on absorbent paper.

Sweet and Pungent Sauce
    (page 311)

In a baking dish, arrange the meatballs. Over them, spoon the Sweet and Pungent Sauce. Bake the dish, covered, at 350° F. for ½ hour.

Serve the dish with Boiled Rice, page 303.

BASIL

Ground Lamb with Onion: India
Serves 6 ■ Doubles ■ Refrigerates

Preparation: 30 minutes ■ Cooking: 15 minutes

4 tablespoons margarine 4 onions, chopped	In a large skillet, heat the margarine and in it cook the onion, stirring often, for 15 minutes. Remove and reserve it.
2 onions, chopped 1 clove garlic, chopped 2 teaspoons ground ginger 1 teaspoon salt	To the remaining fat add the onion, garlic, ginger, and salt. Cook the onion, stirring often, for 5 minutes.
1½ pounds ground lamb 1 teaspoon ground coriander 1 teaspoon ground cumin 1 teaspoon turmeric 3 tomatoes, peeled, seeded, and chopped ⅓ cup water ½ cup yogurt	To the skillet add the meat and brown it, stirring often. Stir in the spices, tomatoes, water, and yogurt. *At this point you may stop and continue later.*
Reserved cooked onion	Simmer the lamb mixture, uncovered, for 15 minutes, stirring it frequently. Garnish the dish with the reserved onion.

Serve the dish with Tomato Pilaf, page 306.

Ground Meat and Bean Cassoulet

Serves 6 generously ■ Doubles ■ Refrigerates ■ Freezes

Preparation: 30 minutes ■ Cooking: 1 hour in a 350° F. oven

6 slices bacon, diced	In a flameproof casserole, cook the bacon until it is golden but not fully crisp; remove it to absorbent paper and reserve it.
1½ pounds meat-loaf mix (page 138)	In the remaining fat, brown the meat; discard the drippings.
1 20-ounce can red kidney beans 1 20-ounce can white kidney beans 1 1-pound can stewed tomatoes ¼ cup chopped parsley 1 teaspoon thyme 1½ teaspoons salt ¼ teaspoon pepper Reserved bacon bits	In a colander, drain the beans; rinse them with cold water. Add them to the meat, together with the tomatoes, parsley, and seasonings. Gently stir the mixture to blend it. Over the top, sprinkle the reserved bacon. *At this point you may stop and continue later.*
	Bake the casserole, covered, at 350° F. for 1 hour.

Serve the dish with Mixed Green Salad, page 298.

Chili Pie: Follow first step as directed; in next step, add 2 onions, chopped, to the meat when browning it; in third step, use *only* 1 can of red kidney beans and add 2 teaspoons chili powder and 2 teaspoons Worcestershire sauce to the suggested ingredients. Simmer the meat mixture for 15 minutes. Over the top arrange the dough from an 8½-ounce package of corn-bread mix, prepared as directed on the packet. Bake the chili pie at 450° F. for 20 minutes, or until the corn bread is golden brown.

Soups

Meatball Soup I: America
Serves 6 ■ Doubles ■ Refrigerates

Preparation: 30 minutes ■ Cooking: 10 minutes

1½ pounds ground beef
1   egg
¼   cup milk
¼   cup cracker crumbs
¼   teaspoon basil
¼   teaspoon marjoram
¼   teaspoon rosemary
¼   teaspoon thyme
1   teaspoon salt
¼   teaspoon pepper

In a mixing bowl, combine the meat, egg, milk, crumbs, and seasonings. Knead the mixture until it is blended. Form it into 36 small balls and reserve them.

5   cups water, in which
    3 beef bouillon cubes
    have been dissolved
2   carrots, sliced very thinly
3   scallions, chopped
1   10-ounce package frozen
    peas

In a large saucepan, bring the liquid to a boil and in it cook the vegetables for 5 minutes.

At this point you may stop and continue later.

Return the broth to the boil and add the reserved beef balls, a few at a time so that the liquid continues to boil. Cook the meatballs for 5 minutes.

Serve the soup with Crusty Bread, page 300.

Meatball Soup II: Italy

Serves 6 ■ Doubles ■ Refrigerates

Preparation: 30 minutes ■ Cooking: 20 minutes

1½ pounds ground beef
1 egg
4 tablespoons grated Parmesan cheese
2 tablespoons bread crumbs
1 tablespoon chopped parsley
Salt
Pepper

In a mixing bowl, combine the meat, egg, cheese, bread crumbs, parsley, and salt and pepper to taste. Knead the mixture until it is well blended. Form it into 36 small balls.

6 cups water, in which 6 beef bouillon cubes have been dissolved

Bring the water to a boil and add the beef balls, a few at a time so that the liquid continues to boil. Reduce the heat and simmer the meatballs 5 minutes.

At this point you may stop and continue later.

½ pound ribbon noodles (*tagliatelle*)
Grated Parmesan cheese

Return the broth to the boil, add the pasta and cook it 12 minutes, or until it is tender but *al dente*. Serve the cheese separately.

Serve the dish with Crusty Bread, page 300.

VARIETY MEATS

"Variety meat" is the term applied to organ and glandular meats, the edible parts of beef, lamb, pork, and veal that are not skeletal muscle (which is usually called just "meat"). Thus, variety meats include brain, heart, kidney, liver, tongue, tripe, and, for some reason unknown to me, oxtail — albeit this is most surely a "skeletal" meat. They are more economical than regular cuts, and they are also remarkably nutritious and easily digested. Carefully prepared, they produce main dishes attractive to both taste and eye. Use them with courage and invention!

Brains

Before being used in a particular dish, brains require to be well rinsed under cold water; they should then be precooked in acidulated water (below) to improve their taste and texture. They should be very fresh when bought and used shortly after purchase. Precooked brain may be safely kept for 24 hours under refrigeration, or in the freezing compartment for 2 weeks, or in a home freezer for 6 weeks; frozen brain should be rapidly thawed in warm water. One quarter of a pound of brain yields one serving; for people who are especially fond of them — who could not be? — a larger helping of this economical high-protein food is welcome. Beef, lamb, pork, and veal brains are all suitable for these recipes. Although of different sizes, they may be purchased by weight, thus assuring the amount you require. Please note that the preparation times given in the following recipes do not include the time required to prepare the brains for cooking. It is hoped that these recipes will please those already familiar with brain and will open new culinary doors to those unfamiliar with the delicacy.

To Prepare Brains for Cooking
Serves 6 ■ Doubles ■ Refrigerates

Time: 15 minutes

1   quart water
2   tablespoons lemon or
      lime juice or
      cider vinegar or
      ½ cup dry white wine
2   teaspoons salt
1½ pounds brains

In a saucepan, combine the water and either the lemon or lime juice or cider vinegar or white wine; add the salt. Bring the liquid to a boil, add the brains, and cook them briskly, uncovered for 10 minutes. Drain them in a colander and plunge them into very cold water.

When the brains are cool, drain them on absorbent paper and remove any skin and veins. Cut the brains in ½-inch slices.

Preparation: 20 minutes ■ Cooking: 20 minutes in a 450° F. oven

Baked Brains Creole: In 2 tablespoons margarine, brown 1 onion, chopped. Add 1½ tablespoons flour; stir in gradually 1½ cups water, in which 2 chicken bouillon cubes have been dissolved, 1 rib celery, chopped, and 3 tablespoons chopped parsley. Simmer the mixture, uncovered, for 10 minutes. Stir in ½ cup evaporated milk. Season the sauce to taste with salt and pepper. Arrange the slices of brain in a greased baking dish. Over them pour the sauce. Garnish the dish with bread crumbs and bake it, uncovered, at 450° F. for 20 minutes, or until the crumbs are browned. Serve the dish with Hot Potato Salad, page 302.

Preparation: 15 minutes ■ Cooking: 20 minutes in a 350° F. oven

Baked Brains with Yogurt: In a greased baking dish, arrange the slices of brain. In a mixing bowl, blend 1 cup yogurt, 2 beaten eggs, 1 tablespoon flour, ½ teaspoon each ground coriander and mace, ½ teaspoon salt, and a pinch of pepper. Pour the sauce over the brains. Bake the dish at 350° F. for 20 minutes, or until the custard is set and lightly browned. Garnish the dish with chopped parsley and serve it with Baked Sweet Potatoes, page 301.

Preparation: 10 minutes ■ Cooking: 10 minutes

Brains with Black Butter: In a skillet, melt 8 tablespoons margarine and, over gentle heat, cook it until it is brown. Meanwhile, in seasoned flour, lightly dredge the slices of brain. Increase the heat and, in the bubbling margarine, sauté the brains. When they are thoroughly heated through and have a slight crustiness, remove them to a serving dish. To the margarine in the skillet add the juice of ½ lemon and ¼ cup finely chopped parsley. Stir the sauce briefly and pour it over the brains. Serve the dish with Boiled White Potatoes, page 301.

Preparation: 10 minutes ■ Cooking: 10 minutes

Brains with Curry Sauce: In 4 tablespoons margarine, sauté the slices of brain. Remove them to a serving dish and keep them warm. To the remaining margarine, add 2 tablespoons flour, stirring. Stir in 1 tablespoon curry powder, or more, to taste. Gradually add 1 cup hot water in which 1 chicken bouillon cube has been dissolved; then add 1 cup hot milk. Cook the mixture, stirring constantly, until it is thickened and smooth. Pour the sauce over the brains. Serve the dish with Boiled Rice, page 303.

Brain Salad: On a bed of salad greens of your choice, arrange the slices of brain, 3 tomatoes, peeled and sliced, 1 green pepper, cut into julienne, 18 pitted ripe olives, 12 scallions, and 1 cucumber, peeled and sliced. Sprinkle over salt and pepper to taste. Dress the salad with olive oil and fresh lemon juice. This is a pleasant summer supper dish from Turkey. Serve it cold, accompanied by Crusty Bread, page 300.

Preparation: 10 minutes ∎ Cooking: 15 minutes

Brains with Vinaigrette Sauce: In seasoned flour, dredge the brain slices and, in 4 tablespoons very hot olive oil, brown them quickly. Arrange the brains in a baking dish. To the remaining olive oil add ¼ cup chopped parsley, 3 tablespoons very finely chopped sweet pickle (optional), and ½ cup All-Purpose Vinaigrette Salad Dressing, page 299. In this mixture, heat the brains in a 350° F. oven for 15 minutes. Serve the dish with Boiled White Potatoes, page 301.

Heart

Hearts of beef, lamb, pork, and veal are used throughout Europe as familiar components of cookery, especially in Scandinavia. Beef heart, the largest, may weigh as much as 5 pounds; it may be stuffed and braised for a delicious main dish. Regardless of which variety of heart you buy, allow about ½ pound per serving. One lamb heart, whole, makes an adequate and attractive single serving. It is not necessary to slice lamb heart, unless so desired; beef, pork, and veal heart may be sliced for quicker cooking. Refrigerate it no longer than 4 days before cooking it; it may be stored in a freezer for as long as 6 months. Nutritious and inexpensive, heart, cut in bite-size pieces, may be used in any recipe in this book for stews. Before starting a particular recipe, wash the heart and, with sharp kitchen scissors or small knife, remove the fat, veins, and arteries. Please note that the preparation times given in the following recipes do not include the time required to prepare the hearts for cooking. Beef heart, the firmest-fleshed, will require 3 to 4 hours to cook, covered, in a 300° F. oven, or at the simmer on top of the range; lamb, pork, and veal heart will require 2½ to 3 hours, under the same conditions.

Sautéed Lamb's Heart
Serves 6 ■ Doubles ■ Refrigerates

Preparation: 30 minutes ■ Cooking: 20 minutes

Only lamb's heart, the tenderest of all, works well in this simple but tasty recipe.

Seasoned flour
6 lambs' hearts, prepared for cooking (page 175) and cut in thin slices
6 tablespoons margarine
¼ cup chopped parsley

In the seasoned flour, dredge the pieces of heart. In a skillet, heat the margarine and in it, over gentle heat, cook the heart, stirring often, for 20 minutes, or until it is well browned but still tender. (Overcooking will toughen the heart.) Garnish the meat with the parsley.

Serve the dish with Baked Acorn Squash, page 294.

Roasted Heart: Italy
Serves 6 ■ Doubles ■ Refrigerates

Preparation: 30 minutes ■ Marination: 1½ hours
Cooking: see page 175

½ cup olive oil
Grated rind and juice of
   1 lemon
½ teaspoon oregano
½ teaspoon thyme
1   teaspoon salt
¼ teaspoon pepper
3   pounds heart, prepared
   for cooking (page 175)

In a mixing bowl, combine these 7 ingredients and in the mixture marinate the heart for 1½ hours.

¼ cup water

Remove the heart to a roasting pan, pour the marinade over it, and bake it, *uncovered*, according to the directions on page 175. Baste it often with the marinade. Remove the heart to a serving dish and keep it warm. With the water, deglaze the roasting pan, and pour the sauce over the heart.

Serve the dish with Spaghetti, page 307.

Hearts with Parsley: Denmark
Serves 6 ■ Doubles ■ Refrigerates ■ Freezes

Preparation: 30 minutes ■ Cooking: see page 175

Perhaps the most "elegant" of these recipes for heart, this dish is good party fare!

¾ cup parsley, chopped
3 onions, chopped
3 pounds whole heart, prepared for cooking (page 175)

In a mixing bowl, toss together the parsley and onion, and with the mixture, stuff the heart. Skewer or sew the heart closed.

3 tablespoons margarine
3 onions, chopped
3 carrots, scraped and sliced
3 ribs celery, chopped
1 bay leaf
1½ teaspoons salt
¼ teaspoon pepper

In a flameproof casserole, heat the margarine and in it lightly brown the heart. Add the vegetables and seasonings.

1½ cups hot water, in which 1 beef bouillon cube has been dissolved

Prepare the bouillon.

At this point you may stop and continue later.

Add the bouillon and cook the heart according to your preferred method (page 175). Remove the heart to a serving dish and keep it warm. Sieve the cooking liquid (the vegetables may be puréed in the container of an electric blender and added to soup stock). Return the liquid to the casserole.

2 tablespoons flour	Shake together the flour and evaporated milk. To the contents of the casserole add the flour mixture and, over medium heat, cook it, stirring constantly, until it is thickened and smooth. Slice the heart and pour the sauce over it.
1 5⅓-ounce can evaporated milk	

Serve the dish with Noodles, page 307.

A variation on the recipe: In first step, in a mixing bowl, cream 3 tablespoons margarine and to it add the parsley and onions; blend the mixture well before stuffing the heart; dredge the heart in seasoned flour. Follow second and third steps as directed. In last step, reduce the flour to 1 tablespoonful. This is essentially the same dish, except that it is richer.

Heart Stew: America

Serves 6 ■ Doubles ■ Refrigerates ■ Freezes

Preparation: 30 minutes ■ Cooking: see page 175

Seasoned flour
2½ to 3 pounds heart, prepared for cooking (page 175) and cut in thin slices
4 tablespoons margarine

In the seasoned flour, dredge the heart. In a flameproof casserole, heat the margarine and in it lightly brown the heart. Remove the heart and reserve it.

3 onions, sliced
2 carrots, thinly sliced
2 tablespoons remaining seasoned flour

In the remaining fat, cook the onion and carrot until the onion is translucent. Over the vegetables, sprinkle the seasoned flour. Replace the heart.

2½ cups hot water, in which 2 beef bouillon cubes have been dissolved

Prepare the bouillon.

At this point you may stop and continue later.

To the contents of the casserole add the bouillon, and cook the heart according to your preferred method, page 175.

Serve the dish with Mashed White Potatoes, page 302.

This simple, bland, and appetizing dish is capable of variations:

Ragout of Lamb Heart: In first step, add ¾ teaspoon thyme to the seasoned flour; in third step, combine 1 cup water with 1 1-pound can tomatoes and 1 tablespoon Worcestershire sauce; in last step, after the first hour of cooking, add 6 carrots, scraped and thinly sliced.

Heart Stew with Vegetables: In first step, use unseasoned flour; in second step, omit the carrots. In place of the water, use 1 29-ounce can tomatoes, to which is added 1 teaspoon basil, 2 bay leaves, ½ teaspoon marjoram, ½ teaspoon thyme, 1 teaspoon sugar, 1½ teaspoons salt, and ¼ teaspoon pepper; in last step, add, for the final hour of cooking, 4 carrots, scraped and cut in ½-inch rounds, 3 ribs celery, coarsely chopped, and 3 medium-sized potatoes, peeled and quartered. This dish requires no accompaniment.

Heart and Kidney Stew: In first step, use only 1½ pounds of heart and add to it 1 veal kidney, prepared for cooking, page 175; in second step, omit the carrot but add 2 cloves garlic, chopped; in third step, add a bay leaf, crumbled.

Braised Stuffed Heart
Serves 6 ■ Doubles ■ Refrigerates ■ Freezes

Preparation: 30 minutes ■ Cooking: see page 175

1   3-pound beef heart *or*
    3 veal hearts, prepared
    for cooking (page 175)
Salt

Sprinkle the cavity of the heart lightly with the salt.

2   cups prepared stuffing
1   onion, grated
½ cup celery, chopped
½ teaspoon thyme
4   tablespoons margarine,
    melted
Warm water

In a mixing bowl, combine the stuffing, onion, celery, and thyme. Toss the mixture with the margarine and a little warm water to moisten the dressing. With this mixture, stuff the heart. Skewer or sew it closed.

At this point you may stop and continue later.

3   tablespoons margarine
1   cup hot water, in which
    1 beef bouillon cube is
    dissolved

In a flameproof casserole, heat the margarine and in it brown the heart. Add the bouillon and cook the heart, closely covered, according to your preferred method (page 175). More water may be added as necessary.

1   tablespoon flour, mixed
    with ¼ cup cold water

Remove the heart and keep it warm. To the liquid in the casserole add the flour and, over high heat, cook the mixture, stirring constantly, until it is thickened and smooth. Slice the heart in serving portions and pour the sauce over it.

Serve the dish with Cabbage, page 294.

Braised Heart with Fruit Stuffing: In second step, make a stuffing of 1 cup tenderized pitted prunes or apricots, chopped, ½ cup golden raisins, 2 onions, chopped, and 1 teaspoon rosemary, crumbled. In third step, add the grated rind and juice of 1 lemon to the liquid ingredient.

Braised Heart with Sausage Stuffing: In second step, make a stuffing of 2 onions, chopped, and 1 rib celery, chopped and cooked until they are translucent in 1 tablespoon margarine; add ½ pound pork sausage meat, cooked and crumbled until it is browned; add 1 cup bread crumbs and ½ teaspoon each sage and thyme.

Kidney

I do not sing — a fact for which my reader should be duly thankful! — but if I *did*, I would sing the praises, loud and lustily, of kidneys. Perhaps no economy meat, with the possible exception of lamb shanks (pages 64 to 69) gives me such pleasure at table. I once thought that preparing kidneys for cooking was a frightful bore. That was only because I had not learned the technique of doing so, nor had I developed a rhythm for it. (If my reader reflects a moment, it will be clear that easy, efficient use of the kitchen and one's time spent there are the results of having established a rhythm for whatever work is at hand. Bread-kneading has its own rhythm. Vegetable peeling and chopping have their particular tempo. I can recall that, when a novice in the kitchen — and surrounded by dirty utensils and confusion — I tried to do everything in one rhythm: fast! One's kitchen sets up its own rhythms, just as life does; when we learn to follow them, kitchen procedures become easy, effortless, and fun.)

But to return to kidneys. One of the glandular organs of all vertebrates, the kidney functions as part of the water-filtering system of the body. As a food, it is a good source of iron, phosphorus, protein, riboflavin, thiamine, and vitamin A. Beef, lamb, pork, and veal kidneys are all available, albeit lamb kidneys are often difficult to find, being the most delicately flavored and therefore, in the public mind, the most desirable. Pork kidney, like pork liver, is the most strongly flavored. Do not believe, however, that pork kidneys cannot be used just as the others are; properly prepared for cooking, they are as good sautéed or broiled as beef, lamb, or veal kidney.

The basic preparation for cooking of kidney is the same: cut the kidneys in half lengthwise so that the veins of fat are seen; with one hand hold the "foot" of the fat mass and, using a very sharp knife, cut out the fat. Beef and veal kidneys are usually cut into bite-size pieces. The smaller lamb and pork kidneys may be left halved or may be cut, as desired. Soak prepared lamb and veal kidney in cold salted water for 1 hour; soak prepared beef and pork kidney in cold salted water for 1½ to 2 hours. Dry them on absorbent paper before proceeding with the recipe of your choice. Please note that the preparation times given in the following recipes do not include the time required to prepare the kidney for cooking.

Overcooking kidneys toughens them. All kidneys properly prepared may be pan-fried (sautéed), broiled, or braised with other ingredients. When buying them, be sure they are fresh — like all glandular meats, they spoil rapidly. Either use them the day you buy them or prepare them for freezing and store them in the deep-freeze. One beef kidney will serve 3 people, perhaps 4; 3 lamb kidneys are an adequate portion per person; 1 or 1½ pork kidneys will suffice for a service; 1 veal kidney yields 2 servings. In stews and braised dishes, it is best to allow 2 pounds of kidney for 6 persons.

Kidney Soup: Ireland

Serves 6 generously ■ Doubles ■ Refrigerates

Preparation: 30 minutes ■ Cooking: 1 hour

A fine wintertime supper, warming and satisfying.

6 tablespoons bacon fat
6 onions, sliced
6 carrots, scraped and cut into ¾-inch rounds
6 white turnips, scraped and cut into ¾-inch rounds
3 medium-sized potatoes, peeled and coarsely chopped

In a soup kettle, heat the bacon fat and to it add the vegetables, stirring to coat them.

1 beef kidney, prepared for cooking (page 184) and cut into 1-inch pieces
8 sprigs parsley, tied
1 bay leaf
1 teaspoon marjoram
8 peppercorns
1 teaspoon thyme
1 teaspoon sugar
2 teaspoons salt
6 cups cold water

To the contents of the kettle, add the kidney. Add the seasonings and, finally, the water. Bring the liquid to a boil, reduce the heat, and simmer the soup, covered, for 1 hour, or until the vegetables are tender. Before serving, remove the parsley.

Serve the soup with Crusty Bread, page 300.

Broiled Kidney
Serves 6 ■ Refrigerates

Preparation: 30 minutes ■ Cooking: 5 to 8 minutes

Kidney for 6 persons,
    prepared for cooking
    (page 184)
Salt
Pepper
Thyme (optional)

In a lightly greased shallow baking pan, arrange the kidney, cut side up. Season the meat with salt, pepper, and, if desired, a sprinkling of thyme.

At this point you may stop and continue later.

¼ cup chopped parsley

Place the pan on the broiling rack of an oven, preheated to broil, and cook the kidneys for 5 to 8 minutes, or until they just begin to draw in. Do not overcook them. Garnish them with the parsley.

Serve the dish with Hot Potato Salad, page 302.

If desired, omit the salt, pepper, and thyme, and marinate the prepared kidneys for 10 minutes in All-Purpose Vinaigrette dressing before broiling them. A pleasantly piquant flavor.

Lamb and pork kidneys should not be turned. Beef and veal kidneys in large pieces may be turned over. If you are lucky enough to be able to buy veal kidney encased in its fat, do not clean the kidney but *bake* it, as is, at 350° F. for 1 hour, or until the fat has become brown and crisp; 1 kidney will serve 2 people. This is perhaps the best kidney recipe of any I know.

Sautéed Kidney
Serves 6 ■ Refrigerates

Preparation: 30 minutes ■ Cooking: 8 to 10 minutes

3 tablespoons margarine
Kidney for 6 persons,
   prepared for cooking
   (page 184)
Salt
Pepper
Thyme (optional)
¼ cup chopped parsley

In a skillet, heat the margarine. Add the kidneys and season them with salt, pepper, and, if desired, a sprinkling of thyme. Over gentle heat, cook them, stirring often, until they lose their redness but are still tender. Garnish them with the parsley.

Serve the dish with Dried Bean Casserole, page 309.

If desired, the prepared kidney may be lightly dredged in ¼ cup seasoned flour. In a skillet, combine 4 tablespoons olive oil, add 1 clove garlic, put through a press, ¼ cup chopped parsley, and 2 teaspoons Worcestershire sauce; add the kidney and, over high heat, brown it quickly. Add ½ cup hot water in which 1 beef bouillon cube has been dissolved; stir the kidney gently until the sauce is thickened.

The flavor of herbs is a pleasant addition to kidney. In a mixing bowl, combine 4 tablespoons soft margarine, ¼ cup minced scallions, ¼ cup chopped parsley, the juice of ½ lemon, ¼ teaspoon marjoram, ½ teaspoon thyme, ¼ teaspoon salt, and a grating of pepper. Blend the mixture well and use it to sauté prepared kidney or to baste kidney when broiling it.

A piquant Italian variation: Sauté the kidney in olive oil to which has been added 1 clove garlic, put through a press. Add to the kidneys, as they cook, chopped anchovy fillets, to taste, ¼ cup chopped parsley, and 3 tablespoons wine vinegar. Adjust the seasoning with salt and pepper to taste.

Kidney with Cream Sauce: France
Serves 6 ■ Refrigerates

Preparation: 30 minutes ■ Cooking: 15 minutes in a 350° F. oven

Ready all ingredients and then "stop and continue later." Cook the dish in one rapid operation. This method assures the best results.

Rognons de veau Dijonnaise is a well-known dish in French cooking.

Salt
Pepper
Nutmeg
Kidney for 6 persons
    prepared for cooking
    (page 184) and cut into
    thin slices
4   tablespoons margarine

With the seasonings, sprinkle the kidney. In a skillet, heat the margarine and in it, over high heat, quickly brown the kidney, stirring to sear it evenly. Remove the kidney to a lightly greased baking dish.

1   tablespoon flour
1½ cups dairy half-and-half
1   small onion, grated
¼   cup chopped parsley
Juice of ½ lemon
2   teaspoons prepared
    mustard
2   teaspoons Worcester-
    shire sauce
Salt
Pepper

To the remaining fat, add the flour and, over gentle heat, cook the mixture, stirring, for 3 minutes. Gradually add the liquid, stirring constantly, until the sauce is thickened and smooth. Stir in the onion, parsley, lemon juice, mustard, and Worcestershire sauce. Add salt and pepper to taste. Over gentle heat, cook the sauce for 2 minutes, pour it over the kidneys, and bake the dish, uncovered, at 350° F. for 15 minutes.

Serve the dish with Noodles, page 307.

Kidney with Onion Sauce: In first step, cook the kidney as directed, adding at the same time 3 onions, coarsely grated; season the mixture with salt and pepper. In second step, in place of the flour and half-and-half, use 2 tablespoons cornstarch mixed until smooth with 1 10½-ounce can condensed chicken broth. Omit all the other ingredients of second step, except the parsley, which is increased to ½ cup. Adjust the seasoning with salt and pepper to taste. Proceed as directed.

Kidney with Sour Cream — *Germany:* In first step, dredge the prepared kidney in seasoned flour and proceed as directed. In second step, add to the remaining fat ¼ cup wine vinegar, 1 small onion, grated, and 1 tablespoon dillweed. Stir in the flour and 1 10½-ounce can condensed chicken broth; when the mixture is thickened and smooth, stir in 1 cup sour cream and adjust the seasoning with salt and pepper, to taste. Omit all the other ingredients of this step, except the parsley. Proceed as directed.

Lamb Kidneys with Curry Sauce: India

Serves 6 ■ Doubles ■ Refrigerates ■ Freezes

Preparation: 35 minutes ■ Cooking: 20 minutes

A delightful dish for a late supper party, this recipe may also be made with 2 or 3 veal kidneys, cut in bite-size pieces.

2 tablespoons margarine 1 tablespoon oil 2 onions, chopped 3 cloves garlic, minced	In a deep skillet, heat the margarine and oil and cook the onion and garlic until translucent.
½ teaspoon ground cardamom ½ teaspoon ground clove 1½ teaspoons ground coriander 1½ teaspoons ground cumin ½ teaspoon ground ginger 1 teaspoon turmeric 1½ tablespoons flour	Into the onion, stir the spices and flour. Cook the mixture gently for 5 minutes, stirring.
1 cup yogurt 1 cup hot water	Stir in the yogurt and water and cook the curry, stirring constantly, until it is thickened and smooth. *At this point you may stop and continue later.*
12 lamb kidneys, prepared for cooking (page 184)	To the hot sauce add the kidneys, stirring. Simmer the kidneys, covered, for 20 minutes.

Serve the dish with Tomato Pilaf, page 306.

Kidney with Peas: Italy

Serves 6 ■ Refrigerates

Preparation: 20 minutes ■ Cooking: 15 minutes

This recipe is adapted from a contribution of my neighbor and close friend Edward Giobbi.

Ready all the ingredients and then "stop and continue later." Cook the dish in one rapid operation. This method assures the best results.

2 tablespoons margarine
2 tablespoons oil
Kidney for 6 persons, prepared for cooking (page 184) and cut into small pieces
2 onions, chopped
1 teaspoon rosemary, crumbled

In a large skillet, heat the margarine and oil; add the kidney and, over high heat, brown the meat, stirring often. Add the onion and rosemary and, over medium heat, cook the mixture, stirring, until the onion is translucent.

½ cup hot water, in which 1 chicken bouillon cube has been dissolved
2 tomatoes, peeled, seeded, and chopped (canned tomatoes, well drained, will do)
2 10-ounce packages frozen peas, fully thawed to room temperature

Add the bouillon and, over gentle heat, simmer the kidney, covered, for 4 minutes. Add the tomato and peas and simmer, covered, for 10 minutes.

Serve the dish with Molded Rice, page 305.

Kidney Stew

Serves 6 ■ Doubles ■ Refrigerates ■ Freezes

Preparation: 30 minutes ■ Cooking: 30 minutes

This very simple dish is surprisingly satisfying; it "feels good."

3 slices bacon, diced 3 onions, chopped 1 clove garlic, chopped	In a skillet, render the bacon; remove it to absorbent paper and reserve it. In the fat, cook the onion and garlic until translucent.
2 pounds kidney, prepared for cooking (page 184) Seasoned flour	Dredge the kidney in the seasoned flour and add it to the onion. Cook the kidney until it is lightly browned. *At this point you may stop and continue later.*
2 cups hot water, in which 2 beef bouillon cubes have been dissolved ¾ teaspoon salt ¼ teaspoon pepper ¼ cup chopped parsley	Add the bouillon, salt, and pepper. Simmer the kidneys, covered, for 30 minutes. Garnish the stew with the parsley.

Serve the dish with Mashed Turnips, page 296.

Braised Kidney with Tomato Sauce: Italy
Serves 6 ■ Refrigerates

Preparation: 20 minutes ■ Cooking: 20 minutes

This recipe is particularly good prepared with pork kidney. If desired, the prepared kidney, halved, need not be cut into small pieces.

2 tablespoons olive oil
Kidney for 6 persons,
    prepared for cooking
    (page 184) and coarsely
    chopped
2 onions, chopped
1 clove garlic, chopped
	In a skillet or heavy saucepan, heat the olive oil and in it cook the kidney, onion, and garlic, stirring, until the kidney has lost its reddish color.

1 1-pound can tomato
    sauce
¾ teaspoon rosemary,
    crumbled
¾ teaspoon salt
¼ teaspoon pepper
	Add the tomato sauce and seasonings.
	
	At this point you may stop and continue later.

¼ cup chopped parsley	Simmer the kidney, covered, for 20 minutes. Garnish with the parsley.

Serve the dish with Spaghetti, page 307.

A traditional recipe from Bavaria offers a pleasant variation: In first step, in place of the olive oil, use 3 tablespoons bacon fat; increase the onions to 4; omit the garlic. In second step, in place of the tomato sauce, use ½ cup each wine vinegar and water; season the liquid with 2 bay leaves, crumbled, 2 tablespoons sugar, and ¼ teaspoon pepper; omit the rosemary and salt. In last step, after simmering the kidney, thicken the sauce with 4 teaspoons flour, blended until smooth with a little cold water. Garnish the dish with the parsley, as directed, and serve it with Mashed White Potatoes, page 302.

Broiled Kidney with Savory Sauce: France
Serves 6 ■ Refrigerates

Preparation: 30 minutes ■ Marination: 1 hour ■ Cooking: 10 minutes

Rognons grillés chantecler is a well-known dish in French cooking. It is especially successful made with veal kidney.

1 cup hot water, in which 1 beef bouillon cube has been dissolved
3 tablespoons olive oil
1 small onion, grated
1 teaspoon finely chopped chives
1 scallion, finely chopped, with as much green as possible
1 clove garlic, put through a press
½ teaspoon powdered basil
1 bay leaf, crumbled
½ teaspoon ground mace
½ teaspoon thyme
½ teaspoon salt

In a mixing bowl, combine and blend thoroughly these 11 ingredients.

Kidney for 6 persons, prepared for cooking (page 184)

To the marinade, add the kidney. Marinate the meat, stirring it often, for 1 hour.

At this point you may stop and continue later.

Remove the kidney from the marinade and wipe it clean. Sieve the marinade into a saucepan.

Bread crumbs

Into the sieved marinade, dip the kidney pieces. Dredge them lightly in the bread crumbs, and, on a rack, broil them for 5 minutes, turning them once.

4 tablespoons tart preserve
   or jelly
1 teaspoon prepared
   horseradish
1 tablespoon margarine

To the marinade add the preserve or jelly, the horseradish, and the margarine. Bring the sauce to a boil, stirring to melt the preserve.

Buttered toast or
   English muffins

Serve the kidney on buttered toast or English muffins. Pour the sauce over each serving.

Serve the dish with Carrots, page 295.

Kidney with Savory Sauce: China
Serves 6 ■ Refrigerates

Preparation: 30 minutes ■ Marination: 1 hour ■ Cooking: 5 minutes

This recipe is especially successful made with pork kidney.

1 tablespoon oil 1 tablespoon ginger root, grated 6 scallions, finely chopped, with as much green as possible ¼ cup soy sauce ¼ cup vinegar 1 tablespoon sugar Dash cayenne	In a mixing bowl, combine and blend thoroughly these 7 ingredients.
Kidney for 6 persons, prepared for cooking (page 184) and cut into ½-inch julienne	To the marinade add the kidney. Marinate the meat, stirring it often, for 1 hour. *At this point you may stop and continue later.*
2 tablespoons oil	In a wok or flameproof casserole, heat the oil. Add the kidney and the marinade. Over high heat, stir-fry the kidney for 5 minutes, or until it has just lost its pink color.

Serve the dish with Tomato Pilaf, page 306.

Liver

The liver, largest of the glandular organs in all vertebrates, is truly one of the most important, converting sugars into glycogen for release into the bloodstream. The livers we eat (beef, lamb, pork, veal, and poultry — the latter dealt with under the section on poultry) are delicious, rich in vitamins A and C, iron, riboflavin, niacin, and thiamine.

Once considered a "waste meat" (I remember my grandmother saying that she paid five cents a pound for calf's liver in a little upstate New York village), liver is now a delicacy eagerly sought to grace any table. In these recipes, calf's liver may be used, but the focus is upon the less expensive beef, lamb, and pork liver — just as healthy and equally tasty if prepared with care.

These three varieties are generally available in the supermarket and are usually sold in slices, either fresh, frozen, or thawed. Beef liver is less tender than that of lamb and has a more definite flavor; its color varies from light to dark red. Pork liver, the strongest flavored of the three, is best used in ragouts or casseroles, but, if soaked in salted cold water for an hour or so, it may be used in delicate liver recipes. All, however, are interchangeable in these recipes.

Liver, like all glandular tissue, should be used shortly after purchase. One or 2 days' storage, uncooked, in the refrigerator is about as long as it should be kept; even when cooked, it should not be stored longer than 3 or 4 days. In a regular home freezer, uncooked liver may be kept, well covered in moisture-proof wrapping, for as long as 6 months.

All liver may be pan-fried in margarine; it is tenderest when cooked medium to rare. All liver may be broiled; place ½-inch slices 4 inches from the broiler for a total of about 6 minutes, turning the pieces once. All liver, too, may be braised — a subject that will be treated in individual recipes. One and a half pounds of liver is adequate for 6 persons. To prepare it for cooking, peel off the membrane (if this has not already been done) from the outer edge and cut out such veins as may be present. Incidentally, these recipes for beef, lamb, and pork liver work well with chicken livers; conversely, the recipes devoted to chicken livers may be made with beef, lamb, and pork liver. The cooking time for chicken livers is much less than that for large pieces of liver.

Divorce yourself, as I have done, from the idea that "liver" had to mean "calf's liver," and explore the possibilities of beef, lamb, and pork liver as nutritious, economical, and satisfying main dishes.

Liver with Apples
Serves 6 ■ Doubles ■ Refrigerates

Preparation: 30 minutes ■ Cooking: 40 minutes

Seasoned flour
1½ pounds liver, cut
    into 6 servings
3   tablespoons margarine
2   onions, sliced

In the seasoned flour, dredge the liver. In a large skillet, heat the margarine and in it brown the liver. Add the onion.

1½ cups apple juice
1   teaspoon sugar
1½ teaspoons salt
¼   teaspoon pepper

Over the contents of the skillet, pour the apple juice. Sprinkle over the seasonings. Bring the liquid to a boil, reduce the heat, and simmer the liver, covered, for 30 minutes.

At this point you may stop and continue later.

3   ripe tart apples,
    peeled, cored, and
    cut into ½-inch wedges
2   tablespoons brown sugar
Ground cinnamon

Add the apple wedges, and sprinkle them with the brown sugar and a dusting of cinnamon. Cover the skillet and simmer the dish for 10 minutes longer, or until the apples are tender-crisp.

Serve the dish with Mashed Sweet Potatoes, page 302.

Liver with Onions I: France

Serves 6 ■ Doubles ■ Refrigerates

Preparation: 30 minutes ■ Cooking: 30 minutes in a 350° F. oven

1 1½-pound piece liver
Ground allspice
Sage
Thyme
Salt
Pepper
3 tablespoons margarine

Sprinkle the liver with the seasonings. In a flameproof casserole, heat the margarine and in it, over high heat, brown the liver on both sides.

2 cups hot water, in which
   2 beef bouillon cubes
   have been dissolved
12 small onions, peeled
4 ribs celery, chopped
¼ cup chopped parsley
1 bay leaf
2 whole cloves
1 clove garlic, put
   through a press

To the contents of the casserole add these 7 ingredients. Bake the casserole, covered, at 350° F. for 30 minutes.

At this point you may stop and continue later.

2 tablespoons margarine
2 tablespoons flour

Transfer the hot meat to a serving platter and surround it with the vegetables. Keep the dish warm while you sieve the broth. In a saucepan, heat the margarine and in it, over gentle heat, cook the flour for 3 minutes. Gradually add the sieved broth, stirring constantly until the sauce is thickened and smooth. Pour the sauce over the meat and serve.

Serve the dish with Crusty Bread, page 300.

Liver with Orange Sauce: In first step, cut the liver into bite-size pieces and dredge it in seasoned flour, to which ¾ teaspoon paprika has been added; brown the liver as directed. Remove and reserve it. To the pan add more margarine, if necessary, and in it cook 3 onions, sliced, until translucent. Add the grated rind and juice of 1 orange, plus orange juice to equal 2 cups, and deglaze the pan. Replace the liver, spooning the onion over it. Simmer the liver, covered, for 8 minutes, or until the sauce is slightly thickened.

Liver with Savory Sauce: In first step, cut the liver into bite-size pieces and dredge it in seasoned flour; after browning it, remove it and cook 2 onions, thinly sliced, and 1 rib celery, chopped, until translucent. Replace the liver, spooning the vegetables over it. In second step, omit the onions and celery and add to the seasonings 1 teaspoon curry powder. To cook the dish, simmer it on top of the stove, covered, for 20 minutes.

Liver with Vegetables: In first step, start by rendering 6 strips bacon, diced; drain them on absorbent paper and reserve them. Discard all but 3 tablespoons of the fat. Dredge the liver in seasoned flour and brown it. In second step, in place of the water, use 1 1-pound can stewed tomatoes; add 6 new potatoes, peeled. Omit last step.

SAGE

Liver with Onions II: Italy
Serves 6 ■ Doubles ■ Refrigerates

Preparation: 20 minutes ■ Cooking: 10 minutes

This recipe is hardly the American liver and onions — also very good — but, rather, a Venetian way of using the same ingredients.

3 tablespoons margarine 3 tablespoons olive oil 5 onions, sliced	In a skillet, heat the margarine and oil and cook the onion until translucent.
¼ cup hot water, in which 1 chicken bouillon cube has been dissolved	To the onion add the bouillon and simmer the onion, covered, for 2 minutes.
1½ pounds liver, thinly sliced and cut into 2-inch pieces	Prepare the liver. *At this point you may stop and continue later.*
Juice of 1 lemon ¼ cup chopped parsley Salt Pepper	To the onion add the liver and, over high heat, cook it quickly, stirring often, for 5 minutes, or until it has reached your preferred degree of doneness. Stir in the lemon juice and parsley. Season to your taste.

Serve the dish with Spaghetti, page 307.

Curried Liver: India

Serves 6 ■ Doubles ■ Refrigerates

Preparation: 30 minutes ■ Marination: at least 45 minutes
Cooking: 8 to 10 minutes

1½ pounds liver, cut into
   ½-inch strips
1   cup yogurt
1   teaspoon salt

In a mixing bowl, combine the liver, yogurt, and salt. Marinate the liver for at least 45 minutes.

4   tablespoons margarine
6   onions, chopped
2   cloves garlic, chopped
1   tablespoon fresh
    ginger, grated

In a large skillet, heat the margarine and in it cook the onion, garlic, and ginger until the onion is translucent.

1   8-ounce can tomato
    sauce
2   tablespoons ground
    coriander
½   teaspoon ground cumin
1   teaspoon turmeric
1½ teaspoons salt

To the onion add the tomato sauce and seasonings. Simmer the sauce, stirring often, for 5 minutes.

At this point you may stop and continue later.

To the sauce add the liver mixture; bring the contents of the skillet to a boil, reduce the heat, and simmer the liver, stirring often, for 8 minutes, or until it has reached your preferred degree of doneness.

Serve the dish with Boiled Rice, page 303.

Liver with Paprika Sauce: Hungary

Serves 6 ■ Doubles ■ Refrigerates

Preparation: 20 minutes ■ Cooking: 30 minutes

Seasoned flour
1½ pounds liver, cut into
    ½-inch strips
4 tablespoons bacon fat
    (or margarine)
3 onions, chopped
1 tablespoon
    paprika (or more,
    to taste)
1 teaspoon salt
¼ teaspoon pepper

In the seasoned flour, dredge the liver. In a skillet, heat the bacon fat and in it cook together the liver and onion for 5 minutes, stirring often. Stir in the paprika, salt, and pepper.

1 8-ounce can tomato sauce

Add the tomato sauce and, over gentle heat, simmer the liver, covered, for 20 minutes.

At this point you may stop and continue later.

1 cup sour cream

Stir in the sour cream and, over gentle heat, bring the mixture to your desired temperature; do not let it boil. Do not cook for more than 10 minutes.

Serve the dish with Mashed White Potatoes, page 302, or Noodles, page 307.

Liver with Vegetables
Serves 6 ▪ Doubles ▪ Refrigerates

Preparation: 20 minutes ▪ Cooking: 40 minutes

Seasoned flour
1½ pounds beef or pork
   liver, cut into 2-inch
   julienne
2   tablespoons margarine

In the seasoned flour, dredge the liver pieces. In a large skillet, heat the margarine and in it lightly brown the liver on all sides.

1½ cups water in which
   1 beef bouillon cube
   has been dissolved
2   tablespoons soy sauce
2   teaspoons brown sugar
1   teaspoon ground cumin
¾   teaspoon ground
   ginger
5   parsnips, scraped and
   thinly sliced

To the liver add these 6 ingredients. Over gentle heat, simmer the liver and parsnips for 35 minutes, or until the parsnips are fork-tender.

At this point you may stop and continue later.

1   10-ounce bag spinach,
   large stems removed,
   rinsed and drained

To the simmering skillet add the spinach and continue cooking the dish, covered, for 3 minutes, or until the spinach is wilted.

Serve the dish with Crusty Bread, page 300.

Chinese-Style Liver with Vegetables
Serves 6 ■ Doubles ■ Refrigerates

Preparation: 25 minutes ■ Cooking: 12 minutes

There is no need for a "stop and continue later" point; prepare all the ingredients ahead of time and, when you are ready, cook them quickly.

1½ pounds liver, cut into ½-inch strips
3 tablespoons cornstarch
3 tablespoons oil

In a mixing bowl, combine the liver and cornstarch. Toss them together to coat the liver thoroughly. In a wok or casserole, heat the oil and in it quickly brown the meat.

8 scallions (or more, to taste), chopped, with as much green as possible
1 10-ounce package snow peas, fully thawed to room temperature
2 cups hot water, in which 2 chicken bouillon cubes have been dissolved
2 tablespoons soy sauce
¾ teaspoon ground ginger
1 teaspoon sugar
¾ teaspoon salt

To the liver, add the scallions and snow peas. Combine the bouillon, soy sauce, ginger, sugar, and salt. Add the liquid and, over high heat, cook the liver and vegetables, stirring constantly, for 3 minutes, or until the sauce is slightly thickened.

1 10-ounce package fresh spinach, rinsed and thoroughly drained

Add the spinach and continue to cook the dish, stirring gently, for 3 minutes, or until the spinach is wilted.

Serve the dish with Boiled Rice, page 303.

Liver Loaf I
Serves 6 ■ Doubles ■ Refrigerates ■ Freezes

Preparation: 30 minutes ■ Cooking: 45 minutes in a 350° F. oven

4 strips bacon, diced
2 onions, chopped
3 ribs celery, chopped

In a skillet, render the bacon dice. Drain them on absorbent paper and reserve them. In the fat, cook the onion and celery until translucent.

1½ pounds liver, coarsely chopped
2 eggs
½ cup tomato juice
½ teaspoon thyme
1 teaspoon salt
¼ teaspoon pepper

In the container of an electric blender, combine the liver, onion, celery, eggs, tomato juice, and seasonings. On medium speed, whirl the mixture until it is well blended.

1 cup bread crumbs

In a mixing bowl, blend thoroughly the liver mixture and bread crumbs. (This may be done in the container of the blender, but is sometimes difficult.)

At this point you may stop and continue later.

Pour the mixture into a lightly greased loaf pan and sprinkle over it the reserved bacon bits. Bake the liver loaf at 350° F. for 45 minutes. Before serving, turn it onto a heated platter.

Serve the dish with Mashed Turnips, page 296.

Liver Loaf II

Serves 6 ■ Doubles ■ Refrigerates

Preparation: 25 minutes ■ Cooking: 1 hour in a 350° F. oven

1½ pounds beef or pork liver
Boiling water

In a skillet, cover the liver with the boiling water and, over high heat, cook the meat for 1 minute. Immediately drain it, reserving the water. Cut the liver into several pieces.

1 cup milk

Into the container of an electric blender, pour the milk. Add the liver pieces and, on medium speed, whirl the mixture until the liver is puréed.

2 tablespoons margarine, melted
3 eggs
1 onion, coarsely chopped

Add these 3 ingredients and, on medium speed, whirl the mixture for 10 seconds. Pour it into a mixing bowl.

¼ teaspoon ground allspice
½ teaspoon nutmeg
2 teaspoons salt
¼ teaspoon pepper
1½ cups dry bread crumbs
¼ cup reserved liver water

Stir in the seasonings, bread crumbs, and liver water. Blend the mixture well.

2 teaspoons margarine

With the margarine, grease an 8-inch loaf pan.

At this point you may stop and continue later.

Into the loaf pan, spoon the liver loaf batter. Bake the loaf, uncovered, at 350° F. for 1 hour, or until a knife inserted at the center comes out clean. Unmold the loaf onto a serving dish.

Serve the dish with Dried Beans with Sour Cream, page 309.

Liver Loaf III: Finland

Serves 6 ■ Doubles ■ Refrigerates

Preparation: 30 minutes ■ Cooking: 1 hour in a 350° F. oven

1   cup raw natural rice
3   quarts (12 cups) water
Salt

In a large kettle, boil the rice in the water, slightly salted, for 12 minutes. Drain and reserve the rice.

4   slices bacon, diced
2   onions, chopped

In a skillet, render the bacon; drain and reserve the dice. In the remaining fat, cook the onion until translucent.

Reserved rice
2   cups milk
2   eggs, lightly beaten
½   cup golden raisins
1   teaspoon marjoram
2   teaspoons salt
½   teaspoon pepper

In a mixing bowl, combine the cooked rice, milk, eggs, raisins, onion, bacon, and seasonings.

1½ pounds liver, puréed
    in the container of an
    electric blender

To the contents of the mixing bowl add the liver and blend the mixture well. Spoon it into a greased 2-quart baking dish.

At this point you may stop and continue later.

Bake the liver loaf at 350° F. for 1 hour, or until a knife inserted at the center comes out clean.

Serve the dish with Eggplant, page 295.

Oxtail

Oxtail has been used for centuries as the basis for various stews and soups. Actually, we buy beef tail, rather than the tail of a true ox. A favorite meat in English cookery, oxtail is not a "variety meat," but it seems to fit comfortably in this section of the book. An oxtail weighs about 1½ to 2 pounds; 4 pounds serves 6 persons generously. Oxtail is very bony and very fatty. It is also very nutritious when cooked slowly, very tasty when properly seasoned, and, happily, it *is* attractively inexpensive. Like most stew-type dishes, those made with oxtail benefit from being prepared a day in advance of serving; this allows the flavors to meld and become richer, and it also facilitates the removal of excess fat from the refrigerated dish before it is reheated for serving.

Oxtail Soup with Barley: Ireland
Serves 6 ■ Doubles ■ Refrigerates ■ Freezes

Preparation: 30 minutes ■ Cooking: 3 hours

2 pounds oxtail, disjointed
1 cup pearl barley
2 onions, sliced
3 ribs celery, chopped
3 carrots, scraped and cut into ¾-inch rounds
½ cup coarsely chopped parsley
2 bay leaves
½ teaspoon thyme
2 teaspoons salt
½ teaspoon pepper

In a large soup kettle, combine these ingredients.

8 cups water
Salt
Pepper

Add the water, bring it to a boil, reduce the heat, and simmer the oxtails, covered, for 3 hours, or until the meat falls from the bones. Remove the oxtails and allow them to cool. Remove the meat from the bones and return it to the kettle. Adjust the seasoning.

Serve the soup with Crusty Bread, page 300.

Oxtail Soup with Vegetables: America

Serves 6 ■ Doubles ■ Refrigerates ■ Freezes

Preparation: 30 minutes ■ Cooking: 3 hours

Seasoned flour
3 or 4 pounds oxtail,
   disjointed
3 tablespoons bacon fat

In the seasoned flour, dredge the oxtail sections. In a large flameproof casserole or soup kettle, heat the bacon fat and in it brown the segments, a few at a time; remove them to absorbent paper and reserve them.

4 cups tomato juice
2 cups water
Juice of 1 lemon
1 bay leaf
2 teaspoons chili powder
1 teaspoon oregano
½ teaspoon rosemary
1 teaspoon sugar
1 tablespoon salt
½ teaspoon pepper

To the fat in the casserole, add the liquids and, over high heat, deglaze the utensil. Add the seasonings and replace the oxtail.

Bring the liquid to a boil, reduce the heat, and simmer the oxtail, covered, for 2½ hours, or until the meat falls from the bones.

At this point you may stop and continue later. (This is an ideal time to cool and refrigerate the soup overnight; remove the solidified fat and proceed as directed.)

3 carrots, scraped and
   diced
3 onions, chopped
3 medium-sized potatoes,
   peeled and diced
1 teaspoon Worcestershire
   sauce

To the contents of the casserole add the vegetables and Worcestershire sauce. Simmer the vegetables, covered, for 30 minutes, or until they are tender.

Serve the soup with Crusty Bread, page 300.

If desired, after the oxtail has simmered for 2½ hours, the meat may be removed from the bones, the bones discarded, and the meat returned to the stock. This step makes for a more elegant soup but does not affect its taste.

Braised Oxtail with Vegetables
Serves 6 ■ Doubles ■ Refrigerates ■ Freezes

Preparation: 30 minutes ■ Cooking: 2½ to 3 hours in a 300° F. oven and 30 minutes simmering

Seasoned flour
3 or 4 pounds oxtail, disjointed
3 tablespoons margarine

In the seasoned flour, dredge the oxtail sections. In a flameproof casserole, heat the margarine and in it brown the segments, a few at a time; remove them to absorbent paper and reserve them.

3 onions, sliced
2 cloves garlic, chopped
4 cups hot water, in which 4 beef bouillon cubes have been dissolved
1 1-pound can tomatoes
1 bay leaf
1 teaspoon marjoram
½ teaspoon thyme
1 teaspoon salt
½ teaspoon pepper

In the remaining fat, cook the onion and garlic until translucent. Add the bouillon and, over high heat, deglaze the casserole. Add the tomatoes and seasonings. Replace the meat.

Bake the casserole, covered, at 300° F. for 2½ to 3 hours, or until the meat separates easily from the bones.

At this point you may stop and continue later. (This is an ideal time to cool and refrigerate the dish overnight; remove the solidified fat and proceed as directed.)

3 carrots, scraped and sliced
3 ribs celery, chopped
3 turnips, scraped and sliced

To the simmering casserole, add the vegetables and continue to cook the dish, covered, for 30 minutes, or until the vegetables are tender.

Serve the dish with Mashed White Potatoes, page 302, or Noodles, page 307.

Braised Oxtail with Barley: In first step, in place of the margarine, use an equal amount of bacon fat to brown the oxtail. In second step, increase the water to 5 cups; do not increase the number of bouillon cubes; add ⅓ cup pearl barley; to the seasonings add 3 whole allspice berries, ¾ teaspoon basil, ¼ teaspoon cayenne, and 3 whole cloves. Serve this Creole dish with Crusty Bread, page 301.

Because the method and timing of braising oxtail remains the same in most recipes, the possible variations of the dish, which are legion, depend for their realization only upon the originality of the cook.

Here are a few ideas to set your imagination working:

Add with the other vegetables 12 white onions, peeled.

Use 3 parsnips, scraped and sliced, as one of the vegetables.

Use 2 green peppers, seeded and chopped, as a color and flavor accent; add them 10 minutes before serving.

Omit the turnips and add ½ cup seedless raisins.

Add with the cooking liquids the juice and grated rind of 1 lemon.

When serving the oxtail, garnish the dish with freshly chopped parsley: I use lots of it, about ½ cup.

In seasoning the casserole, reduce the pepper to ¼ teaspoon and add curry powder to taste (suggested amount, 1 tablespoonful).

Omit the tomatoes and add to the seasonings 1½ tablespoons sweet paprika; omit the turnips; just before serving, stir in 2 cups sour cream.

Add the zest of 1 orange, cut into very thin julienne.

Tongue

The tongue of beef, lamb, or veal is used as a meat food. All tongue requires long, leisurely cooking, for it is a particularly "muscular" muscle in the animals' anatomy. It is, happily, available at all seasons. Beef tongue comes fresh, smoked, and corned; it weighs from 3 to 5 pounds, and a 3-pound tongue serves 6 persons. Lamb tongue is sold fresh, pickled, and canned (actually it is bottled); it weighs about 3½ ounces and you will want 2 tongues per serving. Veal tongue is available fresh; it weighs anywhere from ½ to 2 pounds, thus 2 1½-pound tongues are adequate for 6 portions.

The following recipes are for fresh tongue, which should be kept carefully refrigerated, and for corned tongue. Tongue is a fine source of protein and has good amounts of iron, niacin, and riboflavin. The flavor of tongue is distinctive but subtle, and it is enhanced by the sauce accompanying it. Its texture is firm and pleasant. Like all variety meats, it is a boon to the economy-minded cook because of the seemingly endless variations of which it is capable.

Basic Recipe for Cooking Tongue

Serves 6 ■ Doubles ■ Refrigerates ■ Freezes

Preparation: 10 minutes ■ Cooking: 1 to 1¼ hours per pound

Tongue for 6 persons
   (page 214)
Cold water
1 onion, stuck with 3
   cloves
1 clove garlic, chopped
1 carrot, chopped
1 rib celery
2 bay leaves
6 peppercorns
1 teaspoon sugar
Salt

In a large kettle, arrange the tongue and measure water to cover it by 1 inch. Add the remaining ingredients. Add 1 teaspoon salt for each 2 cups of water.

Rapidly bring the water to a boil, reduce the heat, and simmer the tongue, covered, for 1 to 1¼ hours per pound, or until it is easily pierced with the tines of a fork. Cool the tongue in the cooking liquid, and sieve and reserve the liquid. Remove the bone and tendon at the base of the tongue; slit the skin on the underside and peel it. Cut the tongue into ½-inch slices and reserve them in some of the cooking liquid. Drain the warm tongue only when ready to serve it.

If desired, the tongue may be served cooked this way. Offer it with a good mustard or horseradish and Boiled White Potatoes, page 301.

Please note that the preparation times given in the following recipes do not include the time required to prepare the tongue for cooking.

Sauces for Fresh Tongue: The following sauces are designed specifically for use with fresh tongue prepared in this way; many sauces throughout this book, however, are also tasty with tongue. You should experiment freely; the chances are that if a given sauce appeals to you as a consort for tongue, the marriage will prove a happy one.

Horseradish Sauce: In a large saucepan, heat 3 tablespoons margarine and in it, over gentle heat, cook 3 tablespoons flour for 3 minutes; to the *roux* add 2 cups reserved cooking liquid, stirring until the mixture is thickened and smooth. Stir in 1 5⅓-ounce can evaporated milk and 5 or 6 tablespoons prepared horseradish. Adjust the seasoning with salt and pepper to taste. Pour the sauce over the sliced warm tongue and serve. (If desired, ⅓ cup seedless raisins, plumped for 5 minutes in hot water and drained, may be added to the sauce — a very good addition, I feel.) Serve the dish with Noodles, page 307.

Orange Sauce: In a saucepan, combine 1½ cups reserved cooking liquid and 1 6-ounce can frozen orange juice concentrate. When the concentrate is dissolved, add 2½ tablespoons cornstarch blended with 2 tablespoons water; over high heat, cook the mixture, stirring constantly, until it is thickened and smooth. Stir in 2 tablespoons margarine, the juice of ½ lemon, the zest of 1 orange, cut into very fine julienne, and the juice of the orange. Adjust the seasoning with salt and 1 or 2 drops Tabasco sauce, to taste. Pour the sauce over the sliced warm tongue and serve the dish with Boiled or Baked Sweet Potatoes, page 301.

Raisin Sauce — *Holland:* In a heavy skillet, combine 2 cups reserved cooking liquid, ½ cup brown sugar, ¼ teaspoon ground cumin, and ½ cup seedless raisins; bring the liquid to a boil to dissolve the sugar; reduce the heat and simmer the raisins, covered, for 5 minutes. Blend 2 tablespoons cornstarch with 2 tablespoons water; add it to the liquid and, over high heat, cook the sauce, stirring constantly, until it is thickened and smooth. Stir in 2 tablespoons margarine and 2 teaspoons cider vinegar, and adjust the seasoning with salt to taste. Pour the sauce over the sliced warm tongue and serve the dish with Boiled Rice, page 303.

Tomato Sauce — *Basque Provinces:* In a saucepan, heat 6 tablespoons olive oil and in it cook until translucent 3 onions, chopped, and 3 cloves garlic, chopped. Stir in 2 tablespoons flour. Add 1½ cups reserved cooking liquid and 1 1-pound can tomatoes, chopped, with their liquid. Cook the mixture, stirring constantly, until it is thickened and smooth. Season the sauce with 1¼ teaspoons salt and ¼ teaspoon pepper. Simmer the sauce, covered, for 10 minutes, pour it over the sliced warm tongue, and serve the dish with Spaghetti, page 307.

Sweet and Pungent Sauce: Follow the directions for Sweet and Pungent Sauce, page 311. Pour the sauce over the sliced warm tongue, and serve the dish with Boiled Rice, page 303.

Braised Tongue with Cranberries
Serves 6 ■ Doubles ■ Refrigerates ■ Freezes

Preparation: 25 minutes ■ Cooking: 30 minutes in a 300° F. oven

4   tablespoons margarine
4   tablespoons flour
2   cups reserved cooking
    liquid (page 215)
1   20-ounce can whole
    cranberry sauce
Zest of 1 lemon, cut into
    fine julienne
1   tablespoon cider vinegar
¼   cup brown sugar
1   teaspoon prepared
    horseradish
1   teaspoon Worcestershire
    sauce
1   teaspoon tarragon
½   teaspoon salt
¼   teaspoon pepper

In a saucepan, melt the margarine and in it, over gentle heat, cook the flour for 3 minutes. Gradually add the cooking liquid, stirring constantly until the mixture is thickened and smooth. Add the cranberry sauce, lemon zest, vinegar, and seasonings. Blend the sauce well and simmer it, covered, for 10 minutes.

At this point you may stop and continue later.

Tongue for 6 persons (page
    215), sliced for serving
    and at room temperature

In an ovenproof serving dish, arrange the tongue. Over it pour the sauce and heat the dish at 300° F. for 30 minutes.

Serve the dish with Baked Acorn Squash, page 294.

Braised Tongue with Vegetables
Serves 6 ■ Doubles ■ Refrigerates ■ Freezes

Preparation: 20 minutes ■ Cooking: 30 minutes in a 350° F. oven

2   tablespoons margarine
Prepared tongue for 6
    persons (page 215)
3   carrots, scraped and
    very finely sliced
3   ribs celery, finely
    chopped
3   white turnips, scraped
    and very finely sliced

In a flameproof casserole, heat the margarine and in it brown the tongue slices. Add the vegetables.

2½ cups reserved cooking
    liquid (page 215)
2   tablespoons flour
1½ teaspoons tarragon
¾   teaspoon salt
¼   teaspoon pepper

With a little of the cooking liquid, mix the flour until the paste is smooth. Add it and the remaining liquid to the contents of the casserole. Gently stir in the seasonings.

At this point you may stop and continue later.

Bake the casserole, covered, at 350° F. for 30 minutes, or until the vegetables are just tender.

Serve the dish with Crusty Bread, page 300.

Lamb Tongues with Dates and Raisins: Turkey

Serves 6 ∎ Doubles ∎ Refrigerates ∎ Freezes

Preparation: 2½ hours ∎ Cooking: 1¼ hours in a 350° F. oven

12 lamb tongues
2 onions, quartered
6 whole cloves
½ teaspoon red pepper flakes
1½ teaspoons salt
1 teaspoon sugar
Water

In a soup kettle, combine first 6 ingredients. Add water to cover, bring it to a boil, reduce the heat, and simmer the lamb tongues, covered, for 2 hours, or until they are tender. Cool the tongues, in the broth. Drain them, reserving the broth.

From the tongues remove the skin, bones, roots, and fat.

3 carrots, scraped and sliced
1 cup pitted tenderized dates
1½ cups golden seedless raisins
½ teaspoon thyme

In a casserole, arrange the tongues, carrots, dates, and raisins. Sprinkle the thyme over the raisins.

2 tablespoons margarine
2 tablespoons flour
2½ cups reserved broth, sieved

In a saucepan, heat the margarine and stir in the flour; over gentle heat, cook the *roux* for 3 minutes. Gradually add the broth, stirring constantly to assure a smooth sauce. Cook the mixture until it is thickened and smooth. Pour the sauce over the contents of the casserole.

At this point you may stop and continue later.

Bake the casserole, covered, at 350° F. for 1¼ hours.

Serve the dish with Tomato Pilaf, page 306.

If desired, the dish may be made with a beef tongue; increase the simmering time to 3 hours. Cut the prepared tongue into ½-inch slices.

Tongue with Spinach: France
Serves 6 ■ Doubles ■ Refrigerates

Preparation: 30 minutes ■ Cooking: 30 minutes in a 350° F. oven

Buchettes de langue de boeuf is a well-known dish in French cooking.

2 10-ounce packages frozen chopped spinach, fully thawed to room temperature
Grated rind of 1 lemon
Grating of nutmeg
3 tablespoons melted margarine
½ teaspoon salt
¼ teaspoon pepper

In a mixing bowl, toss together the spinach, lemon rind, and nutmeg. Add the margarine, salt, and pepper, and blend the mixture well.

12 slices cooked tongue

Spread the spinach mixture equally over the 12 slices of cooked tongue. Roll and skewer them with toothpicks. Arrange them in a greased baking dish.

1 cup sour cream
2 tablespoons prepared horseradish
½ teaspoon sage
½ teaspoon salt
Pinch of pepper

Combine the sour cream and seasonings. Spoon the mixture over the tongue rolls.

At this point you may stop and continue later.

¼ cup bread crumbs
¼ cup grated Parmesan cheese

Combine the bread crumbs and cheese and sprinkle the mixture over the tongue rolls. Bake the dish, uncovered, at 350° F. for 30 minutes, or until the crumbs are browned.

Serve the dish with Green Bean Salad, page 299.

Tripe

It is said in France that tripe is eaten by two groups of people — the poor, because they can afford it, and the gourmets, because they can appreciate it. I think I belong to both groups; certainly I am a member of the second, for (together with kidney) no economy meat delights me more. Tripe *does* take long and careful preparation, but the results are worth every effort. As with the section on kidney, I have had trouble containing my enthusiasm and limiting the number of recipes.

Tripe, the inner lining of the stomach of beef, comes in three varieties: honeycomb, pocket, and smooth. All come fresh, pickled, and canned. For the purposes of this book, fresh honeycomb tripe is the variety to buy. Like all organ tissue, it should be carefully refrigerated at once and cooked shortly after it is purchased; cooked tripe may be kept in a freezer for 6 months.

"Fresh" tripe has, indeed, already been cooked before being sold; but it requires more cooking, leisurely and gentle, to perfect its appetizing qualities. On the following page is my favorite recipe for the basic cooking of tripe. Upon this recipe all others in this book are built.

Once the tripe is cooked, it may be dipped in beaten egg and then in bread crumbs and sautéed in hot margarine; serve it with lemon slices. It may be brushed with melted margarine and broiled (for 5 minutes per side); serve it with a good grade of mustard. And it may be enhanced by a number of sauces. Sautéed and broiled tripe are good served with Lima beans made with yogurt (see Dried Beans with Yogurt, page 309).

If the liquid in which the tripe is cooked is not entirely used in a given recipe, reserve it for soup stock, for cooking vegetables, or for use as the liquid ingredient in some other dish. It is flavorful and very nutritious.

Basic Recipe for Cooking Tripe
Serves 6 ■ Doubles ■ Refrigerates ■ Freezes

Preparation: 20 minutes ■ Cooking: 2½ hours

3 or 4 pounds honeycomb
   tripe
3 carrots, scraped and
   sliced
3 ribs celery, chopped,
   with their leaves
3 onions, each stuck with
   2 cloves

2 cloves garlic, split
6 sprigs parsley
2 bay leaves
1 *bouquet garni*
1 teaspoon sugar
2 teaspoons salt
6 peppercorns
Cold water

In a soup kettle, arrange the tripe; add the vegetables, seasonings, and water to cover. Bring the water to a boil, reduce the heat, and simmer the tripe, covered, for 2½ hours, or until it can be easily pierced with the tines of a fork.

Allow the tripe to cool in the broth. Remove it and cut it into bite-size pieces. Sieve the broth and replace the tripe.

At this point you may stop and continue later. (This is an ideal time to refrigerate the tripe overnight; remove the solidified fat and proceed with the recipe of your choice.)

223

Please note that the preparation times given in the following recipes do not include the time required to prepare the tripe for cooking.

Tripe with Beans: Prepare the tripe as directed. Remove it from the defatted liquid and reserve it. In the liquid, bring to a boil for 5 minutes 1 pound white navy beans; remove them from the heat and allow them to sit for 1 hour; return them to the heat and simmer them, covered, for 1 hour or until they are just tender. Sieve the beans and reserve them and the liquid. Over high heat, reduce the liquid to 1½ cups. To the liquid add 1 6-ounce can tomato paste. In a casserole, toss together the tripe and beans; pour over the liquid. Bake the casserole at 300° F. for 1 hour. Serve the dish with Mixed Green Salad, page 298. (*Total time: about 5½ hours,* but you need not spend them all in the kitchen.)

An Italian variation from Lombardy: Render 4 slices bacon, diced, in 2 tablespoons olive oil; remove and reserve the bacon. In the remaining fat, glaze 12 white onions, peeled, and 3 carrots, scraped and thinly sliced; season the vegetables with 1 teaspoon sage. Add the vegetables, bacon, and any remaining fat to the casserole when tossing together the tripe and beans. Proceed as directed above. Serve the dish sprinkled with grated Parmesan cheese.

Tripe with Chick-Peas — *Turkey:* Prepare the tripe as directed. In a saucepan, heat 3 tablespoons margarine and in it cook 3 onions, chopped, until translucent; stir in 1 6-ounce can tomato paste and 1 20-ounce can chick-peas, drained. Add 1 cup of tripe liquid and the prepared tripe. Simmer the dish, uncovered, for 20 minutes and serve it with Crusty Bread, page 300. (*Total time: about 3½ hours.*)

Tripe with Hominy — *Mexico:* Prepare the tripe as directed, adding to the ingredients of the basic recipe 1 veal knuckle, 3 additional cloves garlic, 2 teaspoons ground coriander, and 1 tablespoon chili powder. After discarding the solidified fat, remove and reserve the tripe. Reduce the tripe liquid to 1½ cups; add 1 6-ounce can tomato paste and 1 29-ounce can whole hominy, drained. Replace the tripe and heat it through. Just before serving, stir in ¼ cup chopped parsley, 6 scallions, chopped, with as much green as possible, and the zest of 1 lemon, cut into fine julienne. Serve the dish with Mixed Green Salad, page 298. (*Total time: about 3½ hours.*)

Tripe with Pig's Foot — *Basque Provinces:* Prepare the tripe as directed, adding to the ingredients of the basic recipe 1 pig's foot. Cool, refrigerate;

then remove and reserve the solidified fat; reduce the tripe liquid to 1½ cups. Add the meat from the pig's foot to the tripe; discard the bones. Using the reserved fat, cook 3 onions, chopped, and 3 cloves garlic, chopped, until translucent. Add 4 carrots, scraped and thinly sliced, and 4 white turnips, scraped and thinly sliced. Stir in 1 tablespoon paprika. Combine the onion mixture, the reduced liquid, and the prepared tripe and pig's foot. Simmer the stew, covered, for 30 minutes, or until the vegetables are tender. Serve the dish in soup bowls, garnished with ¼ cup chopped parsley, and accompanied by Crusty Bread, page 300. (*Total time: about 3½ hours.*)

Tripe with Potatoes: Prepare the tripe as directed. In a flameproof casserole, heat ¼ cup olive oil and in it cook 2 onions, chopped, and 2 cloves garlic, chopped, until translucent. Add 1 cup tripe liquid and 1 1-pound can tomato sauce; season the mixture with 1 bay leaf, ¼ teaspoon ground clove, 2 teaspoons marjoram, 2 teaspoons salt, and ½ teaspoon pepper. Simmer the sauce, covered, for 20 minutes. To it add the prepared tripe and 6 medium-sized potatoes, peeled and quartered. Simmer the dish, covered, for 30 minutes, or until the potatoes are tender. (*Total time: about 3½ hours.*)

Tripe with Sausage — *Mexico:* Prepare the tripe as directed. In a large skillet, heat 1 tablespoon lard or olive oil and in it brown well 3 *chorizo* or 3 Italian hot sausages, skinned and sliced; remove the pieces to absorbent paper and reserve them. In the remaining fat, cook 2 onions, chopped, and 1 clove garlic, chopped, until translucent. Add the prepared tripe and cook it for 5 minutes, stirring often. Add 3 tomatoes, peeled, seeded, and chopped (canned tomatoes, drained, will do), ¼ cup chopped parsley, ½ teaspoon each oregano and thyme, ¾ teaspoon salt, and ¼ teaspoon pepper. Add the reserved sausage and, over gentle heat, simmer the dish, covered, for 30 minutes. Serve the dish with Dried Bean Salad, page 309. (*Total time: about 3½ hours.*)

Tripe with Tomato Sauce — *Italy (Trippa alla Livornese* is a classic dish in Italian cooking): Prepare the tripe as directed. In a large saucepan, heat 3 tablespoons margarine and in it cook 3 onions, chopped, until translucent; add 1½ cups tripe liquid, 1 1-pound can tomato sauce, and 1 cup grated Parmesan cheese. Over gentle heat, cook the mixture, stirring constantly, until the cheese is melted. Stir in the prepared tripe and, when it is well heated, serve the dish with Molded Rice, page 305. (*Total time: about 3½ hours.*)

Tripe with Onion: France

Serves 6 ■ Doubles ■ Refrigerates

Preparation: ½ hour ■ Cooking: 30 minutes

Tripes lyonnaise is a national dish in France.

2 tablespoons margarine
2 tablespoons olive oil
Prepared tripe for 6
    persons

In a large skillet, heat the margarine and oil and in it brown the tripe.

2 tablespoons margarine
2 tablespoons oil
3 or 4 large onions, sliced
1 clove garlic, split
    lengthwise

In a skillet, heat the margarine and oil and in it cook the onion and garlic until translucent; remove the garlic.

At this point you may stop and continue later.

Juice of 1 lemon
Salt
Pepper
¼ cup chopped parsley

To the tripe add the onion, and cook the mixture, uncovered, stirring gently, for 30 minutes. Add the lemon juice and salt and pepper, to taste. Garnish the tripe with the parsley.

Serve the dish with Boiled White Potatoes, page 301.

Tripes à la Mode de Caen: France

Serves 6 generously ■ Doubles ■ Refrigerates ■ Freezes

Preparation: 30 minutes ■ Cooking: 9 hours in a 300° F. oven

Perhaps the most celebrated of all tripe dishes, *tripes à la mode de Caen* is usually laced with ¼ cup calvados (the French apple brandy) added to the cooking liquid. The embellishment is not necessary, but it *is* good, if you feel *un*economically-minded.

¼ pound salt pork, diced
3 carrots, scraped and thickly sliced
3 ribs celery, coarsely chopped, with their leaves
3 large onions, thickly sliced
1 green pepper, seeded and chopped
1 bunch scallions, coarsely chopped, with as much green as possible

Over the bottom of a large casserole, sprinkle the salt pork dice. Over them arrange the vegetables in layers.

3½ pounds uncooked honeycomb tripe, cut into bite-size pieces

Over the vegetables, arrange the tripe in an even layer.

2 bay leaves, crumbled
¼ teaspoon ground celery seed
4 cloves garlic, chopped
¼ teaspoon marjoram
¼ teaspoon nutmeg
¼ teaspoon sage
¼ teaspoon thyme
8 peppercorns
1½ teaspoons sugar
8 cups hot water, in which 8 beef bouillon cubes have been dissolved
1 6-ounce can tomato paste

To the contents of the casserole add the seasonings. Combine the water and tomato paste. Pour the liquid over the tripe and bake the casserole, very tightly covered, at 300° F. for 9 hours.

If desired, the cooked tripe may be cooled and refrigerated overnight to facilitate the removal of the fat. Allow the casserole to come fully to room temperature before reheating it at 300° F. for about 1 hour.

Serve the dish with Crusty Bread, page 300.

Tripe and Pumpkin Soup: Curaçao

Serves 6 generously ■ Doubles ■ Refrigerates ■ Freezes

Preparation: 45 minutes ■ Cooking: 4 hours

1½ pounds uncooked
    honeycomb
    tripe, cut into
    bite-size pieces
1   pig's foot
Cold water
½   pound corned beef

In a soup kettle, combine the tripe, pig's foot, and water to cover by ½ inch. Bring the water to a boil, skim it; reduce the heat and simmer the meats, covered, for 2 hours. Add the corned beef and continue to simmer the meats, covered, for 1½ hours longer.

Remove the pig's foot, cut the meat from the bone, chop it, and return it to the broth; discard the bones. Remove the corned beef, dice it, and return it to the broth.

At this point you may stop and continue later. (This is an ideal time to refrigerate the meat overnight; remove the solidified fat and continue with the recipe.)

2 cups pumpkin, peeled and diced (Hubbard squash will substitute)
1 cup potato, diced
2 onions, chopped
1 rib celery, chopped
1 green pepper, seeded and chopped
6 scallions, chopped, with as much green as possible

To the contents of the kettle add the vegetables.

Zest of 1 lime
1 teaspoon chili powder
¼ teaspoon ground clove
½ teaspoon nutmeg
2 teaspoons salt
½ teaspoon pepper

Stir in the seasonings. Simmer the soup for 30 minutes, or until the pumpkin and potato are tender.

Juice of 1 lime

To serve the soup, remove the lime zest and stir in the lime juice.

Serve the soup with Crusty Bread, page 300.

Philadelphia Pepper Pot Soup: America
Serves 6 generously ■ Doubles ■ Refrigerates

Preparation and cooking: 2 hours

This recipe is a simplified version of the American classic dish dating back to Revolutionary times and eaten, so it is said, by General Washington when he was visiting the Quaker City.

3 tablespoons margarine 2 onions, chopped 1 clove garlic, chopped 1 rib celery, chopped, with leaves 1 green pepper, seeded and chopped 3 medium-sized potatoes, peeled and diced	In a soup kettle, heat the margarine and in it cook the onion and garlic until translucent. Add the remaining vegetables and, over gentle heat, cook them 15 minutes, stirring often.
4 tablespoons flour ¼ cup chopped parsley ¼ teaspoon ground allspice 1 bay leaf ¼ teaspoon ground clove ½ teaspoon red pepper flakes ½ teaspoon thyme 1 teaspoon salt ½ teaspoon pepper	Stir in the flour and seasonings.
7 cups hot water, in which 6 chicken bouillon cubes have been dissolved	Add the bouillon and, over high heat, cook the mixture, stirring, until it is slightly thickened.
1½ pounds uncooked honeycomb tripe, cut into 1-inch squares	Add the tripe and, over gentle heat, simmer the soup, covered, for 1½ hours.
1 5⅓-ounce can evaporated milk 2 tablespoons margarine	At the time of serving the soup, stir in the evaporated milk and margarine.

Serve the soup with Crusty Bread, page 300.

POULTRY

Chicken Parts

The following recipes may be made with chicken parts, already packaged at your supermarket; or they may be made with whole chicken, which you dismember yourself. Unless stated to the contrary, the recipes call for broiling fowl, about 3 pounds in weight, requiring 1 hour to cook at the simmer or in a 350° F. oven, depending upon the individual recipe. Allow 2 3-pound chickens for 6 substantial servings. If you use packaged chicken parts, the number of pieces you cook for 6 persons will depend upon that section of the bird's anatomy you choose. I recommend against purchasing chicken breasts, which are expensive and therefore unsuitable to the economic purpose of this book, and which are at their best only when quickly cooked and immediately served; slow cooking or "holding" only toughens and dries them. Legs and thighs are considerably less costly, have far more flavor, do not dry out, and "hold" well. Allow 1 drumstick and 1 second joint per serving. For the very economically minded cook, I suggest chicken wings. The first two wing sections, those closest to the body, are meaty and flavorful; the virtually meatless wing tip, the third section farthest from the body, may be removed and cooked in the same way as chicken giblets (see Basic Cooking of Giblets, page 252). Discard the cooked wing tips after sieving them. In this way, you will have a fine, rich broth to use in chicken dishes or as a base for various soups. Allow at least 3 chicken wings per serving. Necks and backs, while cheap, have insufficient meat to make them suitable for main-course recipes; cooked like chicken wing tips, however, they produce a delicious broth capable of many uses.

In these recipes, the point at which you may "stop and continue later" may also be the best time — if the recipe benefits from doing so — to refrigerate the recipe overnight and remove the solidified fat, if desired, before continuing with the preparation of the dish. When this is the case, indication to this effect is made. For the convenience of the reader, the majority of the recipes have been adapted to casserole cooking, thus reducing the number of utensils required and, at the same time, facilitating the serving. All of these recipes may be made with giblets and hearts.

Chicken Gumbo: America

Serves 6 ■ Doubles ■ Refrigerates

Preparation: 30 minutes ■ Cooking: 2½ hours

A traditional dish from Creole kitchens, chicken gumbo is a satisfying meal, especially welcome on winter evenings.

1   4-pound stewing fowl, cut into 3-inch pieces (if you do not have a meat cleaver, ask your butcher to do this for you)

12 cups water, in which 6 chicken bouillon cubes have been dissolved

3   onions, chopped

2   carrots, scraped and chopped

2   ribs celery, chopped, with their leaves

2   bay leaves

Pinch of cayenne

¾   teaspoon thyme

1   teaspoon sugar

1   teaspoon salt

6   peppercorns

In a soup kettle, combine the chicken, bouillon, vegetables, and seasonings. Bring the liquid to a boil, reduce the heat, and simmer the chicken, covered, for 2 hours, or until the meat falls from the bones. Remove the chicken, and dice and replace the meat; discard the skin and bones.

At this point you may stop and continue later. (Refrigerate the dish overnight; remove and reserve the solidified fat.)

3   tablespoons chicken fat

1   clove garlic, chopped

1½ cups raw natural rice

In a skillet, heat the chicken fat and in it cook the garlic until it is golden; discard the garlic. Add the rice and toast it for 3 minutes, stirring to coat each grain.

3   tomatoes, peeled, seeded, and chopped (canned tomatoes, drained, will do)

1   10-ounce package frozen okra, fully thawed to room temperature

To the contents of the soup kettle, add the rice and tomatoes; simmer the gumbo, covered, for 15 minutes. Add the okra and cook for 5 minutes, or until it is tender.

Serve the gumbo with Crusty Bread, page 300.

Chicken Ragout Soup: Austria
Serves 6 ■ Doubles ■ Refrigerates ■ Freezes

Preparation: 30 minutes ■ Cooking: 1¾ hours

Cook the dumpling dough, as directed, on the surface of the simmering soup. An easy and attractive one-dish meal.

1½ pounds chicken parts (necks, backs, wings, giblets)
1 veal knuckle
10 cups water
2 teaspoons salt
8 peppercorns

In a soup kettle, combine these 5 ingredients. Bring the liquid to a boil, reduce the heat, and simmer the meats, covered, for 1½ hours; skim the surface of the broth as necessary.

4 tablespoons margarine
2 onions, chopped
2 carrots, scraped and thinly sliced
2 ribs celery, chopped, with their leaves
2 parsnips, scraped and thinly sliced
Water

In a saucepan, heat the margarine and in it cook the vegetables, adding a little water as necessary, for 20 minutes, or until they are tender.

When the meat has cooked, sieve it through a colander, reserving the broth. Remove the edible meat from the bones and dice it. Discard the bones, skin, and peppercorns. Remove from the broth as much fat as possible. Return the broth to the kettle.

2 tablespoons flour
2 cups reserved broth

Over the vegetables, sprinkle the flour. Gradually add the broth. Cook the vegetable mixture, stirring, until it is thickened. Stir it into the contents of the soup kettle. Add the diced meat.

At this time you may stop and continue later. (Refrigerate the dish overnight; discard the solidified fat.)

Salt
Pepper
¼ cup chopped parsley

Bring the soup to the simmering point, adjust the seasoning to taste, and stir in the parsley.

Serve the soup with Dumplings, page 307.

Mulligatawny: America
Serves 6 ■ Doubles ■ Refrigerates ■ Freezes

Preparation: 30 minutes ■ Cooking: 1 hour

4 tablespoons margarine
3 pounds chicken parts
(or 1 3-pound fryer,
dismembered)

In a flameproof casserole or heavy soup kettle, heat the margarine and in it brown the chicken pieces.

2 tablespoons flour
2 tablespoons curry
powder
8 cups hot water, in which
6 chicken bouillon cubes
have been dissolved

Combine the flour and curry powder and sprinkle the mixture over the chicken. Gradually add the bouillon.

3 onions, chopped
3 carrots, scraped and
sliced
1 bay leaf
3 whole cloves
6 peppercorns
1 teaspoon sugar
Pinch of cayenne

Add the vegetables and seasonings. Bring the liquid to a boil, reduce the heat, and simmer the chicken for 1 hour, or until the meat falls from the bones. Remove the chicken, and dice and replace the meat; discard the skin and bones.

At this point you may stop and continue later. (Refrigerate the dish overnight; discard the solidified fat.)

2 tablespoons margarine
1 medium eggplant, peeled
and diced

In a skillet, heat the margarine and in it brown the eggplant until tender; margarine may be added as necessary. Add the eggplant to the simmering soup and allow it to cook, uncovered, for 5 minutes.

Serve the Mulligatawny in soup plates over Boiled Rice, page 303.

Chicken with Cheese Sauce
Serves 6 ■ Doubles ■ Refrigerates

Preparation: 30 minutes ■ Cooking: 1 hour in a 350° F. oven

2   tablespoons margarine
2   tablespoons oil
Serving pieces of chicken
    for 6 persons
Salt
Pepper

In a skillet, heat the margarine and oil; brown the chicken and season it. Remove it to a baking dish.

2   tablespoons margarine
1   onion, chopped
1   clove garlic, put
    through a press
2   tablespoons flour
2   teaspoons paprika
2   cups warm milk

To the remaining fat add the margarine and cook the onion until translucent. Stir in the garlic, flour, and paprika. Gradually add the milk, stirring the mixture until it is thickened and smooth.

1   cup grated Gruyère
    cheese

To the sauce add the cheese, stirring until the cheese is melted. Pour the sauce over the chicken.

At this point you may stop and continue later.

Bake the chicken, covered, at 350° F. for 1 hour, or until it is tender.

Serve the dish with Tomato Pilaf, page 306.

Chicken with Cabbage: France

Serves 6 ■ Doubles ■ Refrigerates

Preparation: 30 minutes ■ Cooking: 2½ hours (1 hour in a 350° F. oven)

Potée champenoise is a traditional dish in the Champagne country of France.

2 tablespoons margarine
2 tablespoons oil
Serving pieces of chicken
    for 6 persons
Salt
Pepper

In a flameproof casserole, heat the margarine and oil and brown the chicken; season it. Remove and reserve it.

1 head cabbage (about 2 pounds), shredded
1 teaspoon sugar
1 teaspoon salt
8 peppercorns
1 *bouquet garni* (page 16)
3 carrots, scraped and sliced
Cold water

In the remaining fat, toss the cabbage to coat it well. Over it sprinkle the sugar, salt, and peppercorns; add the *bouquet garni* and carrots. Add water to cover; bring it to a boil, reduce the heat, and simmer the cabbage, covered, for 1½ hours.

½ pound salt pork, cut into 6 slices

Replace the chicken, gently spooning some of the cabbage over it. Tuck in the pieces of salt pork.

At this point you may stop and continue later.

Bake the casserole, covered, at 350° F. for 1 hour, or until the chicken is tender.

Serve the dish with Boiled White Potatoes, page 301.

Chicken with Dried Beans: Alsace

Serves 6 ■ Doubles ■ Refrigerates ■ Freezes

Preparation: 45 minutes ■ Cooking: 5½ hours in a 275° F. oven

Not a true *cassoulet*, which is made with beans and various meats, but a very good dish — and excellent for one-plate buffet supper parties. Inexpensive, too!

1 pound white pea beans Cold water	In a large saucepan, combine the beans and water to cover by a full inch. Bring the liquid to a boil and, over high heat, cook the beans for 5 minutes. Remove the saucepan from the heat and allow the beans to sit, covered, for at least 1 hour.
6 slices bacon, diced	In a flameproof casserole, cook the bacon until the edges curl; it should not be fully crisp. Remove and reserve it.
⅓ cup seasoned flour 1 5-pound stewing chicken, cut into serving pieces	In the seasoned flour, dredge the chicken, rubbing the flour well into each piece. In the bacon fat, brown the chicken. Remove and reserve it.
4 onions, sliced	In the remaining fat, cook the onion until translucent; more fat or margarine may be added, if necessary.
	At this point you may stop and continue later.
	In a colander, drain the beans, reserving the liquid.
1 clove garlic, minced 1 teaspoon sugar 1 teaspoon thyme	Lightly grease the casserole, and in it toss together the beans, onion, garlic, reserved bacon, sugar, and thyme. Add the chicken pieces, spooning the bean mixture over and on top of them.

Reserved bean water
1 tablespoon salt
½ teaspoon pepper

To the bean water add the salt and pepper; bring it to a boil and add it to the casserole just to the level of the contents.

Bake the cassoulet, covered, at 275° F. for 5½ hours, or until the beans are tender and the liquid is absorbed. (The completed dish should be moist, but not soupy; add bean water as needed to maintain the proper consistency.)

Serve the dish with Braised Celery, page 295.

Chicken with Curry: India
Serves 6 ■ Doubles ■ Refrigerates

Preparation: 30 minutes ■ Cooking: 1 hour in a 350° F. oven

Seasoned flour
1 teaspoon ground ginger
Serving pieces of chicken
 for 6 persons
2 tablespoons margarine
2 tablespoons oil

To the seasoned flour, add the ginger and in the mixture dredge the chicken. In a flameproof casserole, heat the margarine and oil and brown the chicken. Remove and reserve it.

2 onions, chopped
1 clove garlic, chopped
1 tart apple, peeled,
 cored, and diced
1 tablespoon curry powder
 (or more, to taste)

In the remaining fat, cook the onion and garlic until translucent. Stir in the apple and curry powder.

1 cup hot water, in which
 1 chicken bouillon cube
 has been dissolved
1 cup warm milk
Grated rind and juice of
 ½ lemon

Gradually add the water and then the milk, stirring constantly, until the mixture is thickened and smooth. Stir in the lemon rind and juice. Replace the chicken, spooning the sauce over it.

At this point you may stop and continue later.

Bake the casserole, covered, at 350° F. for 1 hour, or until chicken is tender.

Serve the dish with Boiled Rice, page 303, and condiments for curries, page 50.

If desired, ⅓ cup seedless raisins may be added for the final 30 minutes of cooking.

Chicken with Chick-Peas: Turkey
Serves 6 ■ Doubles ■ Refrigerates ■ Freezes

Preparation: 45 minutes ■ Cooking: 1 hour in a 350° F. oven

2 tablespoons margarine
2 tablespoons oil
Serving pieces of chicken
  for 6 persons
Salt
Pepper

In a flameproof casserole, heat the margarine and oil and in it brown the chicken; season it. Remove and reserve the chicken.

12 small onions

In the remaining fat, glaze the onions. Remove the casserole from the heat and replace the chicken.

2 1-pound cans tomatoes, chopped, with their liquid
4 tablespoons margarine
½ teaspoon ground cardamom
½ teaspoon ground coriander
½ teaspoon ground ginger

In a saucepan, combine the tomatoes, margarine and seasonings; over gentle heat, simmer the mixture, covered, for 30 minutes.

2 20-ounce cans chick-peas, drained in a colander and rinsed with cold water

To the contents of the casserole add the chick-peas, spooning them around and over the onions and chicken. Over all, pour the tomatoes.

At this point you may stop and continue later.

Bake the casserole, covered, at 350° F. for 1 hour, or until the chicken is tender.

Serve the dish with Mixed Green Salad, page 298.

Chicken with Dressing
Serves 6 ■ Doubles ■ Refrigerates

Preparation: 30 minutes ■ Cooking: 1 hour in a 350° F. oven

2 tablespoons margarine 2 tablespoons oil Serving pieces of chicken for 6 persons Salt Pepper	In a skillet, heat the margarine and oil and brown the chicken; season it.

1 7-ounce package
    prepared
    poultry dressing
½ cup hot water
4 tablespoons margarine,
    melted
1 small onion, grated
¼ cup chopped parsley
1 teaspoon tarragon
	In a mixing bowl, combine these 6 ingredients and, using two forks, toss them together lightly.

2 tablespoons margarine	With the margarine, grease a baking dish. In it, arrange a flat layer of the dressing. Over the dressing, arrange the chicken pieces. Cover the dish with foil. *At this point you may stop and continue later.* Bake the chicken, covered, at 350° F. for 1 hour, or until it is tender.

Serve the dish with Green Bean Salad, page 299.

Chicken Hearts with Dressing: Use 1½ pounds chicken hearts, lightly browned in margarine. Use the essence from the browning as part of the liquid ingredient.

Lamb Chops with Dressing: Trim 6 shoulder chops of excess fat and brown them as directed. Follow remaining steps of recipe as directed. Add a strip of bacon, if desired, to each chop and continue to cook the dish, uncovered, for 15 minutes longer.

Chicken with Fruit I

Serves 6 ■ Doubles ■ Refrigerates

Preparation: 30 minutes ■ Cooking: 1 hour in a 350° F. oven

2 tablespoons margarine
2 tablespoons oil
Serving pieces of chicken
   for 6 persons
Salt
Pepper

In a flameproof casserole, heat the margarine and oil and brown the chicken; season it. Remove and reserve it.

1 onion, chopped
2 tablespoons cornstarch
2 cups orange juice
2 chicken bouillon cubes
¼ teaspoon cinnamon
¼ teaspoon ground clove

In the remaining fat, cook the onion until translucent. Stir in the cornstarch. Gradually add the orange juice, stirring constantly until the sauce is thickened and smooth. Add the bouillon cubes, stirring to dissolve them, and the spices. Replace the chicken.

At this point you may stop and continue later.

1½ cups seedless grapes, stemmed, rinsed, and drained on absorbent paper
2 oranges, sliced paper-thin and seeded

Bake the casserole, covered, at 350° F. for 30 minutes; add the grapes and, in an even layer, the orange slices, and continue to cook the chicken, covered, for 30 minutes longer, or until it is tender.

Serve the dish with Molded Rice, page 305.

Chicken with Fruit II (*Pineapple and Raisins*): Follow first step as directed. Follow second step as directed. In third step, in place of the grapes, use 1 cup golden raisins, plumped for 5 minutes in hot water and drained; add 1 8-ounce can crushed pineapple with its liquid, and the grated rind and juice of 1 lemon. Cook the recipe as directed.

Chicken with Paprika: Austria

Serves 6 ■ Doubles ■ Refrigerates ■ Freezes

Preparation: 30 minutes ■ Cooking: 1 hour in a 350° F. oven

2   tablespoons margarine
2   tablespoons oil
Serving pieces of chicken
    for 6 persons
Salt
Pepper

In a flameproof baking dish, heat the margarine and oil and brown the chicken; season it. Remove and reserve it.

3   onions, chopped
1   clove garlic, chopped
2   tablespoons paprika
3   tablespoons flour

In the remaining fat, cook the onion and garlic until translucent. Stir in the paprika and then the flour.

1   cup hot water, in which
    1 chicken bouillon cube
    has been dissolved
1   8-ounce can tomato
    sauce

Add the bouillon and tomato sauce, and, over moderate heat, cook the mixture, stirring constantly, until it is thickened and smooth.

2   cups sour cream
½   pound mushrooms,
    sliced (optional)

Add the sour cream, stirring to blend the sauce well. Stir in the mushrooms, if desired. Replace the chicken.

At this point you may stop and continue later.

Bake the chicken, covered, at 350° F. for 1 hour, or until it is tender.

Serve the dish with Boiled Rice, page 303, or Noodles, page 307.

The dish may also be made with chicken wings (see page 232) or giblets.

Chicken with Sausage and Rice: Brazil
Serves 6 ■ Doubles ■ Refrigerates ■ Freezes

Preparation: 30 minutes ■ Cooking: 1 hour in a 350° F. oven

½ pound sausage meat, rolled into small balls

In a flameproof casserole, render the sausage balls until they are well browned and crisp; remove them to absorbent paper and reserve them.

Serving pieces of chicken for 6 persons
Salt
Pepper

In the remaining fat, brown the chicken; season it. Remove and reserve it. Discard all but 3 tablespoons of the fat.

2 onions, chopped
1½ cups raw natural rice

In the fat, cook the onion until translucent. Add the rice, stirring to coat each grain.

1 1-pound can tomatoes, drained and chopped (reserve the liquid)

Stir in the tomatoes. Replace the sausage balls and chicken pieces. Spoon the rice mixture over them.

At this point you may stop and continue later.

Reserved tomato liquid
Hot water
3 chicken bouillon cubes

To the tomato liquid, add hot water to equal 3 cups. Add the bouillon cubes and dissolve them. Over the contents of the casserole, pour the mixture. Bake the casserole, covered, at 350° F. for 1 hour, or until the chicken and rice are tender and the liquid is absorbed.

Chicken with Sausage — *Italy:* In first step, use sweet Italian sausage meat. Follow second step as directed. In third step, omit the rice. Follow fourth step as directed. In fifth step, to the tomato liquid, add 1 20-ounce can tomato sauce, 1 8-ounce can pitted ripe olives, drained and sliced, 3 ribs celery, sliced, and ⅓ cup chopped parsley; omit the bouillon cubes; bake the casserole as directed. Serve the dish with Spaghetti, page 307. This dish does not freeze well.

Chicken with Potatoes: Italy
Serves 6 ■ Doubles ■ Refrigerates

Preparation: 30 minutes ■ Cooking: 45 minutes in a 350° F. oven

4   tablespoons olive oil
2   cloves garlic, split
Serving pieces of chicken
    for 6 persons
Salt
Pepper

In a flameproof casserole, heat the olive oil and in it cook the garlic until it is brown; remove and discard the garlic. In the hot oil, cook the chicken until it is well browned and partially done (20 minutes); season it. Remove and reserve it.

2   onions, chopped
4   medium-sized potatoes,
    peeled and cut into
    ¼-inch slices
2   bay leaves
1   tablespoon rosemary,
    crumbled

In the remaining oil, cook the onion and potato, stirring, until the onion is translucent. Add the bay leaves and rosemary. Replace the chicken.

At this point you may stop and continue later.

1½ cups hot water, in which
    2 chicken bouillon cubes
    have been dissolved
¼   cup chopped parsley

Over the contents of the casserole, pour the bouillon. Bake the dish, covered, at 350° F. for 45 minutes, or until the potatoes are very tender. Garnish the dish with the parsley.

Chicken with Dill (a first-century A.D. Roman recipe, adapted from Apicius, the gourmet who, discovering that his banquets had reduced him to comparative penury, committed suicide rather than forego his lifestyle): In first step, dredge the chicken in seasoned flour before browning it as directed. Omit second step entirely. In third step, combine 2 cups hot water, in which 2 chicken bouillon cubes have been dissolved, with 2 tablespoons dillweed (or more, to taste), 1 tablespoon wine vinegar, 1 teaspoon Worcestershire sauce, ½ teaspoon dried mustard, and a generous pinch of dried mint, crumbled. Pour the liquid over the chicken and bake the casserole, covered, at 350° F. for 45 minutes, or until the chicken is tender. Serve the dish with green noodles (see page 307).

Chicken with Peanuts — *Guinea:* In first step, dredge the chicken in seasoned flour before browning it. Omit second step entirely. In third step, reduce the water to 1 cup, mixed with 1 cup sour cream and 1 cup unsalted peanuts, which have been crumbled in the container of an electric blender; proceed as directed. Serve the dish with Boiled Rice, page 303.

Chicken with Okra — *Turkey:* Follow first step as directed. In second step, in place of the potatoes, add 1 29-ounce can tomatoes after the onion is cooked; over high heat cook the sauce, uncovered, for 20 minutes. To the sauce add 1 bay leaf, the rosemary, 2 teaspoons sugar, ½ teaspoon salt, and ¼ teaspoon pepper. Replace the chicken, spooning the sauce over it. In third step, omit the bouillon and parsley; cook the chicken, covered, at 350° F. for 15 minutes. Add, for the final 30 minutes of cooking, 1¼ pounds fresh okra, the stem end removed, and rinsed. If desired, 2 10-ounce packages frozen okra, fully thawed to room temperature, may be used; add them for the final 8 minutes of cooking (*total cooking time: 1 hour*). Serve the dish with Boiled White Potatoes, page 301.

Chicken with Sweet and Pungent Sauce

Serves 6 ■ Doubles ■ Refrigerates

Preparation: 30 minutes ■ Cooking: 1 hour in a 350° F. oven

This recipe, like all recipes in this section, may be made with hearts, gizzards, or wings, as well as with other parts of the chicken's anatomy.

2 tablespoons margarine
2 tablespoons oil
Serving pieces of chicken
  for 6 persons
2 onions, chopped
1 clove garlic, chopped
¾ teaspoon marjoram

In a flameproof casserole, heat the margarine and oil and brown the chicken. Add the onion and garlic and cook them until translucent. Sprinkle the chicken with the marjoram.

Sweet and Pungent
  Sauce, page 311

Over the chicken, spoon the sauce. Bake the dish, covered, at 350° F. for 1 hour, or until the chicken is tender.

Serve the dish with Boiled Rice, page 303.

Chicken with Tomatoes and Onions I: Italy

Serves 6 ■ Doubles ■ Refrigerates ■ Freezes

Preparation: 30 minutes ■ Cooking: 1 hour in a 350° F. oven

4 tablespoons olive oil
Serving pieces of chicken
   for 6 persons
Salt
Pepper

In a flameproof casserole, heat the olive oil and in it brown the chicken; season it. Remove and reserve it.

3 onions, chopped
2 cloves garlic, chopped

In the remaining fat, cook the onion and garlic until translucent.

1 29-ounce can tomatoes
2 chicken bouillon cubes
1 teaspoon rosemary,
   crumbled

To the onion, add the tomatoes, bouillon cubes, and rosemary. Simmer the sauce, uncovered, for 30 minutes. Replace the chicken.

At this point you may stop and continue later.

Bake the chicken, covered, at 350° F. for 1 hour, or until it is tender.

Serve the dish with Spaghetti; page 307.

Chicken with Tomatoes and Onions II — *Italy* (This is chicken *cacciatore* — "hunter's style"): In first step, dredge the chicken in seasoned flour before browning it. In second step, add 2 tablespoons olive oil to the casserole and, in place of the chopped onion, glaze 12 small onions, 3 green peppers, seeded and chopped, and the garlic. In third step, add to the listed ingredients 1 bay leaf, ½ teaspoon thyme, and ¼ cup chopped parsley; proceed as directed. Follow last step as directed. Serve the dish with Crusty Bread, page 301.

Chicken with Peppers and Zucchini — *Italy:* This offers a heartier dish, but one as easily made. Follow first step as directed. Follow second step as directed, adding to the onion and garlic 3 green peppers, seeded and chopped, 4 zucchini cut into ¼-inch rounds, ½ teaspoon marjoram, and ½ teaspoon thyme. Remove and reserve the vegetables. Follow third step as directed. Follow last step as directed, adding, for the final 20 minutes of cooking, the reserved vegetables. Serve the dish with Boiled Rice, page 303. This recipe may also be made with chicken giblets and used as a sauce for Spaghetti, page 307.

Chicken with Yogurt I: Middle East
Serves 6 ■ Doubles ■ Refrigerates ■ Freezes

Preparation: 30 minutes ■ Marination: 6 hours ■ Cooking: 1 hour in a 350° F. oven

2 cups yogurt Juice of 1 lime 1 clove garlic, put through a press 1½ teaspoons ground cardamom 1 teaspoon chili powder 1 teaspoon ground coriander ½ teaspoon ground ginger 2 tablespoons oil 1 teaspoon salt ½ teaspoon pepper	In a mixing bowl, combine and blend thoroughly these 10 ingredients.
Serving pieces of chicken for 6 persons	In a shallow baking dish, arrange the chicken pieces, pour the marinade over them, and allow them to stand for 6 hours (the first 3 hours in the refrigerator); turn them occasionally. Remove the chicken from the marinade and, with a rubber spatula, wipe it clean, reserving the marinade. Dry the chicken on absorbent paper.
2 tablespoons margarine 2 tablespoons oil 2 tablespoons flour Reserved marinade	In a flameproof casserole, heat the margarine and oil and brown the chicken. Remove and reserve it. To the remaining fat, add the flour, stirring. Gradually add the marinade, stirring constantly, until the sauce is thickened and smooth. Replace the chicken. *At this point you may stop and continue later.*

Bake the casserole, covered, at 350° F. for 1 hour, or until the chicken is tender.

Serve the dish with Boiled Rice, page 303.

Chicken with Yogurt II — *Greece:* Omit first three steps. In fourth step, brown the chicken in 4 tablespoons olive oil; season it with salt and pepper. Remove it; pour over it the juice of 1 lemon and reserve it. In the remaining fat, cook 1 onion, chopped, and 1 clove garlic, chopped, until translucent. To the onion add the flour and then 2 cups yogurt. When the sauce is thickened and smooth, stir in ¼ cup water in which a chicken bouillon cube has been dissolved. Replace the chicken. Over the chicken, sprinkle a generous grating of nutmeg. Follow last step as directed. Garnish the dish with chopped parsley and, if available, a little chopped fresh mint.

Chicken Livers and Giblets

Chicken livers, properly prepared, are delicious; they are nourishing; and they are inexpensive. All in all, a very good buy for the budget-minded cook. Six persons are well served by 1½ pounds.

Remove any fat or membrane from the livers and soak them in cold salted water for 1 hour; doing this makes their flavor more delicate. Drain and then dry them on absorbent paper. Chicken livers cook very rapidly; overcooking toughens them. For this reason, it is important, when preparing the following recipes, that you have all ingredients and utensils readied and at hand before you start cooking.

Basic Cooking of Giblets: To 3 cups cold water, add 1 onion stuck with 1 clove, 1 clove garlic, a *bouquet garni* (page 16), 2 teaspoons salt, 5 peppercorns, and 1 teaspoon sugar. Add 1½ pounds giblets of your choice (gizzards or hearts or a combination of both). Bring the liquid to a boil, reduce the heat, and simmer the giblets until they are fork-tender. With a slotted spoon, remove the giblets. Sieve broth and use it as the liquid of the sauce or for some other purpose.

Sautéed Chicken Livers
Serves 6 ■ Doubles ■ Refrigerates

Preparation: 10 minutes, exclusive of soaking the livers ■ Cooking: 10 minutes

3 tablespoons margarine 1½ pounds chicken livers (page 252) Salt Pepper	In a skillet, heat the margarine and in it cook the livers, stirring them gently but constantly, until they are slightly browned. Season them with salt and pepper to taste.

Serve the livers with Hot Potato Salad, page 302.

What could be simpler? The hot potato salad is purely my whim; there is nothing traditional about the combination. This recipe is capable of several variations:

In the hot margarine, cook 1 onion, chopped, until translucent; add the livers and proceed as directed.

Follow the recipe as given, but cook the livers only until they lose their pink color; at that point, sprinkle them with 1 tablespoon flour and gradually add 1 cup hot water in which 1 chicken bouillon cube has been dissolved. Stir the livers gently until the sauce is thickened and smooth. Serve them with Spaghetti, page 307.

Add ¼ cup sherry to the sauce. Or Madeira.

Season the sauce with ¼ cup chopped parsley.

When cooking the onion, add to it 1 teaspoon dried sage; proceed as directed.

In 4 tablespoons melted margarine, cook 2 onions, chopped; add 1½ cups pearl barley, stirring to coat each grain. Add 3 cups hot water, in which 3 chicken bouillon cubes have been dissolved. Bring the liquid to a boil, reduce the heat, and simmer the barley, covered, for 25 minutes, or until it is tender and the liquid is absorbed. Gently toss the sautéed chicken livers with the barley and garnish the dish with chopped parsley.

Chicken Livers with Sour Cream — *Hungary:* Adding ½ teaspoon rosemary, finely crumbled, to the cooking livers. Mix until smooth 1 tablespoon flour with ¼ cup cold water; add this mixture, together with 1 cup sour cream and ¼ cup chopped parsley, to the livers. Stir the mixture constantly until the sauce is thickened and smooth. Serve the dish with Noodles, page 307.

Chicken Livers with Green Beans: Indonesia
Serves 6 ■ Doubles ■ Refrigerates

Preparation: 30 minutes, exclusive of soaking the livers ■ Cooking: 20 minutes

As is true of most Far Eastern dishes, there is here no "stop and continue later" point; ready all the ingredients, then stop, if you desire. Cook the dish rapidly in one operation.

4 tablespoons oil
1½ pounds chicken livers (page 252)

In a flameproof casserole, or wok, heat the oil and in it, over high heat, stir-fry the chicken livers for 2 minutes. Remove them to absorbent paper and reserve them.

2 onions, chopped
6 cloves garlic, chopped
1 teaspoon fresh ginger root, grated (½ teaspoon ground ginger will do)

In the hot oil, stir-fry these 3 ingredients until the onion is translucent; a little oil may be added if necessary.

1 pound green beans, rinsed, the tips removed, and cut into ¾-inch segments

Add the beans and stir-fry them for 3 minutes.

Juice of 2 lemons *or* limes
1½ tablespoons soy sauce
Pinch of cayenne
1½ teaspoons turmeric
1 tablespoon brown sugar
1 cup hot water, in which 1 chicken bouillon cube has been dissolved

To the beans add these 6 ingredients and, over high heat, cook the mixture, stirring, for 10 minutes.

Reserved chicken livers
1½ teaspoons cornstarch mixed with 2 tablespoons cold water

Add the reserved livers and cornstarch mixture and continue to cook the dish, stirring constantly, for 5 minutes, or until the beans are tender-crisp and the sauce is somewhat thickened.

Serve the dish with Tomato Pilaf, page 306.

Chicken Livers with Vegetables — *China:* Follow first step as directed. In second step, in place of the onions and garlic, use 6 scallions, chopped with as much green as possible, 1 green pepper, seeded and cut into julienne, 1 5-ounce can water chestnuts, sliced, 1 8-ounce can bamboo shoots, drained, 1 15-ounce can bean sprouts, drained, 1 9-ounce package frozen pea pods, fully thawed to room temperature, and the suggested ginger. Omit third step. In fourth step, use only 1½ cups hot water in which 1 chicken bouillon cube has been dissolved; over high heat, cook the vegetables for 2 minutes. Follow last step as directed, using 2 tablespoons cornstarch blended with ¼ cup soy sauce. Over high heat, cook the dish, stirring constantly, only until the sauce is thickened and smooth. (The vegetables may be varied as you desire; omit, for example, the bean sprouts and substitute ¾ cup celery, chopped; or use only scallions and pea pods, increasing the latter to 2 9-ounce packages. The possibilities depend only upon your whim.) This recipe may also be made with chicken meat, cut from the bone and sliced into thin julienne; the meat cooks very rapidly. Add 2 green peppers, seeded and coarsely chopped.

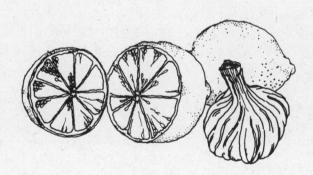

Chicken Livers with Eggplant: America
Serves 6 ■ Doubles ■ Refrigerates

Preparation: 30 minutes, exclusive of soaking the livers ■ Cooking: 30 minutes in a 350° F. oven

12 cups hot water
3 teaspoons salt
1 large eggplant (about 2 pounds), peeled and cut into large cubes

In a large saucepan or kettle, combine the water and salt. Bring the water to a boil, add the eggplant, and cook it, uncovered, for 12 minutes, or until it is tender. Drain it in a colander. In a large mixing bowl, mash the eggplant until it is a smooth purée.

4 tablespoons margarine
1 pound chicken livers (page 252)

In a skillet, heat the margarine and in it, over high heat, cook the chicken livers, stirring them often, until they are slightly browned. Remove and cut them into small dice. Fold them into the eggplant.

2 eggs
1 5⅓-ounce can evaporated milk
Generous grating of nutmeg
1 teaspoon salt
½ teaspoon pepper

In a mixing bowl, beat together the eggs and evaporated milk. Add the seasonings, to taste. Blend the custard with the eggplant mixture. Spoon it into a greased baking dish.

At this point you may stop and continue later.

½ cup bread crumbs
½ cup grated Parmesan cheese

Combine the bread crumbs and cheese and sprinkle them over the top. Bake the dish, uncovered, at 350° F. for 30 minutes, or until it is set and the crumb mixture is browned.

Serve the dish with Mixed Green Salad, page 298.

This recipe from the Southern United States may be varied by the omission of the bread crumb-cheese mixture or by the addition to the eggplant-liver mixture of 1 10-ounce package frozen peas, fully thawed to room temperature. An economical and unusual supper-party dish.

Chicken Livers with Orange Sauce
Serves 6 ■ Doubles ■ Refrigerates

Preparation: 20 minutes, exclusive of soaking the livers ■ Cooking: 5 minutes

2 tablespoons margarine
1 green pepper, seeded and cut into julienne
2 onions, chopped, *or* 6 scallions, chopped, with as much green as possible

In a saucepan, heat the margarine and in it cook the pepper and onion until just translucent.

Seasoned flour
1½ pounds chicken livers (page 252)
2 tablespoons margarine

In the seasoned flour, lightly dredge the livers. To the contents of the saucepan add the margarine and, when it is heated, cook the livers, turning to brown them evenly.

¼ cup chopped parsley
¼ teaspoon marjoram
½ teaspoon rosemary, crumbled
½ teaspoon salt
Pinch of pepper
Grated rind and juice of 1 orange
1 cup orange juice

Add the parsley, seasonings, and orange juice. Over high heat, bring the livers. To the contents of the saucepan add the margarine and, when it is heated, cook the livers, turning to brown them evenly.

Serve the dish with Boiled Rice, page 303.

Chicken Livers alla Primavera: Italy
Serves 6 ▪ Doubles ▪ Refrigerates

Preparation: 20 minutes, exclusive of soaking the livers ▪ Cooking: 15 minutes

This recipe is contributed by Edward Giobbi.

¼ cup olive oil
2 onions, chopped
3 tomatoes, peeled, seeded, and chopped (canned tomatoes, drained, will do)

In a skillet, heat the oil and in it cook the union until translucent. Add the tomatoes and cook the mixture for 10 minutes, or until it is slightly thickened.

At this point you may stop and continue later.

1½ pounds chicken livers (page 252)

To the contents of the skillet add the livers and, over high heat, cook them, stirring constantly, until they have just lost their pink color.

6 scallions, chopped, with as much green as possible
¼ cup chopped parsley
1 teaspoon basil
1 teaspoon oregano
½ cup hot water, in which 1 chicken bouillon cube has been dissolved
Salt
Pepper

Add the scallions, parsley, basil, oregano, and bouillon. Season the mixture with salt and pepper to taste. Simmer the livers, partially covered, for 5 minutes.

Serve the dish with Boiled Rice, page 303, or Molded Rice, page 305.

Chicken Livers with Apples: This is an oriental variant of the recipe. In first step, in place of the tomato, use 3 tart apples, peeled, cored, and diced. Follow second step as directed. For the ingredients of third step, use the juice of ½ lemon, ¼ teaspoon each of ground coriander, cumin, ginger, and turmeric. With the water, mix until smooth 1 teaspoon cornstarch. Stir the livers gently but constantly until the sauce is thickened and smooth. Serve the dish with Rice with Fruit, page 305.

Chicken Livers Risotto — *Italy:* Follow the directions for Chicken Livers alla Primavera. At the same time, cook for 2 minutes 1½ cups raw natural rice in 3 tablespoons margarine, stirring to coat each grain. Add 1 cup tomato juice and 1 cup hot water, in which 1 chicken bouillon cube has been dissolved; bring the liquid to a boil, reduce the heat, and simmer the rice, covered, for 10 minutes. Gently fold in the prepared livers and their liquid and simmer the dish, covered, for 5 minutes longer, or until the rice is tender and the liquid is absorbed. Serve the risotto with Mixed Green Salad, page 298.

Chicken Livers with Spaghetti — *Italy:* Follow the directions given. At the same time, cook 1 pound spaghetti as directed on the box. Be careful not to overcook it; rinse it thoroughly under hot water. To it add 3 tablespoons soft margarine; add the prepared livers and their liquid. Using 2 forks, gently toss the ingredients to blend them. Serve the dish with Mixed Green Salad, page 298.

Chicken Livers with Sweet and Pungent Sauce

Serves 6 ■ Doubles ■ Refrigerates

Preparation: 15 minutes, exclusive of soaking the livers ■ Cooking: 15 minutes

3   tablespoons margarine
1½ pounds chicken livers
    (page 252)
½   teaspoon thyme

In a skillet, heat the margarine and in it, lightly brown the chicken livers. Sprinkle them with the thyme.

Sweet and Pungent Sauce,
    (page 311)

Over the chicken livers, spoon the sauce. Over gentle heat, simmer the dish, covered, for 15 minutes.

Serve the dish with Boiled Rice, page 303.

Chicken Giblet Soup with Barley: Germany
Serves 6 ■ Doubles ■ Refrigerates ■ Freezes

Preparation: 15 minutes ■ Cooking: 1½ hours

1 pound chicken giblets
2 pounds chicken wing
   tips, backs, necks
   (mixed)

Follow the Basic Cooking of Giblets, page 252, adding the wing tips, backs, and wings, and using 8 cups of cold water.

⅔ cup pearl barley, rinsed
   under cold water

To the broth, add the barley and continue to simmer the soup, covered, for 1 hour, or until the barley is tender.

Remove the wing tips, backs, and necks. Discard the skin, pick the meat from the bones, and return it to the broth.

At this point you may stop and continue later. (Refrigerate the soup overnight; discard the solidified fat.)

½ cup coarsely chopped
   parsley

Bring the soup to serving temperature and stir in the parsley.

Serve the soup with Crusty Bread, page 300.

Giblet Soup with Lemon: America
Serves 6 ■ Doubles ■ Refrigerates

Preparation: 15 minutes ■ Cooking: 1 hour

1½ pounds chicken giblets	Follow the Basic Cooking of Giblets, page 252.
	Remove the giblets; sieve the broth. Dice and replace the giblets.
½ pound chicken livers quartered soaked for 1 hour in cold salted water, and drained	Add the livers and simmer them, covered, for 10 minutes.
2 eggs Juice of 1 lemon ½ cup parsley, chopped Pepper	In a mixing bowl, beat together the eggs and lemon juice. Remove the simmering soup from the stove and rapidly stir the egg mixture into it. Add parsley; pepper to taste.

Serve the soup with Crusty Bread, page 300.

Giblets with Paprika Sauce: Follow the Basic Cooking of Giblets (page 252). When the giblets are prepared, remove them from the broth and reserve them; sieve the broth and, over high heat, reduce it by half. In a large saucepan, heat 3 tablespoons margarine and in it cook 3 onions, chopped, until translucent. Add 1 tablespoon paprika, stirring; add the reserved giblets and cook them for 3 minutes. Stir in 1 8-ounce can tomato sauce and 1 cup of reserved broth. Stir together until smooth 1 cup sour cream and 1 tablespoon flour; add the mixture to the giblets, stirring constantly until the sauce is thickened and smooth. If desired, stir in ¼ cup chopped parsley. Serve the dish with Noodles, page 307. (*Total time: 2 hours.*)

Giblets with Noodles: Follow the Basic Cooking of Giblets (page 252). When the giblets are prepared, remove them from the broth and reserve them; sieve the broth and, over high heat, reduce it to 1½ cups. To it add 1 tablespoon flour mixed until smooth with the juice of 1 lemon; stir the mixture until it is somewhat thickened and smooth. Stir in the reserved giblets. Cook until just *al dente* 1 pound white or green noodles as directed on the box. In a colander, drain and rinse the noodles with hot water. In a large bowl, using two forks, toss together the giblets and noodles. Spoon the mixture into a baking dish, sprinkle it with grated cheese, and heat it in a 350° F. oven for 20 minutes, or until the cheese is melted. Serve the dish with Mixed Green Salad, page 298. (*Total time: 2 hours*.)

Giblets with Rice — *Greece:* Follow the Basic Cooking of Giblets (page 252). When the giblets are prepared, remove them from the broth and reserve them; sieve the broth and, over high heat, reduce it to 2½ cups and combine it with 1 6-ounce can tomato paste. In a flameproof casserole, toss together the giblets, 1½ cups raw natural rice, 2 onions, finely chopped, ½ cup chopped parsley, 1¼ teaspoons ground cinnamon, 1½ teaspoons salt, and ½ teaspoon pepper. Add the liquid and bring it to the boil; reduce the heat and simmer the rice, covered, for 15 minutes, or until it is tender and the liquid is absorbed. If desired, yogurt may be spread over the top of the risotto when it is served. Serve the dish with Green Bean Salad, page 299. (*Total time: 1¾ hours*.)

Giblets with Sauerkraut — *Germany:* Follow the Basic Cooking of Giblets (page 252). When the giblets are prepared, remove them from the broth and reserve them; sieve the broth and, over high heat, reduce it by half. In a baking dish, toss together the giblets and 2 pounds sauerkraut, rinsed under cold water and well drained. Sprinkle the mixture with ground celery seed and pepper. Over the top, arrange a layer of 2 onions, sliced. Add the reduced broth and bake the dish, covered, at 350° F. for 30 minutes. Serve the dish with Boiled White Potatoes, page 301. (*Total time: 2 hours*.)

Giblet Fricassee: Follow the Basic Cooking of Giblets (page 252). When the giblets are prepared, remove them from the broth and reserve them; sieve the broth and, over high heat, reduce it to 2 cups. In a mixing bowl, blend thoroughly 1 pound ground beef, 1 egg, beaten, ½ cup bread crumbs, 1 teaspoon oregano, ½ teaspoon salt, and ¼ teaspoon pepper. Roll the mixture into 24 balls. In a flameproof casserole, heat 2 tablespoons margarine and in it cook 2 onions, chopped; stir in 1 tablespoon flour and then, gradually, add the reduced broth, stirring the mixture constantly until it is thickened and smooth. Gently stir in the meatballs and simmer them, covered, for 25 minutes. Stir in the reserved giblets and heat them through. Serve the dish with Molded Rice, page 305. (*Total time: 1¾ hours*.)

FISH

The following recipes are intended for fresh or frozen filets of certain moderately priced white-fleshed fish readily available in your supermarket: cod, flounder, haddock, halibut, scrod, and, somewhat scarcer perhaps, turbot and whiting. In fact, any white-meat fish may be used and, although I find the dishes most successful when prepared with lean fish, I have tried heartier ones with such fat-fleshed fish as bluefish and find that they work well. Frozen fish filets should be fully thawed to room temperature and dried on absorbent paper.

There is a fine rule of thumb for cooking fish, whether in the oven or in the poaching pan. With a small ruler, measure the thickness of the filet at its densest point and allow 10 minutes' cooking time for each inch of thickness. Such thinner filets as flounder, for example, can be pierced at their thickest part with a fork tine and the tine then measured to the depth of its penetration.

Fish is baked, uncovered, in a very hot oven (450° to 500° F.), but when in sauces of cheese, eggs, or milk, it is baked, uncovered, at 350° F. to prevent separation of the sauce; the cooking time will double.

When poaching fish, to preserve shape and texture it is important that the liquid be just below the boiling point (190° to 200° F., so that it barely simmers). It should not cover the fish. If desired, a *court bouillon* may be used in place of plain water; this embellishment brings out the taste of the fish and, when sieved, makes for a more flavorful sauce. To make court bouillon, add to the necessary water a little vinegar or lemon juice, 2 tablespoons each of finely minced carrot, celery, and onion, 4 sprigs of parsley, and a pinch of thyme.

Fish cookery is fascinating to experiment with. For example, try these recipes — and such versions of them that I hope you will invent — with the unhandsome but delectable blowfish, more glamorously known as sea squab, available pan-ready at your fish counter. Again, try rolling and skewering with toothpicks flounder filets so that they are easily and attractively served. (To cook, measure the diameter of the rolled filet.) Two small filets yield 1 good serving and, if the filets are large, allow 1 per serving. Cut them in lengthwise halves before rolling and skewering them.

I should add that many of the sauces used in other dishes throughout this book are very good with fish. If a particular sauce in another recipe appeals to you, make it, pour it over fish filets in a lightly greased baking dish, and cook the dish as directed in the preceding paragraphs.

In the Introduction, an explanation is given for the omission of shellfish (or seafood). It is truly a luxury item and for this reason does not lend itself to the economical purposes of this book.

These recipes may be doubled, but it should be remembered that fish cooks best when arranged in a single layer in the utensil. In these recipes, the "stop now and continue later" phrase applies when the dish is ready for cooking; fish cookery should be done quickly so that the dish may be served at once.

Fish Chowder I: America
Serves 6 ■ Doubles ■ Refrigerates

Preparation: 30 minutes ■ Cooking: 30 minutes

The simple, satisfying New England classic, easily prepared and always delectable. Flounder filets are not practical for this recipe.

¼ pound salt pork, diced
  or 6 strips bacon, diced
6 onions, sliced

In a heavy kettle or flameproof casserole, render the salt pork until it is crisp and golden; remove it to absorbent paper and reserve it. In the fat, cook the onion until translucent.

4 potatoes, peeled and diced

Add the potato, stirring to coat each piece.

4 cups water

Add the water and cook the vegetables for 15 minutes, or until they are just barely tender.

At this point you may stop and continue later.

2 pounds fish filets, cut into bite-size pieces (page 266)

Add the fish and cook it for 12 minutes, or until it flakes easily with a fork.

2 cups milk, scalded
Salt
Pepper
Reserved pork or bacon dice

Add the milk, and season the chowder with salt and pepper to taste. Garnish it with the reserved pork dice.

Serve the dish with Crusty Bread, page 300.

Ideas for flavor accents: Add a bay leaf or 1½ teaspoons paprika, or 1 teaspoon Worcestershire sauce, or use half milk and half clam juice as the liquid (in this case, do not salt the chowder until it is ready to be served).

Fish Chowder II: West Indies
Serves 6 ■ Doubles ■ Refrigerates

Preparation: 25 minutes ■ Cooking: 30 minutes

½ cup olive oil
2 onions, chopped
1 clove garlic, chopped
1 cup raw natural rice

In a heavy kettle or flameproof casserole, heat the olive oil and in it cook the onion and garlic until translucent. Add the rice and cook the mixture for 5 minutes, stirring it often.

2 cups shredded cabbage
3 potatoes, peeled and diced
2 large tomatoes, peeled, seeded, and chopped
8 cups boiling water, in which 4 chicken bouillon cubes have been dissolved

To the contents of the kettle add the cabbage, potato, and tomato. Add the bouillon and bring it to a boil; reduce the heat and simmer the vegetables, covered, for 15 minutes.

At this point you may stop and continue later.

2 pounds fish filets, cut into bite-size pieces (page 266)
Salt
Pepper

Bring the kettle to simmering heat, add the fish, and continue to cook the chowder, uncovered, for 15 minutes, or until the fish flakes easily and the rice and potatoes are tender. Adjust the seasoning, to taste.

Serve the dish with Crusty Bread, page 300.

Baked Fish Chowder: America

Serves 6 ■ Doubles ■ Refrigerates

Preparation: 15 minutes ■ Cooking: 1 hour in a 350° F. oven

3 large potatoes, peeled and thinly sliced

Prepare the potatoes and place them in cold water to prevent their discoloring.

4 large onions, thinly sliced

Prepare the onions and fish.

2 pounds fish filets, cut into bite-size pieces (page 266)

At this point you may stop and continue later.

Margarine
Salt
Pepper
½ teaspoon celery seed
6 cups milk
¼ cup chopped parsley

Grease a large casserole or baking dish with margarine. In it, arrange a layer of potato, then a layer of onion; dot the onion layer with margarine and season with salt, pepper, and the celery seed. Arrange the fish in a single layer, and season it with salt and pepper. Add, in order, the remaining potato and onion. Dot the onion layer with margarine and season it with salt and pepper. Add the milk. Bake the dish, uncovered, at 350° F. for 1 hour, or until the fish flakes easily and the potatoes are tender. Garnish the chowder with the parsley.

Serve the dish with Crusty Bread, page 300.

Another New England classic, very easily made and very good. A richer soup, if desired, may be made by substituting 1 10½-ounce can evaporated milk for an equal quantity of fresh milk.

Fish Soup: France

Serves 6 generously ■ Doubles ■ Refrigerates

Preparation: 35 minutes ■ Cooking: 10 to 15 minutes

In its native Brittany, this soup is called *cotriade*. It is honest peasant fare, very satisfying, very soothing to both stomach and spirit.

6 tablespoons margarine 6 onions, sliced 1 clove garlic, chopped	In a soup kettle, heat the margarine and in it cook the onion and garlic until translucent.
8 cups water 6 medium-sized potatoes, peeled and quartered 2 bay leaves ½ teaspoon marjoram ⅓ cup chopped parsley ½ teaspoon thyme 1½ teaspoons salt ½ teaspoon pepper	Add the water, potatoes, and seasonings. Cook the potatoes, covered, until they are just tender. *At this point you may stop and continue later.*
2 to 3 pounds filets cut into bite-size pieces (page 266).	To the gently boiling broth, add the fish and cook the soup, stirring once very gently, for 10 to 15 minutes, or until the fish flakes easily.

Serve the dish with Crusty Bread, page 300.

Baked Fish Filet: Greece
Serves 6 ▪ Doubles ▪ Refrigerates

Preparation: 30 minutes ▪ Cooking: 20 to 30 minutes (page 266)

A popular way of preparing fish in the Greek islands, this dish is also colorful to the eye. Greek tomatoes, vine- and sun-ripened, are second to none. You will find that the recipe is tastiest when fresh tomatoes are used.

2 pounds fish filets, in serving portions (page 266) Juice of 1 lemon Salt Pepper	Sprinkle the fish with the lemon juice, and season it.
⅓ cup olive oil 6 onions, sliced 2 cloves garlic, chopped ½ cup chopped parsley	In a skillet, heat the olive oil and in it cook the onions and garlic until translucent. Stir in the parsley.
3 tomatoes, peeled, seeded, and chopped (canned tomatoes, drained, will do) ½ cup water, mixed with ½ teaspoon vinegar	Stir in the tomato and cook the mixture for 5 minutes. Add the acidulated water and continue to cook the vegetables for 5 minutes longer.
1 teaspoon olive oil 3 tomatoes, peeled and sliced 1 lemon, sliced paper-thin and seeded	With the olive oil, grease a large baking dish. Spoon into it one half of the sauce. Arrange the fish in the sauce. Over the fish, arrange the tomato slices and lemon in an overlapping pattern. Pour over the remaining sauce. *At this point you may stop and continue later.* Bake the fish, uncovered, at 350° F. for 20 to 30 minutes, or until it flakes easily.

Serve the dish with Rice with Fruit, page 305.

Curried Fish Filets: India

Serves 6 ■ Refrigerates

Preparation and cooking: 35 minutes

Court bouillon (page 266)
2 pounds fish filets, in serving portions (page 266)

In a shallow pan or skillet, bring to a boil the court bouillon. Reduce the heat so that the liquid simmers. In the liquid, poach the fish filets (page 266). Remove them to a serving dish and keep them warm. Strain the broth.

2 tablespoons margarine
1 onion, chopped
½ green pepper, chopped
1 rib celery, chopped
2 teaspoons curry powder (or more, to taste)
2 tablespoons flour

In a pan or skillet, heat the margarine and in it cook the onion, pepper, and celery until they are translucent. Stir in the curry powder and then the flour.

2 cups reserved court bouillon
Salt
Pepper
¼ cup chopped parsley

Add the liquid and cook the mixture, stirring constantly, until it is thickened and smooth. Adjust the seasoning to taste. Pour the sauce over the warm fish and garnish the plate with parsley.

Serve the dish with Boiled Rice, page 303.

Fish Filets with Eggplant: France

Serves 6 ■ Doubles ■ Refrigerates

Preparation: 40 minutes ■ Cooking: 15 to 20 minutes

Filet de poisson aux aubergines is a well-known dish in provincial France. The combination of the two flavors will show you why.

1 medium eggplant, peeled and cut into 6 slices
Seasoned flour
4 tablespoons margarine (about)

Prepare the eggplant and dredge it in the seasoned flour. In a skillet, heat the margarine and in it brown the eggplant on both sides (more margarine may be added as necessary). Over the bottom of a lightly greased baking dish, arrange the eggplant slices. Bake them, covered, at 350° F. for ½ hour.

Milk
2 pounds fish filets, in serving portions (page 266)
Seasoned flour
4 tablespoons margarine, melted

Into the milk, dip the fish filets; then dredge them lightly in the flour. Arrange the filets over the eggplant slices, and over them pour the melted margarine.

At this point you may stop and continue later.

Juice of 1 lemon

Over the fish, sprinkle the lemon juice. Bake the dish as directed on page 266.

½ cup chopped parsley

When serving the fish, garnish it with the parsley.

Serve the dish with Spinach, page 296.

Fish Filets with Orange: Mexico
Serves 6 ▪ Doubles ▪ Refrigerates

Preparation: 20 minutes ▪ Cooking: 10 to 20 minutes

Olive oil
2 pounds fish filets, in
serving portions
(page 266)
Salt
Pepper
½ teaspoon thyme

With the olive oil, lightly grease a baking dish. In it, arrange the filets; season them.

4 scallions, chopped
finely, with as much
green as possible
3 tomatoes, peeled,
seeded, and chopped
1 green pepper, seeded
and cut into 2-inch
julienne
Olive oil

Over the fish, arrange in order the scallions, tomato, and green pepper. Over all, add a drizzle of olive oil.

At this point you may stop and continue later.

Grated rind of 1 orange
¾ cup orange juice
1 orange, sliced
paper-thin and seeded

Over the contents of the baking dish, sprinkle the orange rind; add the orange juice and orange slices. Bake the fish as directed on page 266.

Serve the dish with Green Bean Salad, page 299.

Fish Filets with Paprika Sauce
Serves 6 ■ Doubles ■ Refrigerates

Preparation: 20 minutes ■ Cooking: 10 to 20 minutes

Margarine
2 pounds fish filets, in
   serving portions
   (page 266)
Salt
Pepper
Juice of ½ lemon

In a lightly greased baking dish, arrange the filets. Season them with the salt, pepper, and lemon juice.

3 tablespoons margarine
3 onions, thinly sliced

In a skillet, heat the margarine and in it cook the onion until translucent.

2 tablespoons flour
1½ tablespoons paprika (or
   more, to taste)
½ cup hot water, in which
   1 chicken bouillon cube
   has been dissolved
1½ cups milk

Into the onion, stir the flour and paprika. Add the bouillon and then the milk; cook the mixture, stirring constantly, until it is thickened and smooth. Pour the sauce over the fish.

At this point you may stop and continue later.

Bake the fish as directed on page 266.

Serve the dish with Noodles, page 307.

Fish Filets with Parsley and Tarragon: Mexico
Serves 6 ■ Doubles ■ Refrigerates
Preparation: 30 minutes ■ Cooking: 15 to 20 minutes

Margarine
2 pounds fish filets in
  serving portions
  (page 00)
Juice of 1 lemon
2 teaspoons tarragon
Salt
Pepper

In a lightly greased baking dish, arrange the fish filets. Sprinkle them with the lemon juice and tarragon. Season them. Allow them to stand for 45 minutes.

6 tablespoons margarine
1 onion, grated
1 clove garlic, put
  through a press
½ cup coarsely chopped
  parsley

In a saucepan, heat the margarine and in it cook the onion, garlic, and parsley until the parsley is wilted.

1 cup hot water, in which
  1 chicken bouillon cube
  has been dissolved
1½ teaspoons cornstarch
  mixed with a little
  cold water

To the parsley add the bouillon and then the cornstarch mixture. Over medium heat, cook the sauce, stirring constantly, until it is thickened and smooth. Pour the sauce over the fish.

At this point you may stop and continue later.

Bake the fish as directed on page 266.

Serve the dish with Boiled Sweet Potatoes, page 301.

Fish Filets with Peanut Sauce: East Africa

Serves 6 ■ Doubles ■ Refrigerates

Preparation: 30 minutes ■ Cooking: 10 to 20 minutes

Exotic — a supper-party conversation maker.

Margarine
2 pounds fish filets, in serving portions (page 266)
Salt
Pepper
Sprinkling of basil

With a little margarine, grease a baking dish. In it, arrange the fish filets. Season them lightly.

3 tablespoons margarine
3 onions, chopped
2 teaspoons curry powder (or more, to taste)
2 tomatoes, peeled, seeded, and chopped

In a saucepan, heat the margarine and in it cook the onion until translucent. Stir in the curry powder. Add the tomato and, over medium heat, cook the mixture until the excess liquid is evaporated.

1 cup unsalted peanuts
1½ cups hot water, in which 1 chicken bouillon cube has been dissolved

In the container of an electric blender, combine the peanuts and bouillon and, on medium speed, whirl them until the mixture is smooth. Add it to the contents of the saucepan and cook the sauce, stirring often, until it is the consistency of heavy cream. Pour the sauce over the fish.

At this point you may stop and continue luter.

Bake the fish as directed on page 266.

Serve the dish with Boiled Rice, page 303.

Fish Filets with Potatoes: Netherlands
Serves 6 ■ Doubles ■ Refrigerates

Preparation: 35 minutes ■ Cooking: 45 minutes in
a 350° F. oven

4 potatoes, peeled
Salt
Water

In boiling salted water to cover, cook the potatoes for 12 minutes, or until they are tender. Drain and slice them thinly.

3 tablespoons margarine
2 onions, chopped

In a skillet, heat the margarine and in it cook the onion until translucent.

Margarine
2 pounds fish filets, in serving portions (page 266)
Salt
Pepper

With the margarine, lightly grease a baking dish. Over the bottom, arrange the fish filets in an even layer. Season them. Over them, arrange an even layer of potato slices. Last, spread over all the cooked onion.

3 eggs
½ teaspoon salt
1 cup sour cream
1½ teaspoons dillweed

Beat the eggs with the salt; add the sour cream and dillweed, and mix the sauce well. Pour the sauce over the contents of the baking dish.

At this point you may stop and continue later.

Bake the dish, uncovered, at 350° F. for 45 minutes, or until the potatoes are tender and the sauce is set and lightly browned.

Serve the dish with Spinach, page 296.

Fish Filets with Ravigote Sauce
Serves 6 ■ Doubles ■ Refrigerates

Preparation: 25 minutes ■ Cooking: 10 to 20 minutes

This sauce is very good poured over broiled blowfish (see page 266).

3 tablespoons margarine
6 scallions, chopped finely, with as much green as possible
¾ teaspoon dry mustard
1 cup water, in which 1 chicken bouillon cube has been dissolved
1 8-ounce can tomato sauce
2 teaspoons Worcester-shire sauce
1 teaspoon sugar
1 bay leaf, crumbled

In a saucepan, heat the margarine and in it cook the scallions, stirring occasionally for 10 minutes. Stir in the mustard, then add the bouillon, tomato sauce, and other ingedients. Simmer the sauce, covered, for 25 minutes.

Margarine
2 pounds fish filets, in serving portions (page 266)
Salt
Pepper

In a lightly greased baking dish, arrange the fish filets. Season them.

At this point you may stop and continue later.

Over the fish, pour the hot sauce. Bake the fish as directed on page 266.

Serve the dish with Mashed Turnips, page 296.

Fish Filets with Sour Cream: America
Serves 6 ■ Refrigerates

Preparation: 15 minutes ■ Cooking: 20 minutes

Margarine
1 lemon, sliced
  paper-thin and seeded
2 pounds fish filets, in
  serving portions
  (page 266)

With a little margarine, grease very lightly a baking dish. Over the bottom, arrange a layer of the lemon slices. Over the lemon slices, arrange the fish.

Bake the fish as directed, page 266.

1 cup sour cream
1 small onion, grated
¾ teaspoon prepared
  mustard
½ teaspoon salt
Paprika

Combine the sour cream, onion, mustard, and salt. Spread the mixture over the fish, sprinkle it with paprika, and return the dish, uncovered, to the oven for 5 minutes, or until the sauce is well heated.

Serve the dish with Carrots, page 295.

Fish Filets with Sour Cream and Cheese — *Russia:* Omit the lemon slices, sprinkle the fish with paprika, and add to the sour cream mixture (without paprika) ⅓ cup grated cheese. Garnish the dish with ⅓ cup buttered bread crumbs. Bake the fish as directed on page 266. Serve the dish with Noodles, page 307.

Scalloped Fish Filets: Cut the fish into bite-size pieces (see page 266). In 3 tablespoons butter, cook 1 green pepper, seeded and chopped, and 1 onion, chopped, until the onion is translucent. Add the fish pieces, 1 teaspoon salt, and ¼ teaspoon pepper. Over gentle heat, cook the fish, covered, for 10 minutes. In a saucepan, combine 1 cup sour cream, 1 cup milk, and 3 tablespoons flour; stir the mixture until it is smooth. Add 1½ teaspoons Worcestershire sauce. Cook the mixture, stirring constantly, until it is thickened and smooth. Fold in the fish and vegetables. Into a greased ovenproof baking dish, spoon the mixture, and sprinkle it with ½ cup grated cheddar cheese mixed with ½ cup bread crumbs. Toast the dish, uncovered, under the broiler, for 10 minutes, or until the top is golden brown. Serve the fish with Zucchini, page 296.

The same recipe may be spooned over cooked fresh or frozen broccoli, arranged in an ovenproof baking dish. This method provides a complete entrée in one dish.

Fish Filets with Spinach I: Greece
Serves 6 ■ Doubles ■ Refrigerates

Preparation: 30 minutes ■ Cooking: 10 to 15 minutes

Olive oil
2 pounds fish filets, in
serving portions
(page 266)
Salt
Pepper

With a little olive oil, grease a baking dish. In it, arrange the fish filets. Season them lightly.

3 tablespoons olive oil
2 10-ounce packages frozen
chopped spinach, fully
thawed to room
temperature and drained
6 scallions, chopped,
with as much green as
possible
1 clove garlic, put
through a press
¼ cup chopped parsley

In a skillet, heat the oil, add the spinach, scallions, garlic, and parsley, and cook the mixture, stirring often, until it contains no excess water.

Over each serving portion of fish, spoon some of the spinach mixture. (If flounder filets are used, they may be filled, rolled, and skewered.)

At this point you may stop and continue later.

Bake the fish as directed on page 266.

Serve the dish with Dried Bean Salad, page 309.

If desired, grated cheese may be sprinkled over the spinach before baking the dish, or — a nice Greek touch — when serving the fish, pour over it egg-lemon sauce: beat 2 egg whites with a pinch of salt until stiff. Beat in 2 yolks, singly, then the juice of 2 lemons, mixed with 2 teaspoons cornstarch. Finally, add gradually and while beating constantly, 1 cup boiling water in which 1 chicken bouillon cube has been dissolved. In the top of a double boiler, over hot water, cook the mixture, stirring constantly, until it coats the spoon. When serving, pour the sauce over the dish.

Fish Filets with Spinach II — *France:* Follow first step, using margarine in place of the olive oil; follow second step, using margarine in place of the olive oil, omitting the garlic, and seasoning the spinach with a generous sprinkling of nutmeg; follow third step, arranging the fish on top of the spinach. Bake the dish, covered, as directed on page 266. Add a sauce: into 1 tablespoon melted margarine, stir 1 tablespoon flour; add 1 cup warm milk, 1 small onion, grated, and salt and pepper to taste. Cook the mixture until it is thickened and smooth. Combine ¼ cup milk and 1 egg yolk, and beat the mixture, adding gradually 6 tablespoons grated cheese. Stir this mixture into the sauce; pour the sauce over the fish, sprinkle over ¼ cup grated cheese, and brown the top under a hot broiler for about 1 minute. Serve the dish with Boiled White Potatoes, page 301.

Fish Filets with Sweet and Pungent Sauce
Serves 6 ■ Doubles ■ Refrigerates

Preparation: 20 minutes ■ Cooking: 10 to 20 minutes

Margarine
2 pounds fish filets in serving portions (page 266)
Basil

In a lightly greased baking dish, arrange the filets. Sprinkle them with basil.

Over the fish, spoon the Sweet and Pungent Sauce, page 311. Bake the dish as directed on page 266.

Serve the dish with Boiled Rice, page 303.

Fish Filets Thermidor: France
Serves 6 ■ Doubles ■ Refrigerates

Preparation: 30 minutes ■ Cooking: 15 minutes in a 350° F. oven.

Thermidor, named after the period from July 19 to August 18 of the French Revolutionary calendar, is a classic sauce.

Court bouillon
  (page 266)
2 pounds fish filets, in serving portions
  (page 266)
Margarine

In a large skillet, in court bouillon not quite to cover, poach the fish as directed on page 266. Remove the filets, and arrange them in a lightly greased baking dish. Sieve and reserve the broth.

Reserved broth
1 5⅓-ounce can evaporated milk
1 teaspoon Worcestershire sauce
1 teaspoon salt

To the reserved broth add water, if necessary, to equal 2¼ cups. Combine the liquids and add the seasonings.

6 tablespoons margarine
6 tablespoons flour
½ cup Parmesan cheese, grated

In a saucepan, heat the margarine; stir in the flour and, over gentle heat, cook the mixture for 3 minutes. Gradually add the liquid ingredient, and cook the sauce, stirring constantly, until it is thickened and smooth. Add the cheese, stirring until it is melted.

At this point you may stop and continue later.

Over the fish, pour the hot sauce and bake the dish, uncovered, at 350° F. for 15 minutes, or until the sauce bubbles.

Serve the dish with Boiled White Potatoes, page 301.

Kedgeree: England

Serves 6 ▪ Doubles ▪ Refrigerates (adequately only)

Preparation: 40 minutes ▪ Cooking: 30 minutes in a 300° F. oven

The English classic fish and rice dish is pleasant for brunches, luncheons, and suppers. It is a light dish, welcome for summer eating. If desired, it may be made with smoked fish, soaked, poached, skinned, and boned before flaking.

6   tablespoons margarine
2   teaspoons curry powder
    (optional)
1½ cups raw natural rice

In a saucepan, heat the margarine and to it add the curry powder, stirring to blend the mixture well. Add the rice, stirring to coat each grain. Set the rice aside and reserve it.

2   pounds fish filets, in
    serving portions
    (page 266)

In water barely to cover, poach the fish (for timing, see page 266). Drain it and reserve the broth. Flake the fish and reserve it. To the broth add water, if necessary, to equal 3 cups.

Add the liquid to the rice and bring it to a boil; reduce the heat and simmer the rice, covered, for 15 minutes, or until it is tender and the liquid is absorbed.

Juice of ½ lemon
4 eggs, hard-boiled
½ cup chopped watercress
   or parsley

Prepare the lemon juice. Chop the egg whites and force the yolks through a coarse sieve; reserve both separately. Prepare the watercress.

At this point you may stop and continue later.

Worcestershire sauce

In a large mixing bowl, using two forks, toss together lightly the fish flakes and rice. Add the lemon juice, egg whites, watercress, salt and pepper to taste, and a dash of Worcestershire sauce. Toss the mixture once again to blend it well.

Margarine
Light cream (optional)

With a little margarine, lightly grease a baking dish. Into it, spoon the kedgeree and heat it, covered, for 30 minutes in a 300° F. oven. If desired, a little light cream may be added for extra moistness.

Fish Pudding: Denmark

Serves 6 ■ Refrigerates (adequately only)

Preparation: 30 minutes ■ Cooking: 1 hour in a 325° F. oven

So elegant! Light of texture and delicately flavored, this pudding is a standby at my house for those occasions when I want to offer something rather special.

1 pound fish filets, coarsely chopped (page 266)
1 small onion, coarsely chopped
1 cup milk
2 eggs
2½ tablespoons potato flour
½ teaspoon ground cumin

In the container of an electric blender, combine these 6 ingredients and, on high speed, whirl them until the mixture is smooth.

¼ cup milk
¼ cup water, in which 1 chicken bouillon cube has been dissolved
1 5⅓-ounce can evaporated milk, plus whole milk to equal 1 cup

With the motor running, add the milk and bouillon. If the blender is large enough, add the evaporated milk. Otherwise, empty the container into a mixing bowl and add the evaporated milk to the fish mixture.

At this point you may stop and continue later.

Margarine

With margarine, grease a 1-quart mold or baking dish. Pour the pudding mixture into it. Set it in a pan of hot water and bake the pudding, uncovered, at 325° F. for 1 hour, or until a knife inserted at the center comes out . clean.

1 cup sour cream
2 tablespoons dillweed
¼ teaspoon salt
¼ teaspoon white pepper

Meanwhile, make the dill sauce by combining and stirring well these 4 ingredients. (The sauce improves with standing.)

On a warmed serving platter, unmold the fish pudding and serve it immediately. Offer the dill sauce separately.

Serve the dish with Carrots, page 295.

SIDE DISHES

The following side dishes are offered for their high nutritional value and their low cost. Some are plain, some are fancied up a bit. All are intended as complements to the meat recipes they accompany. I urge you, however, to serve whatever side dish you wish with whatever meat recipe; remember always that a principal idea of this book is experimentation. All necessary ingredients, it is hoped, are available to the food shopper at any kind of market and in virtually every season of the year.

It is too easy, I fear, at the present time in history, to forget or to overlook what is good and simple, or simply good. Anybody who has tasted a properly cooked new potato will not soon forget that flavor. Or the taste of sweet carrots. Or the pleasant crunch of cabbage carefully prepared. Such newly discovered and pleasurable experience is what this section of the book is about: the wonderful memory of tastes past recaptured in basic foods. Even the fancied-up dishes are simple in their ingredients; they are only given more flavorful treatment as an enhancement to milder-tasting main dishes. Some of the following side dishes are not specifically called for by the recipes in the main body of this book; they are included to increase the variety of your menu making.

Vegetables

Acorn Squash: Although a "winter" vegetable, acorn squash is available nearly year round. Allow ½ squash per serving.

For *Baked Acorn Squash*, cut the squash in half vertically, leave the seeds in; arrange the halves on a baking sheet and cook them in a 400°F. oven for 45 minutes, or until they are tender. Remove the seeds and season each half with salt, pepper, and 1 tablespoon soft margarine placed in the cavity. If desired, the seeds may be removed before the squash is cooked; sprinkle each half with salt and pepper, and in each cavity put 1 tablespoon brown sugar and 1 tablespoon margarine.

For *Stuffed Acorn Squash*, follow the directions in previous recipe for baking squash. When the squash is cooked, scoop out and discard the seeds; then scoop out the flesh, reserving the shells. Mash the flesh until it is smooth, adding, as you do so, ¼ cup milk, 6 tablespoons soft margarine, a generous grating of nutmeg, and salt and pepper to taste. Fill the shells, arrange them on a baking sheet, and cook them in a 400°F. oven for 20 minutes, or until the filling is browned.

Cabbage: Too often cabbage is so cooked to death that the resultant "vegetable" is without either taste or texture. Cabbage is capable of a delightful tender-crisp crunch and of a fresh and delicious flavor. The following recipes, favorites of mine, provide both:

In a saucepan, combine 1 cup milk, 2 tablespoons margarine, 1 teaspoon salt, and ¼ teaspoon pepper. Over gentle heat, melt the butter. To the mixture add 1 medium-sized cabbage, finely shredded; pack the vegetable tightly. Bring the milk to a boil, reduce the heat, and, over medium heat, simmer the cabbage, covered, for 20 minutes. Remove the pan from the heat, add 2 tablespoons soft margarine, and toss the vegetable gently. Drain the cabbage, reserving the liquid. Arrange the cabbage in a serving dish and keep it warm. Return the liquid to the saucepan and bring it to a boil. Meanwhile, beat 1 egg yolk lightly. Away from the heat, add the yolk to the liquid and then gently cook the sauce, stirring constantly, until it begins to coat the spoon. Pour the sauce over the cabbage and serve.

A less complicated recipe, but a very good one:

In a large saucepan, arrange 1 medium-sized head of cabbage finely shredded; add cold water to cover. Over high heat, bring the water to a boil; do not cover the pan. When the water reaches the boiling point, the cabbage should be tender-crisp; if desired, cook it a few minutes longer. Drain the vegetable and toss it with 3 tablespoons soft margarine; season it with salt and pepper to taste.

Carrots: Two pounds serve 6 persons. A well-known source of vitamin C.

With a vegetable parer, scrape the carrots; slice them into rounds or lengthwise; cook them, covered, in boiling water for 15 minutes, or until they are tender-crisp. Drain them and season them with soft margarine, salt, pepper, and, if desired, a grating of nutmeg.

Carrots may be mashed, like potatoes; or they may be candied: in a heavy saucepan, melt 8 tablespoons margarine, add ½ cup brown sugar, and when the sugar is melted, add the cooked carrots; over gentle heat, glaze them, stirring them often.

Celery: Two pounds serve 6 persons.

For *Boiled Celery*, cut the vegetable into pieces from 1 to 3 inches long and cook them, covered, in boiling water for 15 minutes or until they are tender-crisp; drain them and add soft margarine, salt, and pepper to taste.

For *Braised Celery*, cook the vegetable in a skillet with only enough water to prevent its burning; season the water with a bouillon cube; when the celery is tender-crisp, add margarine, salt, and pepper to taste. If desired, sprinkle the braised celery with grated cheese and bake the vegetable in a 425°F. oven for 5 minutes, or until the cheese is melted.

Eggplant: Cut 2 medium eggplants lengthwise into equal thirds. With a sharp knife, score the flesh. With a pastry brush, paint the flesh with ⅓ cup olive oil to which 1 clove garlic, put through a press, has been added. Season the eggplants with salt, pepper, and, if desired, a sprinkling of oregano. Arrange the segments, skin side down, in a baking dish and bake them, uncovered, at 350° F. for 50 minutes, or until they are very tender.

A dish from the Middle East calls for pricking the skin of 2 large eggplants, arranging them in a baking dish, and baking them at 425° F. for 45 minutes, or until they are very tender; peel the eggplants and chop the pulp; add 1 cup yogurt, 1 clove garlic, put through a press, and salt and pepper to taste. Spoon the mixture into a greased baking dish and heat it at 350° F. for 20 minutes.

Grilled Onions: Peel 6 large yellow onions and, in boiling water to cover, cook them for 10 minutes (they should be not quite tender). Drain and halve them crosswise. Arrange them in a broiling pan, cut side up. Sprinkle them with chopped fresh parsley and dried basil; add 1 teaspoon olive oil to each half. Season each with salt and pepper. On the lowest shelf of the broiler, cook the onions for 10 minutes, or until they are tender. Serve them sprinkled with lemon juice.

Spinach: Rinse and remove the woody stems from 2 10-ounce packages fresh spinach. Shake off the excess water. In a large soup kettle, arrange the spinach; season it with salt and pepper and over it pour ⅓ cup olive oil flavored with 1 clove of garlic, put through a press. Toss the spinach as you would a salad. Over high heat, cook the spinach, covered, for 2 or 3 minutes, or until wilted; stir it once or twice. Cooked this way, spinach retains all of its nutrients and tastes refreshingly different from the more common boiled spinach.

Turnips: Turnips come in two varieties, the mild white and the more peppery yellow, sometimes called rutabagas; white turnips cook more quickly. Two pounds serve 6 persons.

Scrape them with a vegetable parer and slice them; cook them, covered, in boiling water for 20 minutes, or until they are tender. Season them, to taste, with soft margarine, salt, and pepper.

Or prepare *Mashed Turnips*, following the directions for Mashed White Potatoes, page 302.

A handsome side dish of turnips is *Turnip Pudding*: boil 2 pounds turnips with 3 onions until very tender. Drain and mash them together. Add 1 can cream-style soup of your choice, 3 lightly beaten eggs, 3 tablespoons soft margarine, ¾ teaspoon salt, and ½ teaspoon pepper. Spoon the mixture into a greased baking dish and over the top sprinkle packaged poultry stuffing. Bake the pudding, uncovered, at 350° F. for 30 minutes, or until it is set. If desired, grated cheese may be sprinkled over the top before the dish is baked.

Zucchini: Although zucchini are "summer" squash, they are available — like "winter" acorn squash — virtually year round. I find the following very simple recipe fresh-tasting and satisfying.

Cut 6 medium zucchini in ½-inch rounds. In a skillet, heat 4 table-spoons margarine; add the zucchini; season them with salt, pepper, and a sprinkling of cinnamon. Over gentle heat, cook the zucchini, covered, stirring them occasionally, for 12 minutes, or until they are tender-crisp.

Salads

Salad-tossing should be a last-minute operation, done just before serving, but the preparation of salad greens and of the dressing may be undertaken ahead of time. Salad greens and vegetables may be readied and stored in plastic bags in the refrigerator. Salad greens may be stored together. Their accompaniments (onion, cucumber, etc.) should be kept separately so that each component of the salad will retain its special flavor.

The following salad greens go well together in almost any combination:

Chinese or celery
   cabbage
Endive

Escarole
Lettuce (all kinds)
Rugola (arugola or roquette or rocket)
Watercress

One or more of the following vegetables may be added to the greens:

Canned bamboo shoots
Raw broccoli stalk,
   peeled and cut in
   julienne
Cherry tomatoes, whole
   or halved
Cucumber, sliced

Green pepper, in
   julienne
Radishes, sliced
Red-onion rings
Scallions (I prefer them sliced
   lengthwise in 2-inch strips)
Sweet red pepper, in julienne
Canned water chestnuts, sliced

Bacon bits are particularly flavorful in salad. Three strips, diced, rendered until crisp, and drained on absorbent paper, will give a pleasant accent to salad for 6 persons.

If fresh herbs are available, nothing will give salad more interest than the addition of one or two of the following, cut fine with scissors:

Basil   Marjoram
Chervil   Oregano
Chive   Parsley
Dillweed   Tarragon

Dried herbs will also enhance salad; do not hesitate to use them. It is difficult to say how much, for the quantity used is a matter of personal taste.

You may further embellish your salad with croutons or mimosa egg (hard-boiled egg put through a sieve).

Mixed Green Salad: This, the most familiar of all salads, has no rule of thumb for its preparation; its success depends in large measure upon experimenting with different combinations — all work well, but you will find favorites of your own.

To prepare: select a combination of salad greens that appeals to you (such as iceberg and Boston lettuce with spinach, or celery cabbage with watercress; or romaine and Boston lettuce — the combinations are endless). Rinse the greens well and shake off the excess water (swinging them in a large muslin towel is a good way). Put them in a large salad bowl and, with scissors, cut them through in several directions until they are of uniform size. (Yes, I admit that to cut salad greens is heresy, but the technique works without bruising tender leaves.)

Salad Dressings: *A dependable all-purpose Vinaigrette dressing:* in a jar with a tight-fitting lid, combine 2 teaspoons sugar, 1 teaspoon salt, ½ teaspoon white pepper, ½ teaspoon dry mustard, and ¼ cup lemon juice or vinegar; shake the mixture until the sugar and salt are dissolved. Add ¾ cup oil; shake until well blended.

A cream dressing: in the container of an electric blender, combine 1 clove garlic, 1 teaspoon sugar, the grated rind and juice of 1 lemon, ½ teaspoon salt, ¼ teaspoon paprika, ¼ teaspoon pepper, 4 tablespoons sour cream, and ½ cup oil. Blend the mixture at low speed for 15 seconds.

A slightly sweet dressing for mild-flavored greens: in a jar with a tight-fitting lid, combine ¼ cup honey, ¼ cup olive oil, the juice of 1 lemon, ¼ teaspoon salt, and ¼ teaspoon white pepper. Shake the mixture until thoroughly blended. (If desired, a sliver of garlic may be marinated in the dressing for 1 hour and removed.)

A dressing for calorie-watchers: in the container of an electric blender, combine 1 cup buttermilk, 2 tablespoons sour cream, ¼ teaspoon dry mustard, ½ teaspoon Worcestershire sauce, ¼ teaspoon white pepper, 1 teaspoon powdered cumin, 1 teaspoon dillweed, ½ clove garlic (optional). Blend the mixture at low speed for 15 seconds.

Green Bean Salad: Green beans are inexpensive and healthful — and never more flavorful than when eaten cold.

To prepare: pick over 1½ pounds green beans and rinse them in cold water. In a large saucepan or soup kettle, bring to a boil 4 quarts water, seasoned with 1 tablespoon salt and 1 tablespoon sugar; add 1 teaspoon soda. Add the beans and, when the water returns to the boiling point, cook them uncovered, for 12 minutes, or until they are just tender. Remove them from the heat, drain them, and plunge them in cold water. Drain them thoroughly and chill them.

The beans should be tender but still crunchy; the soda will have turned them a rich green.

Toss the beans with the dressing of your choice.

Garnish the salad with halved cherry tomatoes or red-onion rings.

Crusty Bread

Bread plays a very important part in my history, for my father's family were bakers in a small upstate New York village. The bread was mixed, kneaded, and baked in the cellar of the house where Father was born. As a boy, he delivered the fresh-baked loaves to the local grocer and private customers. Father — as of this writing, a venerable ninety-three years of age— occasionally shares reminiscences of hitching his horse to the cart, loading it with fresh-smelling, still-warm loaves, and plodding off in the snow to make his rounds. Anyone who has experienced the satisfaction of making one's own bread, or the aroma of it, fresh from the oven, or the taste of it, newly cut, will agree that home-baked bread is one of the great culinary and gastronomic experiences.

White Bread: In a large mixing bowl, combine 5 cups unbleached flour, 1 tablespoon salt, 1 tablespoon sugar, and 1 package dry yeast. Stir to blend the ingredients well. Add 2 cups warm water or milk and 3 tablespoons vegetable oil or margarine, melted. Add flour as necessary to make the dough workable. Knead the dough until it is silky and resistant (about 10 minutes). Put it into a greased bowl and, in a warm place, covered with a dampened cloth, allow it to rise until double in bulk (1½ to 2 hours). On a lightly floured surface, knead the dough for 10 minutes. Shape it into 2 loaves; arrange them on a lightly greased baking sheet. In a warm place, covered with a dampened cloth, allow them to rise until doubled in bulk. Bake the loaves at 450° F. for 15 minutes; reduce the heat to 350° F.; remove the loaves to a rack, and continue to bake them for 30 minutes, or until they sound hollow when tapped on top. Cool the loaves on a rack.

Whole-Wheat Bread: Follow the directions in White Bread recipe, using 3 cups whole-wheat flour and 2 cups unbleached white flour. If desired, ½ cup wheat germ may be added.

This recipe is contributed by Mrs. Edward Giobbi, my neighbor in the country. Elinor bakes all the bread for her family's use. The directions given, adapted from her mother-in-law's breadmaking, produce a solid, moist, crusty loaf with a full flavor. It tastes good, is wholesome and satisfying, and is worth every minute required to make it. "And anyway," Elinor says, "kneading bread is the best therapy in the world. It's good exercise and certainly lets off steam. High prices, taxes, children's problems — all are helped by breadmaking."

Potatoes

Rich in vitamins and minerals and low in cost, potatoes may be cooked in virtually countless ways. Although only the simplest methods are offered here, I suggest looking into other sources to discover the variations of which the humble potato is capable and, therefore, the many different ways in which it can enhance your main course.

Sweet potatoes, which belong to a different botanical species from white potatoes, contain more sugar than their "cousins." They are a good source of vitamin A. Yams, a variety of sweet potato, are more moist and sweeter than *their* cousins. All members of the potato family are cooked similarly.

Boiled White Potatoes: One medium-sized potato serves 1 person; 3 or 4 new potatoes, depending upon their size, make 1 serving. Scrub the potatoes, but do not peel them. New potatoes should be left whole; if desired, mature potatoes may be halved. Cook the potatoes, covered, in boiling salted water just to cover for 15 minutes (new potatoes) or 25 minutes (mature potatoes), or until they can be pierced with the tines of a fork. Drain the potatoes thoroughly. Peel them, if desired (I enjoy the peel, myself, and it is especially healthful); new potatoes should not be peeled (my opinion). If the potatoes are to accompany a dish with gravy or sauce, serve them plain; otherwise, toss them with soft margarine and, if desired, garnish them with chopped parsley.

Boiled Sweet Potatoes: Follow the directions for Boiled White Potatoes; allow 20 to 25 minutes' cooking time.

Baked White Potatoes: Allow 1 medium-sized potato per serving. Scrub the potatoes, prick them in several places with the tines of a fork, rub them with bacon fat or margarine, and bake them on the oven rack at 450° F. for 50 minutes, or until they are easily pierced to the center with the tines of a fork. If they are to accompany a dish with gravy or sauce, they may be served plain. Otherwise, serve them with a pat or two of margarine. If desired, they may be served with crumbled crisp bacon, chopped chives or scallions, and sour cream — each condiment offered separately. Thus garnished, the baked potato becomes, by itself, nearly a main course.

Baked Sweet Potatoes: Follow the directions for Baked White Potatoes; bake the sweet potatoes or yams at 375° F. for 50 minutes, or until they test done. Serve them with soft margarine, salt, and freshly ground pepper.

Mashed White Potatoes: Allow 1 potato per serving; follow the directions for Boiled White Potatoes, page 301. When they are very tender, drain and peel them. In a large mixing bowl, mash them until smooth. Add hot milk until they are of the desired consistency. Using a large mixing spoon or an electric beater, beat the potatoes until they are light. As you beat them, season them, to taste, with soft margarine, salt, and pepper. Keep them warm, uncovered, in the top of a double boiler.

Mashed Sweet Potatoes: Follow the directions for Mashed White Potatoes.

Hot Potato Salad: Originally a German idea; this particular recipe is contributed by James Litton, a culinary associate of twenty years' friendship, with whom I have made many memorable, and sometimes disastrous, gastronomic forays.

Prepare 6 potatoes, following the directions for Boiled White Potatoes, page 301, and adding to the water 1 onion, quartered. Cool the potatoes, peel them, dice them into a mixing bowl, and season them with salt and pepper. Discard the cooked onion. Over the potatoes sprinkle ¼ cup finely chopped celery, ¼ cup chopped parsley, and 2 strips bacon, diced and rendered until crisp. In a mixing bowl, blend 1 small onion, grated, the juice of ½ lemon, 3 tablespoons bacon fat, and ¼ cup all-purpose dressing, page 299. Pour the dressing over the potatoes, and toss the mixture gently; spoon it into a baking dish and heat the salad, covered, at 350° F. for 10 minutes.

Rice

Rice, among the most healthful and least fattening of the starches, gives weight to a meal without making the eater feel heavy. Rice is more easily prepared than noodles or spaghetti, for it absorbs the liquid in which it is cooked and thus requires no last-minute draining. There are two readily available kinds of rice at the supermarket. (Wild rice is not rice at all, but a member of the wheat family.) White, or polished, rice is the most used. Brown rice, free of its hull but unpolished, is the second variety. It takes longer to cook than white rice but, I feel, has more body and taste and, if frozen, tends to hold up better. Of the white rices, there are long-grained, short-grained, Italian, Middle Eastern, and domestic varieties; each variety has its own characteristics, but all are cooked identically. I avoid precooked rice. I find natural rice more flavorful and of more pleasing consistency than precooked varieties. Preparing raw natural white rice requires at most only 25 minutes, and while the grain is actually cooking, you can do other things.

A word about refrigerating and freezing rice: both may be done successfully (I find the casserole method of cooking best). Before reheating to serve, however, the grain must reach room temperature. Reheating must be done over gentle heat. Heating cold cooked rice over high heat will result in an unappetizing mush. Use a fork to stir the grain.

Boiled Rice: In a heavy saucepan with a tight-fitting lid, heat 2 tablespoons margarine or oil. Add 1½ cups rice, stirring it with a fork until each grain is coated. Add 3 cups water and 1 teaspoon salt; bring the liquid to a boil, stir it once, reduce the heat, and simmer the rice, covered, for 15 minutes, or until it is tender and the liquid is absorbed.

Rice en Casserole: In a flameproof casserole with a tight-fitting lid, heat 2 tablespoons margarine or oil. Add 1½ cups rice, stirring it with a fork until each grain is coated. Add 3 cups boiling water and 1 teaspoon salt, stir once, and bake, covered, at 350° F. for:
  18 to 25 minutes for white rice
  50 minutes for brown rice

The flavor of rice may be enhanced by various seasonings. Before adding the water, season the grain with one or two of the following (suggested quantities are for 1½ cups, or 6 servings):

1 teaspoon ground allspice
½ teaspoon dried basil
1 bay leaf, broken
½ teaspoon dried chervil
1 or 2 tablespoons minced onion
Grated rind of ½ orange
¼ teaspoon dried rosemary, crumbled

1 teaspoon curry powder
½ teaspoon dried dillweed
1 teaspoon dried marjoram
½ teaspoon dried sage
½ teaspoon dried thyme
¾ teaspoon turmeric (for color)

BAY LEAVES

In place of water, you may use: chicken broth or bouillon, beef broth or bouillon, consommé, homemade chicken or meat stock, clam juice, or orange juice.

To the cooked grain, you may add:

½ cup yogurt (a typical Middle Eastern treatment)

¼ cup currants or seedless raisins, plumped in boiling water and well drained

2 or 3 tablespoons minced parsley

3 scallions, finely chopped (with as much green as possible)

Small jar pimientos, chopped

The different flavors possible with rice are virtually endless, dependent only upon your desire to experiment. The quantity of liquid must be twice that of the grain; the liquid must be completely absorbed by the cooked grain. Given this rule, any individuality you care to give rice will only enhance your meal; here is a challenging example of the creativity of cooking!

For the cook who would enjoy offering a more festive presentation of rice, here are three particular recipes for doing so:

Rice with Fruit: Combine ¼ cup currants, 6 prunes, cut in julienne, 6 apricot halves, cut in julienne, 4 tablespoons slivered blanched almonds, and 1½ cups raw natural rice. In a saucepan, heat 2 tablespoons margarine and, over medium heat, cook the rice mixture, stirring to coat each grain, for 3 minutes. Add 3 cups hot water, in which 3 chicken bouillon cubes have been dissolved. Bring the liquid to a boil, reduce the heat, and simmer the rice, covered, for 15 minutes, or until it is tender and the liquid is absorbed.

Molded Rice: In the usual way, cook 1¼ cups raw natural rice. In a mixing bowl, combine 1¼ cups milk, 4 tablespoons margarine, melted, 1 egg, 1 onion, grated, ½ teaspoon paprika, and 1 teaspoon salt. With a rotary beater, blend the mixture well. Stir in ½ cup grated cheese and ½ cup parsley, chopped. Pour the mixture into the rice, stirring gently to blend the ingredients. Into a greased casserole or ring mold, spoon the rice and bake it, uncovered, at 350° F. for 40 minutes, or until it is set.

Tomato Pilaf: Turkey
Serves 6 ■ Doubles ■ Refrigerates (adequately only)

Preparation: 45 minutes ■ Cooking: 15 minutes in a 350° F. oven

1 tablespoon olive oil
1½ cups raw natural rice
1½ teaspoons salt
Boiling water

In a large saucepan, heat the olive oil and in it cook the rice for 2 minutes, stirring to coat each grain. Stir in the salt and add boiling water to cover. Stir the liquid, allow it to cool, and drain the rice.

4 tablespoons olive oil
4 tomatoes, peeled, seeded, and chopped (canned tomatoes, drained, will do)
2½ cups hot water, in which 2 chicken bouillon cubes have been dissolved
½ teaspoon ground cumin
½ teaspoon salt
¼ teaspoon pepper

In a flameproof baking dish, heat the oil and in it cook the tomatoes, stirring, for 30 minutes, or until the mixture is pastelike. Add the water and seasonings. Boil the sauce for 2 minutes.

At this point you may stop and continue later.

To the boiling sauce add the rice, stirring once. Bake the rice, covered, at 350° F. for 15 minutes, or until it is tender and the liquid is absorbed.

Pasta and Dumplings

Noodles and Spaghetti: Noodles and spaghetti come in a bewildering variety of sizes and shapes. I prefer the thinner noodles and am especially fond of green noodles, which are made with spinach. Spaghetti no. 8, fettucini, vermicelli, and linguine are all excellent accompaniments to main dishes.

To prepare: in a large saucepan or soup kettle, bring to a boil 4 quarts (or more) salted water. Add the pasta of your choice. Immediately remove the utensil from the heat, stir the pasta once, and allow it to stand, covered, for 20 minutes. Drain it, add soft margarine, if desired, and serve. For the most part, however, I find it unnecessary to add butter or any flavoring agent, preferring to use the noodles or spaghetti as a bed for the main-dish sauce. An 8-ounce box of noodles or a little more than half a 1-pound box of spaghetti serves 6 persons.

Dumplings: A fine addition to any dish cooked in its sauce, dumplings are inexpensive, and satisfying without being heavy. Although "Serve the dish with Dumplings" is suggested for only certain dishes, there is every reason for your serving them whenever and with whatever you wish.

To make 6 large dumplings: in a mixing bowl, combine 1 cup unbleached flour, 2 teaspoons baking powder, ½ teaspoon sugar, and ½ teaspoon salt; gradually add ½ cup milk, stirring the batter well.

Onto the surface of the cooking casserole, spoon the dumpling dough. Cook the dumplings, covered, for 20 minutes.

If desired, you may make richer dumplings by adding to the milk 2 tablespoons melted margarine or salad oil and 1 egg, well beaten.

Chopped parsley may also be added, or a generous pinch of celery seed or marjoram or thyme, or 1 teaspoon onion flakes.

Dried Beans and Canned Beans

Always available, always inexpensive, and always nourishing, dried beans are capable of many tastes and textures. Four of my favorite recipes for them follow.

The *basic preparation* of dried beans is the same for each recipe: put 1 pound dried beans in a saucepan; add 2 teaspoons salt and cold water to cover by 1 inch; bring the water to a boil, and, over high heat, cook the beans for 5 minutes; remove the saucepan from the heat and allow the beans to stand, covered, for 1 hour. Over medium heat, cook the beans, covered, until they are tender (30 minutes for Lima beans; 45 to 60 minutes for other varieties). Drain the beans, but do not discard the bean water until you are sure you have no use for it; it contains many nutrients and may be used in soup or as the liquid ingredient of other dishes.

Dried Bean Casserole — *Turkey:* In a flameproof casserole, put 4 onions, chopped, 2 gloves garlic, chopped, 2 tomatoes, peeled, seeded, and chopped (canned tomatoes, drained, will do), 1 carrot, scraped and thinly sliced, 2 ribs celery, diced, ¼ cup olive oil, and cold water just to cover. Bring the water to a boil, reduce the heat, and simmer the vegetables, covered, for 30 minutes. Add 1 potato, peeled and finely diced, the juice of ½ lemon, ¼ cup parsley, chopped, 1 teaspoon sugar, 1 teaspoon salt, and a pinch of cayenne. Continue simmering the vegetables, covered, for 15 minutes. Add the prepared beans, stirring gently to blend the mixture. Over the top arrange a layer of lemon slices, cut paper-thin. Bake the casserole, covered, at 350° F. for 30 minutes. This dish may be served hot or cold. If desired, it may be made with canned white kidney beans, well drained in a colander and rinsed under cold water.

Dried Bean Salad — *Italy:* Cook the beans as directed, adding to the bean water ⅓ cup olive oil, 1 bay leaf, and 2 cloves garlic, split; when draining the beans, discard the bay leaf and garlic. Put the beans in a mixing bowl. Combine ½ cup olive oil, ¼ cup wine vinegar, ¼ cup chopped parsley, ½ teaspoon basil, ½ teaspoon oregano, 1 teaspoon tarragon, ½ teaspoon salt, and ¼ teaspoon pepper. Pour the dressing over the beans and, using two forks, gently toss them to coat them well. Refrigerate the beans, covered, overnight. If desired, this dish may be made with canned white beans, well drained in a colander and rinsed under cold water.

Dried Beans with Sour Cream: Arrange the prepared beans in a casserole. In 3 tablespoons margarine, cook 3 onions, chopped, until translucent; remove the onions from the heat and stir in 1 cup sour cream, ¾ teaspoon salt, and ¼ teaspoon pepper. Pour the sour cream over the beans, stirring them gently to blend the mixture. Bake the casserole, covered, at 350° F. for 30 minutes.

Dried Beans with Yogurt — *India:* In 4 tablespoons margarine, cook 2 onions, chopped, until translucent; add 1 teaspoon ground coriander and 1 teaspoon salt. In a mixing bowl, combine 1 cup yogurt, 1 glove garlic, put through a press, ¼ teaspoon ground allspice, ¼ teaspoon ground glove, ¼ teaspoon ginger, ¼ teaspoon peper. Blend the onion and yogurt, pour the mixture over the beans, stirring gently to coat them well. Over gentle heat, simmer the beans just long enough to heat them through. If desired, this dish may be made with frozen lima beans, prepared as directed on the package.

"Dressed-up" Canned Baked Beans: Canned baked beans are very good when doctored a bit; using ready-cooked beans is a tremendous time-saver. I do not pretend that beans prepared in the following way compare with those cooked from scratch; they do not. But they are nonetheless tasty *and* inexpensive. In a mixing bowl, to 1 35-ounce can of baked beans with pork and molasses sauce add 1 onion, chopped, ¼ cup dark molasses, ¼ teaspoon ground clove, ½ teaspoon salt, and ½ teaspoon pepper. Stir the mixture gently to blend it. Spoon the beans into a baking dish and heat them, covered, in a 350° F. oven for 30 minutes.

TARRAGON

Sauce

Sweet and Pungent Sauce
For Use with Various Meats: China
Serves 6 ■ Doubles ■ Refrigerates

Preparation: 15 minutes

For meat, poultry, and fish. There are various ways of making sweet and pungent (sweet and sour) sauce. All share in common the characteristic flavor of pineapple combined with aromatic vinegar.

Please note that this sauce is rather highly seasoned; therefore do not season with salt and pepper. In using Sweet and Pungent Sauce, follow instructions given for particular recipes.

3 tablespoons sugar ½ teaspoon ground ginger (or more, to taste) 3 tablespoons cornstarch	In a saucepan, mix these three ingredients.
1 cup hot water in which 2 chicken bouillon cubes are dissolved 1 20-ounce can pineapple chunks ¼ cup cider vinegar 3 tablespoons soy sauce	Stir in the boullion, the pineapple and its liquid, the vinegar, and soy sauce. Over high heat, cook the mixture, stirring constantly, until it is thickened and smooth.

If desired, the grated rind and juice of 1 orange and/or 1 green pepper, seeded and chopped, may be combined with the pineapple, vinegar, and soy sauce, and added to the cornstarch mixture. Cook the sauce as directed. A clove of garlic may be put through a press and added to the sauce.

With meat, poultry, or fish cooked with Sweet and Pungent Sauce, serve Rice (page 303 to 305).

INDEX

Nationalities of dishes, listed by the principal meat or fish ingredient, are given under names of specific countries.

Acidulated water, 171–72
Acorn squash, baked, 294
  stuffed, 294
Ale with beef stew, 44
America, United States of
  beef, corned, with vegetables, 32
  chicken, giblet soup with lemon, 262
    gumbo, 233
    livers with eggplant, 256
  fish, chowder, 267
    chowder, baked, 269
    filets with sour cream, 280
  ham hock and bean soup, 104
  heart stew, 180
  lamb, breast with orange sauce, 60
    breast with vegetables, 63
    shanks with lentils, 65
  meatball soup, 167
  mulligatawny, 235
  New England boiled dinner, 32
  Philadelphia pepper pot, 230
  pig's feet with sauerkraut, 109
  pork chops with sour cream, 97
  pot roast, baked, 23
    with cabbage and potatoes, 24
    with cream sauce, 26
  sausage, pudding, 127
    with rice and eggplant, 129
  short ribs, braised, 37
  soup, chicken giblet with lemon, 260
    ham hock and bean, 104
    meatball, 167
    oxtail with vegetables, 211
    Philadelphia pepper pot, 230
Appicius, 246
Apples, with chicken livers, 259
  with liver, 198
Arab States
  lamb, with green beans, 76
  lamb shanks with tomatoes, 68
Austria
  chicken, ragout soup, 234
    with paprika, 244

Barley, and chicken giblet soup, 261
  with lamb and orange, 87
  and lamb soup, 71
  with oxtails, braised, 213
  with oxtail soup, 210

  with pot roast and lima beans, 31
  with short ribs and lima beans, 31
Beans, baked, canned, 310
  dried, 308
    basic preparation, 308
    casserole, 309
    with chicken, 238–39
    and ham hock casserole, 105
    and ham hock soup, 104
    with lamb, 74
    with pork, 111
    salad, 309
    and sausage soup, 121
    with sour cream, 309
    with tripe, 224
    with yogurt, 309
  green, salad, 299
    with chicken livers, 254
    with Italian sausage, 124
    with lamb, 76
  and ground meat cassoulet, 165
Beef, 21
  corned, with vegetables, 32
  curried, stews, 50–53
  ground. See Ground meats
  pot roasts, 22
    baked, 23
    with barley and lima beans, 31
    with cabbage and potatoes, 24–25
    with carrots and turnips, 28
    with cream sauce, 26
    with currant and horseradish sauce, 27
    with dried fruit, 29
    with eggplant and peppers, 30
    with ginger sauce, 27
    with horseradish and currant sauce, 27
    with lima beans and barley, 31
    with sweet and pungent sauce, 23
  short ribs, 36
    braised, 37
    with chick-peas, 38
    with lima beans and barley, 31
    savory, 39
    with sweet peppers, 40
  stews, 41
    with ale, 44
    curried, 50–53
    with figs, 44
    with grapes, 45

Pot roast. *See* Beef
Poultry. *See* Chicken
Primavera, chicken livers *alla*, 258
Prunes with pork chops, 95
Pudding, fish, 288–89
    sausage, 127
Pumpkin soup with tripe, 288–89

Ragout, lamb heart, 180
    soup, chicken, 234
Raisin sauce with tongue, 217
Raisins with tongue and dates, 220
Ravigote sauce with fish filets, 279
Rice, 303
    boiled, 303
    casserole, 303
    with chicken and sausage, 128, 245
    with chicken giblets, 263
    with eggplant and sausage, 129
    flavorings for, 304–305
    with fruit, 305
    with lamb, 87
    with lamb breast, 62
    with lamb shanks, 67
    liquids for cooking, 304
    molded, 305
    with pork chops, 96
    with sausage and chicken, 128, 245
    with sausage and eggplant, 129
    tomato pilaf, 306
Risotto, chicken liver, 259
    ground beef, 151
    sausage, 130
Roux, 17
Rumania
    beef with sour cream, 47
    beef stew with grapes, 45
Russia
    fish filets with sour cream and cheese,
        281
    pork with sour cream and sausage, 135
    pork with stroganoff sauce, 119

Salads, 297–99
    bean, dried, 309
    bean, green, 299
    brain, 174
    greens for, 297
    herbs for, 298
    mixed green, 298–99
    potato, hot, 302
    vegetables for, 297
Salad dressings, 298
Sauces
    cheese with chicken, 236
    cream, with kidney, 188
        with pot roast, 26
    curry, with brains, 173
        with lamb kidneys, 190
    dill, with lamb, 79
        with pork chops and paprika, 94
    fruit with spareribs, 100

ginger with pot roast, 27
horseradish, and currant with pot roast,
    27
with pork, 115
with tongue, 216
onion, with kidney, 189
orange, with chicken livers, 257
    with lamb breast, 60
    with liver, 200
    with meatballs and spinach, 160
    with tongue, 216
paprika, with chicken giblets, 260
    with fish filets, 275
    with liver, 203
peanut, with fish filets, 275
    with lamb, 96
piquant, with braised kidney, 193
raisin, with tongue, 217
ravigote, with fish filets, 279
sausage, for pasta, 132
savory, with kidney, 196
    with kidney, broiled, 194–95
    with liver, 200
stroganoff with pork, 119
sweet and pungent, 311
    with beef, 48
    with chicken, 248
    with chicken livers, 260
    with fish filets, 284
    with ground beef, 163
    with pot roast, 23
    with sausage, 131
    with spareribs, 102
tomato, with braised kidney, 193
    with swiss steak, 35
    with tongue, 217
    with tripe, 225
vinaigrette with brains, 174
Sauerkraut, with chicken giblets, 263
    with frankfurters, 134
    with meatballs, 157
    with pig's feet, 109
    with pork, 118
    with pork hocks, 101
    with spareribs, 101
Sausages, 120
    with beans, 124
    with bean soup, 121
    with chicken, 245
    with chicken and rice, 128, 145
    with eggplant, 123
    with eggplant and rice, 129
    frankfurters, and corn chowder, 136
        with noodles, 133
        with sauerkraut, 134
    knackwurst, 135
        with potatoes, 93
    with lentils, 125
    with Lima beans, 125
    with meat loaf, 142
    and onion tart, 126
    with pork and sour cream, 135